D1374522

Flight to the Sun

ALSO AVAILABLE FROM CONTINUUM:

Clift and Carter (eds): *Tourism and Sex*
Foley and Lennon: *Dark Tourism*
Godfrey and Clarke: *The Tourism Development Handbook*
Hudson: *Snow Business*
Law: *Urban Tourism*
Lumsdon and Swift: *Tourism in Latin America*

FLIGHT TO THE SUN

The Story of the Holiday Revolution

Roger Bray and Vladimir Raitz

Continuum
London and New York

Continuum

The Tower Building	370 Lexington Avenue
11 York Road	New York
London SE1 7NX	NY 10017-6503

www.continuumbooks.com

© 2001 Roger Bray and Vladimir Raitz

First published in 2001

British Library Cataloguing-in-Publication Data
A catalogue record for this book is available from the British Library

ISBN 0–8264–4829–1 hb

Typeset by YHT Ltd, London
Printed and bound in Great Britain by
Creative Print and Design, Wales

Contents

Figures   vii
Foreword
Sir Richard Branson   ix

1 The Birth of Horizon
   Vladimir Raitz   1

2 The Pre-history of Tourism
   Roger Bray   21

3 The 1950s
   Roger Bray   34

4 Growth of Horizon
   Vladimir Raitz   55

5 The 1960s: how the Wild West was tamed
   Roger Bray   80

6 Skiing and Cruising
   Roger Bray   99

7 Horizon at its Peak
   Vladimir Raitz   127

8 The Rise and Fall of Clarksons
   Roger Bray   140

CONTENTS

9 The End of Horizon
Vladimir Raitz   161

10 The 1970s: prices tumble, bonding is born
Roger Bray   172

11 The Latter Years: from free spirits to flotation
Roger Bray   199

Epilogue, June 2000
Vladimir Raitz   223

Chronology of the Industry
Roger Bray   226

Index   239

Figures

1.1 Horizon's office at 146 Fleet Street   6
1.2 An early group of Horizon holidaymakers, Calvi, 1950   12
1.3 An early group of Horizon holidaymakers making themselves at home, Calvi, 1950   13
1.4 Vladimir with Horizon's first handling agent in Calvi   15
1.5 Horizon's first air service to Sardinia, 1954   19
2.1 Harry Chandler   30
3.1 British TV star Hughie Green appearing on the cover of the Universal Sky Tours brochure, 1959   35
3.2 A BOAC Comet   37
3.3 Passengers at Palma Airport, Majorca, 1954   43
3.4 A page on Benidorm from Horizon's 1963 brochure   50
3.5 An early holidaymaker submits to a local sunburn treatment   51
3.6 The interior of a BEA 'Elizabethan' aircraft   53
4.1 A Pilgrim Tours departure from Gatwick to Lourdes   57
4.2 A page on Ibiza from Horizon's 1963 brochure   71
4.3 Vladimir with Honor Blackman and Bernard Braden   78
5.1 Holidays behind the Iron Curtain in 1963   89
5.2 Illustration from a 1960s British Eagle flight information leaflet   91
6.1 The first winter sports inclusive tour, organized by Sir Henry Lunn, Grindelwald, Switzerland, 1892   102
6.2 The front of Inghams' 1975/6 winter brochure   105
6.3 An 18–30 age-group skiing holiday, from Hotel Plan's 1962/3 brochure   108

7.1 Vladimir suffering through one of the more mundane days
     in the Horizon office   136
8.1 A page from the 1968 Clarksons brochure   145
8.2 The ticket of Clarksons' one millionth passenger, 1970   151
9.1 Tom Gullick, of Clarksons   164
9.2 The cover of Horizon's silver jubilee (and final) brochure,
     1974   168
10.1 One of Freddie Laker's Skytrain DC-10s   192
11.1 A Dan-Air Comet and 727   215

Foreword

SIR RICHARD BRANSON
CHAIRMAN, VIRGIN ATLANTIC AIRWAYS

I was one of the first children of the charter holiday revolution. My parents ended up with a holiday house on Menorca and we were able to get there thanks to entrepreneurs like Vladimir Raitz and Sir Freddie Laker.

Meanwhile, crossing the Atlantic still cost the same price as buying a small car. Just as Virgin Records were getting off the ground I watched with awe as Sir Freddie Laker took on the IATA cartel and turned Laker into a household name at the same time as giving ordinary people their first taste of 'the land of the free'.

There is no doubt in my mind that the effects of the package holiday have been far greater in a social and economic sense than most people realize. The story of this fascinating book is also the story of the rebirth of British entrepreneurship.

My admiration for Laker was one of the reasons that Virgin Atlantic got off the ground in 1984. He was enormously helpful at the time, and he gave me tips which prepared us for British Airways' attempts to put the airline out of business. However, he also gave us an understanding of the need to compete on quality as well as price, after his own bitter experiences.

It is often better to follow a pioneer than be a pioneer, and I am sure I would not be in business today without the pioneers whose story is told on the pages that follow.

To the six women in my life
Toni, Lucy, Sophie, Sarah, Hannah and Becky

Vladimir Raitz

1

The Birth of Horizon

VLADIMIR RAITZ

Early August, 1949. I was standing on the deck of the SS *Ile de Beauté* bound from Nice to Calvi – a sleepy little fishing village on the nort-west coast of Corsica.

I was 27 years old and working for Reuters, the news agency. It was my first holiday after the war. I'd chosen Corsica (and specifically Calvi) because a friend of mine, a fellow Russian colleague at Reuters, not only knew Calvi well but had taken part in 1938 in organizing a holiday camp at Calvi run by an émigré Russian water polo club called 'Les Ourses Blancs' – the White Bears. Now, after the war and the occupation, this idea had been revived. One of the original White Bears, Dimitri Filipoff (known to one and all as 'Poff') had formed the Club Olympique – a tented village on the superb Calvi beach. A friend of mine from Reuters, Baron Nicholas Steinheil, was staying there and had invited me for a fortnight's vacation.

And there they both were on the quayside as the *Ile de Beauté* majestically swung round the fourteenth-century Genoese citadel of Calvi, preparing to dock after the six hour journey from Nice. Nicholas, six foot three, a land owner's son from Vladikavkaz in the Caucasus; and little Poff, heir to the biggest bakery fortune in Czarist Russia and now Chef de Camp of the Club Olympique in Calvi.

Besides Nicholas and Poff there was a welcoming committee with a large banner proclaiming 'Club Olympique', and a small but extremely noisy jazz band blaring out current hits and the Club song.

As the ship discharged its cargo, all of us (including the jazz band) piled into two coaches, our luggage stowed in a lorry. We roared out

1

of the port of Calvi towards the 'pinède', the pine-covered stretch of beach where the US Army's war surplus tents provided the living quarters of the Club.

To say that the installations and living conditions were primitive would be putting it mildly. The tents were 'furnished' with camp beds: two, three or four to each tent, standing directly on the sand. You were expected to keep your gear in your suitcase throughout the stay. Ablutions and other essential human functions were performed in a 'bloc sanitaire' consisting of washing and showering cubicles, and toilets. Naturally, there was no main drainage. If the toilets were all occupied, one simply went out into the maquis – the sweet smelling Corsican shrubbery – to relieve oneself.

The bar, thankfully, functioned beautifully. We paid by means of coupons that were purchased by the booklet from Mario, the head barman. Prices were extremely low, and after half a dozen pastis (the aniseed flavoured drink that was a favourite apéritif) and a few cognacs after dinner, you were past caring about the sanitation. There was also wine that was included in the overall price and that flowed freely.

In addition to the tents, the sanitary block, the bar, and the 'restaurant' (a few large tables and long wooden benches), there was a tiny and perpetually crowded dance floor where the band that had greeted the new arrivals was performing vigorously after dinner to an appreciative audience. This was 1949, and tangos, paso dobles and slows were much in demand. Naturally, romance flourished.

Despite the various shortcomings, everyone seemed to have a wonderful, carefree holiday. The beautiful Calvi beach of fine sand was almost deserted although it was August, and the Mediterranean was clear and unpolluted. A short distance away, there was magnificent rock swimming to be had, and snorkels and underwater spearguns were just making their appearance in France. At night there was the Club bar and dance floor, or the opportunity of visiting 'downtown' Calvi. Here, you had a choice of two bars. The first, 'Au son des Guitares' featured two boys from Ajaccio singing Corsican love songs à la Tino Rossi. The second bar, 'Chez Tao', had been set up by Tao Khan from Tadjikistan, a former member of a Cossack riding and dancing team. He was financially assisted by his patron Prince Youssupoff – renowned for having led the assassination of Rasputin.

Although a few White Russians (survivors of the original White

Bears) were still in evidence at the Club Olympique, most of the clients were French or Belgian. There was even a tiny British contingent. The Belgian agent of the Club, who used to pay flying visits to Calvi, was a huge man, a powerful swimmer and international water polo player named Gérard Blitz. It was as a result of seeing the Olympique in operation that he set up in 1950 his own company. He called it Club Méditérranee. Today, it straddles the world. Holiday camps and hotels, cruise ships and an airline are part of the conglomerate now. Winter sports have been added, and locations (apart from many in France) include Italy, Spain, Greece, Portugal, Switzerland, Egypt, Israel, Martinique, Guadeloupe and Tahiti. There is even a luxury hotel in the heart of Paris.

As for the Club Olympique, it functions in Calvi to this day. The tents have been replaced by wooden chalets and Poff, alas, is dead. For years it was run with an iron hand by Mme Filipacchi of the famous French publishing dynasty. She died in 1960 but her partner Lionel Marcu, now 80 years old and looking 60, is still in total command.

CONCEPTION

Towards the end of my vacation at the Club in 1949, I was having a drink with Nicholas Steinheil in the bar.

'Listen, Vova' (the Russian diminutive for Vladimir) Nicholas said. 'My father, the old Baron, and Tao Khan have excellent connections with the Calvi Mayor and the Municipal Council, and can get a concession on a large piece of land right on the beach between the Club and the town. We'll get some tents and equipment, and you can get us some British clients to supplement the French. We'll advertise in the Metro stations in Paris, and it's up to you how you get your clientele. If you want, we'll even call it the Club Franco-Britannique. You can do the work in your spare time, and we'll pay you a commission on each client.'

'Sounds exciting,' I said. 'But it's going to be a long and tedious journey for the Brits to even get here. Train and boat, then train and boat again – the best part of 48 hours in each direction. I know, I've just done it! Isn't there an airport anywhere nearby?'

'Not exactly an airport, but there's a runway built by the American

Seabees, the Construction Battalions, in 1943, when they invaded from North Africa. Mind you, there are no airport buildings – not even a shack. I'm sure the Municipality could provide something, though. Why don't you just charter some planes when you get back to London? We'll be opening the Club in May next year, and you can have sole rights for the UK.'

My holiday was drawing to a close and I was excited by the opportunity that was being offered to me. But before returning to London I decided, out of sheer curiosity, to take a look at another Mediterranean island – Majorca. Nicholas too was keen to see it. So, after a prolonged and somewhat drunken Russian farewell party in Tao Khan's bar, we lurched down to the port and boarded the overnight boat to Marseilles. This was followed by a train journey to Barcelona and then a short hop to Palma de Mallorca in a converted Bristol freighter of the Spanish airline Aviaco.

Upon arrival, Majorca made a gentle impression. Certainly it was an attractive island, with high mountains and deserted beaches. There was a charming little airport with a terminal building resembling a country house, and there were innumerable windmills pumping water for the fertile plains around Palma. I decided there and then that after Corsica (which I still consider the more beautiful of the two), the island offered great potential for tourism.

One problem was the lack of hotels. All of them were of pre-war vintage, and the large, comfortable ones could be counted on the fingers of one hand. Nicholas and I stayed in a magnificent old pile, the Hotel Mediterraneo in the Terreno district of Palma. It has since been modernized several times, and is now an apartment building. Next to it was a tiny open-air nightclub, called Tito's. There was a four piece band to dance to, and plenty of cheap drinks. Within 20 years it had become the largest and plushest nightclub on the entire Mediterranean, seating a thousand clients, with a floor show of top international performers. The drinks were no longer so cheap.

After two days of exploring the island, I returned to London via Barcelona, Paris, Calais and Dover. My own holiday had finished, but my enthusiasm for the concept of holidays was just beginning.

GESTATION

Back in London, the idea of supplying clients to my friends in Corsica was increasingly appealing. It would be straightforward and uncomplicated, a sideline to my day job at Reuters. What could be simpler? Charter a plane, put a couple of ads in the papers, and the public would come rolling in. So, taking a few hours off from work, I decided to call on a firm of air brokers that had been recommended to me, Instone Air Transport. I would get the first part of the equation, chartering a plane, quickly out of the way.

An appointment was duly made, and I turned up in Instone's City office to be greeted by an affable and courteous Frenchman. He was the Managing Director, Monsieur Gaston Levi-Tilley. I explained my idea, and was heard out politely.

'You mean you want to charter a plane, do a series of weekly flights to Corsica, more or less as one hires a taxi?'

'Precisely,' I replied.

'My dear fellow, have you not heard that there is a monopoly by British European Airways regarding British carriers for holiday services? The Ministry of Transport will never allow you to compete! I don't think your friends in Calvi had any idea what they were letting you in for.'

'Surely there's something I can do? BEA don't even fly to the capital of Corsica, let alone to godforsaken Calvi. I don't want our clients to spend 48 hours each way getting to their destination.'

'Oh, I can get you the planes, all right. They'll be converted DC3s – Dakotas – with 32 seats. I can even recommend a good air company: Air Transport Charter (Channel Islands) Ltd. They have three of the planes and precious little work. But I'm afraid you'll be stopped by the powers that be. Still, you might as well try. Go to the Ministry, and I'll wish you the best of luck. And by the way, in the unlikely event that you succeed, the cost of the return flight from Gatwick to Calvi would be £305 – not bad divided by 32 passengers.'

I left Gaston's office rather crestfallen. BEA monopolies and Ministry licences were not obstacles I'd counted on. Still, I was 27 years old, full of optimism, and determined to see this matter through to the end. What was more, I had a promise to keep.

One thing at least had become crystal clear to me. This was going to be a far more complicated business than I'd envisaged. The idea of it

Figure 1.1   Horizon's office at 146 Fleet Street. Vladimir's secretary, Connie Everest, can be seen in the window. Horizon were subsequently ordered to remove their 'brash' advertising from the building.

being a sideline was definitely out. I was going to have to devote all my time to it. That meant leaving Reuters, finding an office, registering a company, getting a secretary, and above all starting seriously to lobby the Ministry of Transport to let me carry out my original plan.

Hiring a secretary was the easiest part. Miss Connie Everest, aged 24, had an enthusiasm for the scheme that persisted even after I told her that her job (and mine) could be rather short-lived if the professionals were right and the flights to Calvi were never going to leave the ground. So far, so good, but I still had no office, no company, no name and no licence to fly. What I did have was some money. My grandmother had left me just under £3000, and I decided to risk it all on this venture. Incorporating a £100 company was easy, but choosing a name proved a considerable headache. At least a hundred were thought up and then rejected.

Finally, I hit upon one that expressed exactly the right ideas: Horizon Holidays. The blue horizon that the clients could contemplate out of the windows of their aircraft or looking out to sea from their Calvi beach, the alliteration of the two words, the easy abbreviation to HH – all of this seemed just right.

Finding an office proved, in the end, remarkably easy. Riding on the top deck of a number 15 bus en route to see my bank manager in the City, I saw a To Let sign on the first floor of a tiny building on Fleet Street, just before the Daily Telegraph. On my way back from the bank I stopped off to have a look. One hundred and forty six Fleet Street proved to be a 200-year-old house, and the modest publisher who occupied it was ready to sublet one room on the first floor, facing Fleet Street. The rent was a very reasonable £8 per week. The ground floor at the time was occupied by the Olde Snuffe Shoppe, as patronized by Dr Johnson. The entrance was in Wine Office Court, and a few steps further along was Ye Olde Cheshire Cheese pub – also reputedly patronized by the good doctor. The next day, I bought two second-hand desks, some third-hand chairs, and a brand new typewriter and filing cabinet. The day after that, the office was open. It was October 12th, 1949. All that was needed now was a licence to fly.

LICENSING

The Ministry of Transport told me that the relevant department was the Ministry of Civil Aviation at Ariel House in Holborn. On telephoning them to request an appointment, I was put through to a polite, public school voice.

'What did you have in mind, sir?' it enquired.

I explained the situation. There was a long and ominous silence. Finally, the voice replied. 'Well, you'd better come along and see me tomorrow. I'll try and explain to you the regulations regarding flights.'

At 11 a.m. the next day, I presented myself at Ariel House. I was received by a helpful civil servant who proceeded to enlighten me, at great length, on the impossibility of my scheme, as defined in the Civil Aviation Act 1947. I refused to give up hope.

'But surely this cannot apply to me! BEA have no service whatsoever to Corsica.'

'I know, sir, but I'm afraid the rules still don't allow that kind of operation.' There was a pause while he appeared to weigh up his options. 'However, I shall put your proposal to my superiors. You'll be hearing from me.'

This was the middle of October. I heard nothing from the Ministry for weeks. They didn't call, they didn't write. I telephoned them again and again, always to be told that the matter was 'under consideration'. Christmas and New Year came and went. Still no news. I was getting mildly desperate. There was no work being done in the office. No brochure could be printed, no adverts designed or placed. Meanwhile, the Calvi contingent were busy with their preparations to set up the Club Franco-Britannique. 'We shall add the name Club de l'Horizon, in your honour', they gleefully informed me. 'You're sure to get the licence!' Sure was the one thing that I wasn't.

January and February dragged by. Eventually, in early March 1950, I received a phone call from the civil servant at the Ministry of Civil Aviation.

'Come round as soon as possible,' he said, 'we have a decision for you.'

I grabbed a taxi to Ariel House.

'I'm not sure whether you'll like the decision, or even if you'll be able to proceed at all,' the civil servant said. 'But you can operate your flights if you carry students and teachers only.'

'Students and teachers only?' I repeated stupidly.

'That's right, sir. And we are making a considerable concession in your case as it is.'

I stumbled out of Ariel House in a daze. I didn't know whether to feel elated for achieving something, or dejected because we were limited to such a small sector of the public. It didn't take me long to make up my mind, though. Too much time and money had been invested to stop now because of this student/teacher limitation. After all, how many clients were actually required to break even? Only 350, it was reckoned.

After months of waiting, speed was now of the essence. Easter was near, and the first flight was scheduled for the middle of May. Back at the office, Connie was elated that we were on our way. I called Gaston Levi-Tilley, the air broker.

'Gaston, it's Vladimir. We're going to fly teachers and students to Calvi. Please make a firm commitment with Captain Gratrix for weekly flights over 16 weeks, plus two 'empty leg' flights at the end of the season to bring back the last two groups.'

'So you've got some sort of a licence after all!' said the astonished Gaston.

'Yes, and I don't know whether to be pleased or sorry – but I'll do my damnedest to fill those planes!'

Easier said than done.

PUBLICIZING

Now that Horizon Holidays knew where it stood, life in the office changed abruptly. The brochure – a four page leaflet – had to be got out as quickly as possible, with the text adapted to the 'teachers and students' angle. Emphasis was placed on 'plentiful food at the Club', including meat twice a day. This was a big selling point in a Britain that was still under strict rationing, particularly where meat was concerned. In France and Corsica, everything seemed to be obtainable very soon after the end of the war, and certainly by 1950.

Where to advertise was a tricky question. The mass circulation media were out – first because of the expense and also because we were aiming at such a limited market now. I finally chose three publications: *The Teacher's World*, *The Nursing Mirror* and the *New Statesman*, explicitly inviting their teacher and student readers to have a marvellous holiday in the sun. They would sleep under canvas, enjoy delicious meat-filled meals and as much local wine as they could put away, and would have return flights to Corsica for the all-inclusive charge of 32 pounds and 10 shillings.

9

The adverts were placed, the brochures were printed. Two days after the first ad appeared, three postcards and one letter arrived in the office, requesting particulars of the holiday. Connie and I were beside ourselves with joy and almost disbelief. People had actually seen the small ad and were interested enough to contact us: it was incredible!

I vividly remember posting off the brochure to these first potential clients. It was the day before Good Friday. The Easter weekend was a nailbiting time. Then, Tuesday's post brought a batch of fresh enquiries, as well as some phone calls.

'Is the aircraft safe?'

'How can it be so cheap?' (Actually, £32 then was no small amount – but air fares in those days were extremely expensive. BEA charged £70 return to Nice, their nearest destination to Calvi.)

After the questions, the miracle occurred. An elderly gentleman presented himself in our office. He produced a booking form and filled it in for himself, his wife, and his stepdaughter. He handed it to Connie with a cheque for three deposits: £9. He was called Mr Pike, and he said that as a retired teacher he surely qualified as a *bona fide* participant. We were only too glad to accept him, and he and his family were to travel with Horizon for the next dozen years, until he died.

This glorious moment was followed by quite a few enquiries, but a paucity of actual bookings. I alternated between elation (when, for instance, a booking for seven clients named Galloway arrived in the post) and black despair when there was nothing at all for three days, and the deadline for the first flight grew ever nearer. I'm still not sure why the bookings were so few in number. Was the teacher/student qualification just too tight? Was it the very late start with our marketing? Was it mistrust that a holiday could be sold so cheaply? Was it perhaps a fear of flying, or an aversion to living in tents in an unknown resort? It was probably a combination of all of these factors.

TAKE-OFF

The day of the first flight, the third Saturday in May of 1950, arrived. The tally of clients for the season at that stage stood at about 180. The first plane was about one third booked with paying clients, but it went out full with 32 bodies on board. (The other two-thirds being made up by friends who were to fly back on the empty return flight after a two hour stay in Calvi to look over the amenities of the Club Franco-Britannique and have a quick swim in the Med.)

The group assembled in the early morning at King's Cross Coach Station, where a chartered coach took us out to Gatwick. I was there early to see that everything went off smoothly. So were a number of my friends from University days, including Norman Mackenzie, later a professor at Sussex and a prolific author, and Oliver McGregor, later a professor at Bedford College and Chairman of the Royal Commission on the Press and subsequently Lord McGregor.

The DC3 Dakota was ready and waiting at Gatwick. There was hardly another plane on the tarmac. The twin-engined, propeller driven, unpressurized marvel of the skies took off, and we quickly reached our prescribed altitude of 3000 feet and top speed of 170 miles per hour. We reached Lyons in three hours, where we refuelled the plane and our stomachs. Then it was on to Calvi, passing over Villefranche and Cap Ferrat. We touched down at Calvi St Catherine Airport six hours after leaving Gatwick, to be greeted by friends, flowers and the Municipal band.

The friends I had invited took it all in their stride. The paying clients, intrepid pioneers that they were, looked somewhat bewildered and apprehensive. Their adventure – and Horizon's even greater adventure – had begun.

THE CAMP FRANCO-BRITANNIQUE

The Camp Franco-Britannique was just as we had described it in the Horizon brochure – it was, effectively, a smaller version of the Club Olympique. There were tents, a primitive open-air dining room, a sanitary block, a dance floor and a pleasant bar built from bamboo canes. The bar was presided over by Jean Zemette and his companion Christine, whom I had wooed away from the Bar Montana on Paris's Left Bank. Jean and Christine were not employed by the Camp but were concessionaires – having provided the capital for the bar, the dance floor installations, and all the sound equipment. From the word go, the bar was doing a roaring business, especially with my friends who were on the day trip and who were drinking on the house.

Figure 1.2 An early group of Horizon holidaymakers, sheltering from the sun under the wing of their aeroplane, Calvi, 1950.

The handful of paying clients seemed to be settling in and liking the place. At least no one asked to be flown home immediately! Soon, however, it was time for myself and the daytrippers to leave. I would dearly have liked to stay for the first week at least to see how the clients were being treated. I also wanted to see if they would get on with the French holidaymakers at the Camp (of whom there were not many either); to see if the food was of the standard promised in the brochure; and to see if the sun was going to continue shining as brightly as it was doing now – another thing the brochure had guaranteed. But it was imperative to get back to the office to stimulate the booking season. While the high season was looking quite good, the June departures looked dismal.

The next plane to Corsica was two-thirds empty, and the one after that was destined to carry three passengers only. It was, of course, impossible to cancel any flight. Once the series had begun, each aircraft had a return load of passengers to carry.

As the season progressed, it became clear that we were not going to reach the magic target of 350 bookings. On the plus side, however,

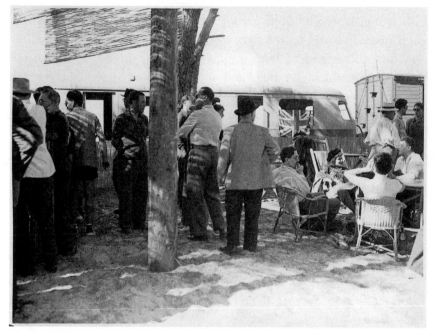

Figure 1.3 An early group of Horizon holidaymakers making themselves at home, Calvi, 1950.

the returning clients were delighted with their holiday. Almost without exception, those who wrote in (and in those early, pioneering days, very many did) said it was the best holiday of their lives and the best value for money they had ever experienced. We replied to these letters, and urged them all to tell their friends.

Meanwhile, there were ominous rumblings from the owners of the Franco-Britannique: they were facing an acute cash crisis. The supply of both British and French clients was way off expectations. Much of the equipment had been bought on the never never, and the chief supplier, a M. François Luciani, was demanding payment and threatening to stop the Camp's food deliveries. I was summoned urgently to Calvi for discussions. At least there was no problem about getting a seat on the plane.

Arriving at the Camp, I could see that the clients, both British and French, were having a fabulous time. The management, though, were wearing gloomy expressions. I was whisked off to the village for a confrontation with Luciani. I told him of the excellent bookings we had for August and September. He was unimpressed. Waving a stack of bills at me, he roared in his strong Corsican accent: 'Qui va me payer ça et quand?' I told him not to worry, that everything would be fine and that, if necessary, fresh capital would be found. He appeared somewhat mollified by this, and our delegation departed. We felt relieved – not knowing what the wily Corsican bandit was planning.

After the meeting with Luciani was over, I spent a curious week at the Club. Half the time I was worrying about finances and the other half I was enjoying the fabulous weather, the superb swimming and the charming café life on the quayside promenade. After dinner at the Club, having consumed a good quantity of the local Patrimonio wine, we would progress to Jean Zemette's speciality drink. It was made of white rum, lime juice, sugar and ice, and he called it a Zem. 'Zemette, encore un Zem,' I would call out, while the latest Edith Piaf number came over the loudspeaker. Needless to say, after a succession of Zems, bookings, supplies, break-even points and even Lucianis were forgotten – only to rear their heads the following morning together with the hangover.

As I flew back to London at the end of the week, the returning clients were full of praise for their fortnight at the Club. Their comments were an enormous satisfaction. By the end of that first season, the position of Horizon Holidays was as follows. The booking target had not been reached: we had fallen about 50 short of our break-even point. The air charter fees had all been paid, as had all other bills for which Horizon was responsible. Connie's salary was secure for another six months. But there was no capital left for next year's operation. As for M. Luciani, his strategy had now become clear. 'As you cannot pay my bills on time,' he informed us, 'I have reluctantly decided to take ownership of the Camp Franco-Britannique Club de l'Horizon.'

TAKEOVER

Luciani did take over the Club, having first secured another investor in the shape of a Polish gentleman as fat and unscrupulous as himself, named Wiszniewski. His name was soon Corsicanized by the locals to Vinceschi. From my point of view, the Luciani–Vinceschi axis, although obnoxious, did at least secure the continuity of the Club without the constant financial crises.

Figure 1.4 Vladimir (left) with Horizon's first handling agent in Calvi – a man of considerable girth named Mr Casanova.

It was Horizon Holidays that was now in a state of cashless anxiety. A brochure for 1951 had to be produced, and working capital had to be found for advertising and the day-to-day running of the office. Even though I was forced to live as frugally as possible, the idea of giving up was never even contemplated. Fortunately, those were the days when every branch of every bank had a Manager to whom one could talk about one's problems. Mr Whitbread, Manager of the Westminster Bank in Lombard Street, was a gentleman of the old school, who had followed the fortunes – or misfortunes – of Horizon throughout 1950. I told him with certainty that the second year of operations would yield enough extra bookings not only to break even but to make a profit. He kindly agreed to a £2000 credit line – and that without collateral.

His faith in the company was vindicated. Four hundred and twenty bookings were achieved that year, with the Pike family being the first in line. We were still using the same aircraft company, the same itinerary, the same teacher/student clause. The only difference was a small hike in the price of a holiday, from £32 10s to £35 10s. This was due to an increase imposed by Luciani and Vinceschi.

By the end of 1951, Horizon's modest success had yielded enough surplus cash to enable me to look forward with some confidence. At the same time, there was a revolutionary change in the licensing of air routes. No longer did you have to apply to the Ministry of Civil Aviation. The newly installed Conservative government had set up the Air Transport Advisory Council (ATAC), with the genial Lord Terrington as its first chairman. The council met in a sparsely furnished room overlooking Dean's Yard next door to Westminster Abbey – handy for a quick prayer before putting one's case before Lord T. and five or six members of his committee.

ATAC functioned in a most informal manner, quite unlike the procedures of its successor, the Civil Aviation Administration. The applicants for air licences sat around a table with the council members. Smoking was permitted, and jovial banter was the order of the day. Few, if any, applicants were legally represented, and even the objectors to the granting of licences (usually British European Airways) were on the friendliest of terms with the applicants. The best news for Horizon was the abolition of the student/teacher clause. This was the breakthrough the company had been waiting for. It would obviously revolutionize the whole concept of marketing the holidays, especially as far as advertising was concerned. But it would also, I knew, attract the attention of the large, established travel companies like Thomas Cook, Polytechnic, Sir Henry Lunn, Global and others, as well as newcomers who would sense opportunities.

Another change was that there were now considerable numbers of aircraft available for charter, chasing – at that time – few takers. In fact, the supply of planes outstripped demand to such an extent that many of the small airlines were going out of business. They included, much to my regret, Air Transport Charter (Channel Islands) Ltd, who had given such sterling service to Horizon in its first two years of operation.

Levi-Tilley, the air broker, soon came up with a replacement. It was a new company that operated two DC3s and one Viking, the latter being pressurized and thus able to fly twice as high as the Dakota although still at roughly the same speed. This company, with which Horizon was to work for many years, was called BKS. The initials stood for the three partners: Barnby, Keegan and Stevens. Captain Stevens, a former chief pilot, was Managing Director. Many years later, BKS was absorbed into British Airways.

When Captain Stevens and I went to the first joint hearing before ATAC, two applications were submitted: Calvi and Palma de Mallorca. As soon as the government liberalization policy had been announced, I had made a quick trip to Majorca to look at a hotel in the north-west corner that had been recommended to me. It was run by a colourful and highly unconventional Englishwoman named Noreen Harbord: a woman who worked hard, but played and drank even harder. It was called the Hotel Costa Brava. I made a provisional contract with the hotel, subject to the air licence being granted. Much Spanish brandy and 'champagne' was consumed in anticipation of a successful season.

British European Airways opposed both applications on the grounds of 'material diversion of traffic'. This despite the fact that BEA still did not fly to Corsica. It did not even fly to Palma. The nearest airport to Palma it flew to was Barcelona. ATAC thankfully ruled BEA's objection as unreasonable, and granted Horizon a seven year licence to each of the two airports. (This was the first and only occasion on which a seven year licence was ever granted for an inclusive tour. After that, the standard form was for licences to be granted for one year only.)

So 1952 found Horizon taking holidaymakers to Corsica and Majorca. Not all of our clients found Noreen's exuberance and salty language exactly their cup of tea, but the vast majority of them enjoyed their Majorca holidays. There was a young engaged couple who had insisted on booking two single rooms. On arrival, they were told by Noreen not to be 'so bloody silly', and to anticipate their forthcoming nuptials in a room with a large double bed. 'They'll have a great time, and it'll help me with my room problem,' she told me. Noreen was years ahead of her time. It was she who called our clients 'the Horizontals' to their faces, and regaled them with tales of her amorous experiences, and of the time she spent in prison after being caught with an ex-lover, a racing driver, smuggling watches from Switzerland into the UK.

In Calvi, meanwhile, a revolution was in progress. Jean and Christine Zemette had had a bitter quarrel with the new owners of the Club, threatening to pull out of the operation, taking their bar equipment with them. I too was getting fed up of Luciani and Vinceschi. Greedy to make more money, the standard of the food they were providing was slipping constantly. Also, I felt it was time to provide better accommodation than US Army tents. So I encouraged the Zemettes to raise a loan from the Crédit Hotelier, a semi-government agency, and buy some land in a beautiful spot on rocky terrain on the other side of the Citadel. There, they should build a series of wooden bungalows and call this camp 'The Chalets Tamaris', after the tamarisk shrubs that grew there in profusion.

When I told Luciani and Vinceschi that the deal with the Club Franco-Britannique was over, their reaction was one of disbelief. They thought it was merely a ploy to get the food improved. When they finally realized I was earnest, their fury was something to behold. Their chief ire, however, was not directed at me but at the Zemettes, for having 'betrayed' them by setting up in opposition. Another part of the Calvi saga was over.

The following year, 1953, was one of consolidation. Calvi was now served by two flights a week, to fill the Chalets Tamaris – which relied exclusively on a British clientele. Noreen's hotel in Puerto de Soller received just one 36-seater Viking load each week, as she could accommodate no more than 72 clients. From the financial point of view, the high load factor achieved for both destinations (about 90 per cent) meant that it was a great year. There was now capital available to hire extra staff, and to rent an additional room in 146 Fleet Street. The stage was set for 1954 – a breakthrough year.

EXPANSION

Horizon Holidays now had to find other resorts in order to expand upon a formula which appeared to have great promise. To stand still at that time would have been fatal, especially since competition from the established companies as well as newcomers was becoming increasingly inevitable. For the first four years, we had had the field to ourselves. It couldn't last.

The new destinations I had in mind were Sardinia and the Costa Brava, which ran from the French-Spanish frontier to within about 100 miles of Barcelona. Sardinia, a region of Italy with semi-autonomous status, had been the granary of Ancient Rome. It had fallen on hard times in the last few centuries, as the population had been decimated by malaria. But in 1946, a joint programme by UNRRA and the Rockefeller Foundation carried out a huge, vastly expensive mosquito-

Figure 1.5 Horizon's first air service to Sardinia, 1954. A local girl (left) presented each passenger with a bouquet of flowers. On the right is Doris Jones of Tewkesbury, in the centre is air hostess Joyce Ambler.

killing operation which had totally eradicated the disease. The island was now ready to receive tourists. One of our Calvi clients had recently returned from Sardinia and he too thought it was a logical extension for Horizon. He was an able and forceful barrister named John Parris, who was to make his name in the famous murder trial of Craig and Bentley.

The town we picked in Sardinia was Alghero: on the north-west of the island, it was a delightful port with many ancient buildings, a lovely sandy beach, and just enough hotel accommodation for one planeload per week. I signed it up immediately I went to the island, at the end of the 1953 season. Horizon was to popularize Sardinia many years before the Aga Khan launched his Costa Smeralda development on the north-east coast of the island.

As for the Costa Brava on mainland Spain, it was not easily accessible from any Spanish airport. The road from Barcelona was terrible – the motorways which now criss-cross Spain were still many years off. The modern airport in Gerona would not be constructed for another six or seven years. The most ideal entry point seemed to be Perpignan airport in France. It took some time to convince ATAC, and especially the French Civil Aviation authorities, to allow Spanish holidays for British clients to arrive at a French airport. Fortunately, Perpignan airport at that time was as busy as an outdoor pool in January, and the Commandant there welcomed the Horizon initiative with enthusiasm. A French coach company was equally keen, and promised that we could make the journey to the Costa Brava in two hours. Our two chosen resorts were Tossa de Mar and San Feliu de Guixols: sleepy little fishing villages with magnificent beaches and very few hotels.

It was not easy to explain the concept of a back-to-back charter to the local hotel owners.

'You see, Señor, the plane arrives with a load of holidaymakers. They come to your hotel in the same coach which, a few hours earlier, has taken your departing guests to the airport. So, you see, you will never have a gap between the parties.' It was lucky that I spoke Spanish.

It was exhilarating and immensely satisfying to go to new resorts, where the locals had no concept whatsoever of this form of tourism. I signed up their hotels, and added further arrangements to Horizon's ever-growing roster. As Wordsworth had said in a somewhat different context:

> Bliss was it in that dawn to be alive
> But to be young was very heaven!

I was 31 at the time – presumably I could still call myself young.

2

The Pre-history of Tourism

ROGER BRAY

Resorts with no concept of tourism? For those familiar with today's busy Mediterranean resorts they may be hard to imagine. In the second year of Vladimir's new adventure, only two million Britons travelled abroad on holiday, by train, car and scheduled airline services. As the new millennium arrived, that figure was closer to 30 million – which included package holidays by charter aircraft.

Perversely, Corsica has remained one of the places in which it is easiest to picture the tourist world of the early 1950s. True, it has moved on from 1936, when Eugene Fodor's guide noted that the island had only just been cleared of bandits and warned that it remained, 'considering its inaccessibility, one of the most backward spots in Europe from the point of view of luxurious accommodation for travellers'. But there are still resorts untouched by high rise development which are remarkably quiet when the French have returned to work at the end of August, and peaceful beaches where it is possible to be alone and which can be reached only by clambering over rocks or getting one's legs scratched in the remorseless maquis.

It was Spain, to which the young Vladimir turned his attention in 1954, which proved the most fertile ground for the package holiday revolution. Try to imagine, as you drive down the main coastal road from Malaga to Marbella, how it looked fifty years ago. Then, the country's Mediterranean littoral was much as it had been for centuries. There were hardly any hotels. The sea lapped and sucked at dreaming, empty beaches, unviolated by roasting sunbathers and noisy jet skiers. Fishermen went after shoals in boats painted with an eye on the prow, to ward off malign spirits. In small, dark bars, behind beaded curtains which prevented flies from buzzing through open doors, Andalusian guitarists of sublime dexterity plucked and strummed with no inkling even of the looming tidal wave of rock and roll, let alone the pulsing strobe lights and mechanical beats of a later generation. And in the evenings, on dusky promenades, the daily *paseo* remained a bashful rite of courtship, boys following breathless girls until their passions were silently declared with no sunburnt, skimpily dressed British or German alternatives, caution loosened by cheap alcohol and the heady escape from dreary jobs, to divert their intentions and provide release from stifled sexual desires.

Foreign women daring to venture out in revealing clothes would have found their holidays quickly terminated. Spain was in the firm grip of General Francisco Franco's dictatorship, and, for some years to come, to dress indiscreetly away from the beach was to risk arrest by the pervasive Guardia Civil. It was little more than a decade since Mussolini's Italian troops, sent to aid Franco's Nationalist cause, had marched into what is now the important tourist centre of Alicante at the end of a civil war of extreme atrocity, which had divided families and friends and channelled all the polemic of twentieth-century politics – fascism, republicanism, communism, anarchy – into a bloody conflict which has been estimated to have cost over 400,000 lives. In Barcelona the Catalan language and the stately dance known as the *sardana*, which visitors may now see performed in quiet squares, were banned. The pornography currently on plain view on the Ramblas was unthinkable and the handbag snatchers who spoil tourists' innocent pleasure today simply did not exist. Indeed, even as late as the mid-1960s, regular visitors to Spain claimed you could leave a wallet on a café table and return, hours later, to find it still there.

How did the great change come about? It cannot simply have been, as Vladimir is inclined to believe, that Britain was fed up with the grief of war and the rationing which lingered on after it. And there must have been more to it than the fact that Britons had travelled abroad to fight, and were anxious to do so in peacetime, which has been suggested as one prime motive by Vladimir's great rival Tom Gullick, founder of the huge but ill-fated Clarksons Holidays operation. There is some truth in both theories but, more likely, there was a cocktail of reasons. Holidays with pay had been introduced in 1938, but the opportunity to enjoy them had been nipped cruelly in the bud by Hitler's invasion of Poland. The Education Act of 1944 raised the school leaving age to 15 (in 1947) and resulted in a burgeoning of grammar schools, which raised the aspirations of a whole new stratum of society. Though its impact has probably been exaggerated by some observers, the melting pot of conflict had undoubtedly helped to erode class barriers. Demand for labour created greater bargaining power for workers immediately after the war, pushing up their wages sharply. In 1954, the Tory Chancellor, R. A. Butler envisaged Britain doubling its standard of living in 25 years, and three years later Harold Macmillan, in an often misquoted speech, was telling the electorate that 'most of our people have never had it so good'. Between 1955 and 1960, average weekly earning, including overtime, rose by 34 per cent, while retail prices increased by only 15 per cent. Television – particularly commercial television which encouraged the 'live now pay later' society – fanned the flames of longing for destinations more exotic than the British seaside. And into this general atmosphere of opportunity, the feeling that suddenly, anything was possible for any members of society, from any background, burst the rise of youth culture and the sexual revolution of the 1960s. By 1959 a survey was noting that teenagers spent an average of 4s 6d a week (just over £11 a year) on holidays – or 7 per cent of their total annual expenditure. That compared with 6s 10d a week (about £17.50 a year in today's decimal currency) on cigarettes, 4s 3d on going to the cinema and 3s 10d on alcohol. Research the following year showed that teenagers represented one in ten of British European Airways' customers.

The other reasons for the travel boom were technological, rather than purely social. It took 66 days for the Pilgrim Fathers to reach Cape Cod in 1620. The first transatlantic Cunarder, the 1135 ton wooden paddle steamer *Britannia*, on which Charles Dickens sailed when he went to America in 1842, took 14 days. Passengers got fresh food for the first three days, he wrote 'and thereafter the fish and meat is salted. *Britannia* has two ice rooms and the fruit is stored there. At least we are sure of avoiding scurvy.' By 1924, the Zeppelin LZ126 airship had crossed from Friedrichshafen in Germany to Lakehurst, New Jersey non-stop in three and a half days. By 1936, the *Queen Mary*, a long time holder of the Blue Riband for the fastest Atlantic crossing, was making the trip in just under five days.

But while those who ran the shipping lines may have hoped against hope that it would not happen, may even have buried their heads in the sand, passenger liners were threatened already with the fate of the dinosaurs. The following year saw what was, for them, an ominous event, when the de Havilland Albatross flew for the first time. It carried 22 passengers on 1000 mile stages at a cruising speed of 210 mph but its real significance was as forerunner to the Lockheed Constellation. The beautiful Constellation, with its characteristic curved back and its four 2200 hp Wright engines, which could carry 45 passengers in pressurized luxury at 260 mph for 3000 miles, was to revolutionize north Atlantic travel. In June 1946, BOAC's first 'Connie' flew from New York to London in 11 hours 24 minutes, putting paid to the era of flying boats, which made the first scheduled commercial flights in 1939.

Advances in transport technology were quickened by the need to defeat Germany and Japan. Demobilization left large numbers of surplus bombers and transport planes, which could be acquired cheaply and turned into passenger aircraft. Pan American, for example, bought 45 C54 land planes which were slow and unpressurized but offered transatlantic capability. They included the Halifax bomber which was converted into a peacetime workhorse, able to carry ten passengers and called the Halton. The Avro Lancastrian, a version of the Lancaster, the aircraft flown by the Dambusters, slashed the journey time from Britain to Sydney, Australia from nine days to just 63 hours.

THE DEVELOPMENT OF LEISURE TRAVEL

But we are running ahead of ourselves. Where did leisure travel begin? It is not the intention of this book to look in any depth at the distant past but nothing in history begins or ends abruptly and to gain a full appreciation of the astonishing expansion of tourism in the past half century it is useful to consider how slowly it had grown until then.

There is some evidence that wealthy Romans and Greeks visited the Pyramids of Egypt for pleasure. In the Middle Ages, it seems logical that pilgrimages to great cathedrals, such as that at Santiago de Compostela in northern Spain, were also stimulated partly by a desire to see extraordinary works of architecture massively bigger than anything which existed where most people lived. Originally ordered as penance for the expiation of sins or undertaken in the hope of a miracle cure, pilgrimages appear to have metamorphosed into an early form of escape, interludes in a dreary existence. Chaucer captured some of this early feeling of release in the prelude to his *Canterbury Tales* whose opening sees the coming of April, with its 'sweet showers' stirring restlessness in medieval souls. Certainly pilgrimages stimulated the growth of souvenir sales, a phenomenon more readily associated with the modern T-shirt and Flamenco doll, for pilgrims brought home badges as mementos of their trips: the scallop shell of St James with a face at the narrow end, for example, or a metal moulding of St Michael slaying the dragon.

The pilgrimage period, which petered out with Henry VIII's dissolution of the monasteries, was still going strong in the fourteenth century, when a Venetian, Agostino Contarini, provided what could be seen as an early package tour, laying on transport to the Holy Land and back for 60 ducats a day, or around £3000 at today's currency values (Brendon 1991). Early tourists sought not only the curative power of saints but the healing power of spa waters. Kaiser Friedrich III is recorded as visiting Bad Gastein in Austria's Salzburg province, though it was Paracelsus, who knew the place well, who carried out the first analysis of its spring water in the early sixteenth century.

Travel may also have been stimulated by Renaissance painters, who depicted lush landscape and mountains as the background for religious subjects. It has been argued that this encouraged an interest in the Alps which had been suppressed by fears of deep cold, avalanche and the suspicion that fearsome beasts lurked there, fears reflected in surviving folk custom, such as the grotesque masks worn at the Gasteiner Perchten festival in Austria's Gastein Valley.

In 1724, Daniel Defoe published the first volume of his *A Tour Through the Whole Island of Great Britain*. It was described on the title page as 'A particular and Diverting Account of whatever is Curious and worth Observation', which was 'Particularly fitted for the Reading of such as desire to Travel over the Island'. It may have been a forerunner of later travel books containing a certain artistic licence, for some have questioned whether he really visited all the places described.

By then the Grand Tour was reaching its peak of popularity, largely as a means of bashing some culture into young, aristocratic brains.

Many of these travellers resented being dragged around the churches and palaces of Italy with their tutors, known as 'bear leaders'. Itineraries foreshadowed those later, hectic American tours of Europe, which prompted the 1969 film: *If it's Tuesday, this must be Belgium*, whose stars included Suzanne Pleshette and whose plot followed the adventures and mishaps of just such a whistle-stop holiday group. Samuel Johnson observed that the Grand Tourist, in a rush to take in as many sights as possible, left with 'a confused remembrance of palaces and churches'. Already there were businessmen arranging group tours, but the phenomenon came to an abrupt halt with the French Revolution.

Sea bathing became popular, not least through the example of George III, who went to Weymouth in Dorset and was made cross, so the story goes, because the white horse subsequently carved into the hillside at Osmington, showed him riding out of town, rather than into it. The word 'hotel' appeared in the English language in 1765.

The defeat of Napoleon and the arrival of steamers across the English Channel brought a sharp increase in tourism in the nineteenth century, though the proportion of those going abroad (still an activity for the wealthy) was probably only about one in 200 against today's figure of over 50 per cent. These tourists drew on the services of the courier, an early equivalent of the travel agent, whom John Ruskin described as an important figure who knew the best hotels on a route and the choicest rooms in them – and opened the eyes of travellers to sights of interest along the way. The courier ran ahead of coaches to book accommodation, checking the guest list for eminent names at high class establishments such as the Drei Konige in Basle and the Albergo Svizzero in Lugano. The fact that couriers also steered lady travellers towards the best shopping en route suggests that, like their modern counterparts, they were adept at raking off commission.

Rail travel

It was the coming of the railways which brought the next – and thus far the biggest – explosion in travel. Until then the only way to cut journey times had been to improve roads and change coach horses regularly. In 1844, the number of foreign guests at the inn which had been built on the Rigi, an already famous mountaintop viewpoint in central Switzerland, was 1589. Following the opening of a railway line to Basle the total in 1852 had jumped by around one third, to 2199 (Bernard 1978).

From station hotels to resorts, the railways created new demand for accommodation. Sometimes hotels were constructed simply to persuade more passengers to ride the rails. William Cornelius Van Horne, who became vice president of the Canadian Pacific Line in the 1880s is credited with telling colleagues: 'Since we can't export the scenery, we'll have to import the tourists'. As early as 1883 he was urging the creation of a national park in the Rocky Mountains, east of Banff in Alberta – a wish which was fulfilled four years later. And in 1888 the opening of the Banff Springs, later re-built as a Scottish baronial castle but then described by one guest as 'something like the combination of a Tudor hall and Swiss chalet', gave passengers somewhere grand to stay.

The railways, or more specifically, the Midland Counties Railway Line between Leicester and Derby, prompted what is often seen as the real genesis of mass tourism – Thomas Cook's decision in 1841 to drum up enthusiasm for the temperance movement by organizing an excursion (from Leicester to Loughborough for one shilling and sixpence, including a 'ham tea') as a healthier alternative to drink. This could be seen as ironic, in view of the role played by cheap alcohol in attracting later generations to Spain. Cook, a printer, was 33 and had been a Baptist preacher. In 1855 he took his first groups abroad, sailing from Harwich and visiting cities including Brussels, Cologne, Heidelberg and Paris. Eight years later, he was organizing trips to Paris via Newhaven and Dieppe. A new rail link created extensions from the French capital to Switzerland opening the way for a wave of tourism to the Alps.

Thomas's son John Mason Cook, whose initials are now the name of a major holiday brand operated by the company, was more entrepreneurial than moral. He expanded the business and by 1868 the firm was claiming to have organized travel for some two million people. He introduced vouchers, which were sold for 8 shillings (40p) and entitled the purchaser to a night's accommodation, two meals and service. The idea was not so very different from today's system of holiday deposits, in that the vouchers brought the benefit of cash flow before hoteliers had to be paid.

Hotels

The nineteenth century saw the birth of a galaxy of great hotels such as Raffles in Singapore and Shepheard's in Cairo. Richard d'Oyly Carte, a flautist's son turned theatrical impresario teamed up with W. S. Gilbert and Arthur Sullivan to launch London's Savoy Theatre in 1881 with a performance of *Patience*. Having observed the success of hotels such as the Palace in San Francisco and the increasing number of Americans coming to Britain, he opened the Savoy Hotel in 1889 (a double room then cost 12 shillings (60p). It had 70 bathrooms, which prompted the builder to wonder whether d'Oyly Carte expected his guests to be amphibious. Two years later came the opening of Reid's in Madeira, where early visitors were carried in hammocks, which they hired at rates from £5 10s a month and which were 'most ably handled by muscular and gentle bearers, to the great advantage of delicate people, who are thus enabled to spend their entire days in passive, unfatiguing exercise' (Weaver 1991).

Between the wars

Between the First and Second World Wars, the growth of mass travel was clearly impeded by the Depression, yet the internal combustion engine began to affect travel habits in a way which was to prove more dramatic even than the growth of railways. Even in 1939, less than half the British population (Taylor 1965) left home even for one night, but the number of private cars registered had soared from under 200,000 in 1920 to some two million. The car was no longer just a plaything of the rich, though the many people who did not have or could not afford cars got their first taste of travel on a charabanc or open topped bus.

Only a few had the wherewithal to travel abroad. In 1932, Imperial Airways started offering sixteen-day air cruises – including hotels and first class sleeping compartments on the train from Paris – to Brindisi in Italy. From there, passengers went by Kent flying boat to Athens, Castelrosso and Galilee, with side excursions to Damascus and Jerusalem. They continued to Cairo and after four days in Egypt flew via Crete to Athens and returned from there to London. The price was £80, an immense sum in real terms compared to the amount now charged for a Nile cruise package.

But while foreign travel remained an indulgence mainly of the middle classes, by the 1930s its magnetism was now slowly drawing in entrepreurs from humbler backgrounds. In 1934, the Cape Town-born Billy Butlin first had the idea of building a holiday camp which would draw together all the attractions he had observed at similar establishments in Canada, including swimming, entertainment and funfairs. Two years later he bought 40 acres of land at Skegness for £3000, built his first camp and advertised it at £500 for a half page in the *Daily Express*. Within a few days he had received over 10,000 enquiries. It opened on Easter Saturday with a sign at reception saying 'Our true intent is all for your delight' – a quotation from *A Midsummer's Night Dream*. An all inclusive holiday cost between 35 shillings and £3 a week, depending on the season. Dan Maskell, later the BBC's commentating voice of Wimbledon, coached campers at tennis. Joe Davis demonstrated snooker techniques. The singer Gracie Fields made a guest appearance as entertainer. Butlin's proved percipient.

At that time, only about three million Britons had holidays with pay but in 1938 Parliament passed an act which gave a week's paid annual leave to all industrial workers. Confident that this would happen, Butlin opened a second camp, at Clacton in Essex. He used the slogan: 'Holidays with pay: holidays with play. A week's holiday for a week's wage'. In 1939, when some 11 million Britons had holidays with pay, his two camps drew almost 100,000 customers.

Harry Chandler

In the same year that Butlin had his inspiration, a young Harry Chandler took his first trip abroad. When he told workmates he was planning to take his bicycle across the Channel they 'started off being impressed but then pulled my leg unmercifully, because the idea of a kid like me taking a holiday "on the continong" just like the swells was absolutely ridiculous' (Chandler 1985).

Harry, who later founded a successful tour operation still called the Travel Club of Upminster and who, as a leading light in the creation of financial protection for package holidaymakers, will figure frequently in this story, was an East End boy who had started cycling to get away

Figure 2.1 Harry Chandler.

from it. In 1934, aged 21 and in a state of high excitement, he set sail with a friend from London for Hamburg on a Russian ship called the *Co-operazia*. From Hamburg they spent some of their savings on a flight by Heinkel He70 to Berlin. It was the start of a lifelong love affair with travel which saw Harry largely responsible for the development of the Portuguese Algarve to mass tourism.

It was in the following year, 1935, that Harry stumbled on a wheeze for getting free holidays, which was to change his life. He bumped into some Britons holidaying with the Workers' Travel Association, an offshoot of the trade union movement, at Schwangau in Bavaria. He went to another pension in the village, got a rate of 6 shillings for room and full board, negotiated a 25 per cent discount on the rail fare – and a free place if he took fifteen people. He advertised, attracted only five customers and had to pay the full whack. The lesson for an embryonic tour operator was the same as it is now: you have to get the load factor up. But his clients, disappointingly few though they were, went anyway.

Harry's breakthrough came, oddly, when he made a speech to members of his Old School Association at Stratford in the East End. They were not the sort of people who felt they could afford holidays abroad but he told them they could. Unwittingly he had stumbled upon another *sine qua non* of the package travel business – a good mailing list. Gradually the bookings began to flow in.

For ten guineas customers got third class rail travel between London and Augsburg, ferry crossings and full board in Schwangau. Later, he offered second class travel at a supplement of £2 10 shillings. A brochure followed. He began to organize excursions. In 1939 he was selling holidays to Sarnen, some twenty miles south of Lucerne in Switzerland. Harry guaranteed that if the man who ran the local horse drawn post buses would buy a 30 seat motor coach, he would provide enough tourists to make it worthwhile. It was an early example of the way the package holiday industry would become inextricably intertwined with business interests in European holiday destinations, making and losing fortunes for those abroad who became caught up in it, affecting the economic destinies of towns, regions and whole countries.

After the war

The war put everything on hold. On New Year's Day, 1946, the ban on civilian flying was lifted, but while Britain may have been nursing a pent-up desire to travel, the omens for a mass holiday exodus were hardly auspicious. In 1947, following Prime Minister Clement Atlee's warning of 'peril and anxiety' over Britain's inability to pay her import bill, the country found itself in the grip of a severe austerity clampdown. Ration books would need to be used at hotels after a two night stay, motoring for pleasure was stopped, foreign holidays were banned and business travellers going abroad were limited to £8 spending money a day. Thomas Cook, about to fall into the hands of the state as a result of the nationalization of its railway company owners, was forced to restrict its outbound foreign holiday business to the sterling area. Though the foreign travel ban was lifted early in 1948, there was a further setback the following year, with a sharp devaluation of sterling.

Yet there were growing signs that despite its stuttering reluctance, the engine of tourism was about to roar into life. Harry Chandler had started selling holidays again in 1947. Many of those on his original mailing list had been bombed out but his razor sharp business brain came up with an alternative. As an army captain he had been appointed military forwarding officer in Singapore. That made him responsible for arranging the homeward passage of prisoners who had suffered in the notorious Japanese Changi camp there. He collected the names and addresses of officers. Now he sent them details of his trips. In those immediate post-war days, many of his clients were still starved of rich food, but when they reached Basle station in Switzerland, they were confronted with a full eggs and bacon breakfast. So many were sick as a result of this sudden treat that Harry had to agree a fee of one franc per victim with station staff – to cover the cost of cleaning up.

By 1949, BEA was already test flying the turbo-prop Vickers Viscount, which made its first flight for fare payers on 29 July 1950 from Northolt to Paris and its newly appointed chief executive, the young Peter (later Sir Peter) Masefield, who was to become one of the grand old men and great gurus of transport, was predicting that the airline's fare of sevenpence halfpenny a mile would tumble dramatically, to fourpence, within five years – a huge fall in real terms.

The cheapest New York-London round trip in the year that Vladimir visited the Club Olympique was US$466 – or US$630 in high season – at rates agreed by members of the International Air Transport Association and rigorously adhered to. Despite the inflation that has raged since then, in 2000 it was possible to buy a return ticket from London for at least $150 less. The main reason carriers clung to common fares was the paucity of services. A passenger flying out with one airline often needed to return with another – and neither was anxious to see its share of the revenue dragged down by discounting. Airlines had already experimented with return tickets which cost less than the sum of two singles, and discounts for passengers who travelled at night. But it was not until 1950 that they agreed to offer the first economy class seats, with some airlines offering less leg room and abandoning lavish service in favour of simple tray meals.

It was to be many years before the advent of the Boeing 747 and the chill wind of open skies produced today's bargain fares – but the door had creaked open an important inch or two. It would never be pushed shut again.

REFERENCES

Brendon, P. (1991) *Thomas Cook: 150 Years of Popular Tourism*.
Weaver, H. J. (1991) *Reid's Hotel: Jewel of the Atlantic*.
Jackson, S. (1989) *The Savoy: a Century of Taste*.
Bernard, P. P. (1978) *Rush to the Alps*.
Taylor, A. J. P. (1965) *English History 1914–1945*.
Chandler, H. (1985) *Chandler's Travels*, written with John Carter.

3

The 1950s

ROGER BRAY

It is doubtful that anyone, at the dawn of the 1950s, truly foresaw the imminent, mushroom growth of mass travel. A survey by the *Daily Herald* newspaper showed that, in 1952, only half the British population took any kind of holiday and that of those who did, a tiny 3 per cent went abroad. But Vladimir was not the only British entrepreneur poised, unwittingly, on the brink of becoming an air tour operator. Captain Ted Langton, had just turned 30 when he entered the travel business between the wars, setting up a firm called Happiways in his home town of Southport, Lancashire with a capital outlay of £500. It was the result of a conversation in a Liverpool pub, in which a coach operator was complaining that business was painfully slow. Langton asked how much he would charge to provide a coach for the whole summer. He then scoured the West Country for hotels and guest houses similarly in need of business. Thus was born a concept adopted by the package tour business – with coaches taking customers from the north to Devon and Cornwall and bringing home those who had completed their holidays. A one week break – Happiways offered packages to Scotland, too – started at just under £5 a week. The business expanded healthily, and in 1933 he decided to start operating tours to Ostend and Paris. He formed a coach company in Belgium called Les Cars Bleus, to carry customers on the continent. This firm was known in Britain as Blue Cars.

Figure 3.1   An early Sky Tours brochure of 1959.

UNIVERSAL SKY TOURS

By 1950, Langton was 'fed up' with Blue Cars and was eyeing new possibilities in tour operating. He sold the firm to the British Electric

Traction Company for £234,000, and three years later launched what was to become a long lasting and, though the name has been truncated, surviving brand in package tour operating: Universal Sky Tours.

His technique, an associate said later, was to offer to take beds in a hotel for an entire season and then repeatedly chisel away at the price. If the hotelier refused to concede, Langton would simply take his business elsewhere.

When Universal Sky Tours took wing in 1953, the whole of Britain seemed engrossed by preparations for the Queen's Coronation. Millions of children yet to travel abroad made models of the royal coach and its horses and brought home commemorative mugs from school. Thousands bought their first television sets to watch the great event, even though it could be seen only in black and white. Across the Atlantic, President-to-be John F. Kennedy married Jacqueline Bouvier at Newport, Rhode Island but Senator Joseph McCarthy's witch hunt of alleged Communists cast a paranoid shadow across America. Everest was conquered, Stalin died of a cerebral hemorrhage. The Korean War armistice was signed but the French battled on in Vietnam. Ford launched the Popular, a cut price version of the Anglia, which sold for £390 and was reckoned to be the world's cheapest four cylinder car. But while families celebrated their new ability to afford wheels, those who had welcomed the passenger jet age a year earlier, when BOAC operated its first scheduled flight by Comet, were given gloomy cause for concern. May 1953 brought the third Comet crash in eight months. The airliner went down near Calcutta and all 43 people on board were killed.

THE GROWTH OF AIR TRAVEL

The first edition of the industry newspaper, *Travel Trade Gazette*, was published on 20 March, 1953, leading its front page with a story that new tourist fares to Europe were to come into effect on 1 April. BEA expected this to result in a 25 per cent rise in traffic. Only three first class services to the Continent would remain – one of them the Air France Epicurean Service to Paris, operated daily in each direction using DC 4s. That year, Pan Am announced it would no longer require tourist class passengers to buy meal vouchers on its transatlantic flights.

Figure 3.2 A BOAC Comet, the first jet airliner.

With the agreement of IATA, it would charge an extra £1 15s on the London–New York route – where the fare would be £98 5s single – and include the provision of hot meals in the ticket price.

Following a recommendation from the Government's Air Transport Advisory Council, the Ministry of Transport granted Silver City Airways permission to launch passenger and car carrying services between London and Le Touquet, but independent airlines faced a struggle of almost Sisyphean proportions against the state owned BEA (British European Airways) and BOAC (British Overseas Airways Corporation) which, much later, merged to become British Airways. The bulk of their business was still transporting troops. The Government had set out broad policy for civil aviation, indicating that there were glittering prizes to be won by privately owned carriers but statistics suggested that laying hands on them was rather like grasping soap in the bath. In its report for 1952–3, the British Independent Air Transport Association recorded that of 171 route applications by its members, only 78 – plus another eight for flights as part of inclusive tours – were approved.

Conservative though the state airlines may have appeared, they were also experimenting with the extension of travel to a broader public. But they lacked confidence that cheaper travel would attract the mass market. In 1952, European carriers belonging to the International Air Transport Association agreed to introduce tourist class seats at reduced fares. These fares were significantly lower than the best previously available. Those between the UK and Italy were cut by 20–25 per cent, for example. Ticket prices to Spain dropped by 18-21 per cent, to France by 16-21 per cent, to Switzerland by 20 per cent and to Malta by 32 per cent. Some airline executives argued that the changes fell between two stools. As Per Norlin, then president of SAS (Scandinavian Airlines System) noted in 1953: 'The low fare, high density scheme has not been the success expected in European Traffic. The reason for that seems to be that the traffic potential in Europe is not as big as in the United States and that the rate reduction for tourist class in Europe has been too small to reach a broader market. On several routes, only tourist class has been available to the public. The result is that that passengers who have been prepared to pay for a first class ticket have been forced to travel tourist class.' Airlines, he lamented, had been getting less money from passengers ready to part with more. Swissair reported complaints for customers who wanted more comfort. But its president, Walter Berchtold, accepted the inevitability of change: 'Once you have started tourist service, it is difficult to stop it'. This acceptance led his airline to experiment with a seating layout which became standard – offering luxury and tourist cabins on the same aircraft. SAS also introduced 'Combined Class' services. As a flavour of the times, it is worth noting that, as late as 1954, it was still offering a 'toilet lounge' with two dressing tables for first class customers on its London–Stavanger run.

BEA, in contrast, described the new tourist fares as a 'real success'. Its overall passenger traffic soared by 34.7 per cent in June, 1953, compared with the same month the year before. But it agreed that, as a consequence, airlines had not mounted sufficient first class capacity to meet demand.

Foreign exchange allowances for travellers, which had existed since 1945, were still restricted. There was pressure from the trade to get it raised to £35. Such was the pent-up demand for travel that it was estimated this might add £5million to tourist spending abroad in a full year. The pressure paid off. The Government raised the adult limit to

£40 and doubled the child allowance to £30. It was a momentous decision. Agents rubbed their hands in glee. Swans reported an instant rush of customers trying to rearrange their holidays to incorporate more costly itineraries. More British would visit Spain, travel firms predicted – and more would venture away from the Costas to explore inland areas. One company, WTA of London, said people were extending their trips and upgrading to better hotels. Easons of Grimsby reported customers asking for more excursions during their holidays.

The young industry found this upsurge in business hard to handle. A TTG leader writer noted: 'The nightmare of the extended holiday produced by the increase in the travel allowance has been exorcised by the ingenuity of the travel booking clerk'. How? In many instances, customers had been diverted by advice to spend a bit more on drinks and entertainment instead.

But the charter airline business was still in its infancy. The move had only a marginal impact on the rates it could charge, which hardened a little to 6s 6d per mile for Dakotas and from11s to 11s 6d for Avro Yorks.

In April a BOAC Comet broke the record for a flight to Tokyo in 74 hours 45 minutes. Chairman Sir Miles Thomas said the next step would be jets across the Atlantic but first there would have to be trials without passengers. North Atlantic weather was notorious and very little was known yet about flying conditions above 30,000–40,000 feet (9000–12,000 metres).

THE GROWTH OF TRAVEL COMPANIES

The term 'brochure' was not yet in common use but travel company 'books', as they were usually called, were already putting on weight. Cook's wintersports programme for 1953-4, for example, ran to 120 pages and Sir Henry Lunn's covered over 100 resorts in 72 pages. Sex, in the shape of bikini clad cover girls, was not yet used as a marketing magnet, although, by the following year, Eagle Aviation advertisements pictured the reigning Miss Sweden, 'lovely Ulla Sandklef', wearing a demurely cleavage-covering dress. She had been taken on as the regular air hostess on the airline's twice weekly London–Gothenburg service. Though some of today's airline advertising still exploits the image of the beautiful stewardess, the copy writing which was accepted nearly a half century ago now seems excruciatingly unsubtle: 'Businessmen will need no second bidding to find good reasons for regular visits to Gothenburg. Probably their wives will insist on accompanying them!'

HAROLD BAMBERG

Eagle, later to become British Eagle, had been founded by another man who was to make a giant impact on the travel industry – Harold Bamberg. In the summer of 1953, he began operating aerial cruises around the Mediterranean. It was a suggestion from one of his pilots that set Bamberg on course to become a holiday charter operator. 'Why don't we run bus tours?', the pilot mused. 'We've got buses with wings'. So they did. But not before they had engaged in a heroic struggle against entrenched interests.

Today's travellers, accustomed to a jungle of bargain fares, may find it hard to imagine the sternly restricted regime of the immediate post-war years. This protectionism was not quite as outrageous as it looks at first glance, for the scheduled air travel industry was still in vulnerable adolescence and there were fears that the USA, with its massive power and huge fleets of aircraft left over from the war, could establish a hegemony. In 1953, airlines belonging to the International Air Transport Association carried only 50 million passengers world-wide. In the year 2000 they were forecast to have carried just over 1.5 billion. Nevertheless, IATA's zeal in policing the industry sometimes verged on the paranoid. The Association, originally set up to supervise European air agreements between the wars, had been revived in 1945 as a curious hybrid – a trade club sanctioned by governments to agree fares. While its senior officials denied heatedly that it existed only to keep fares high, it certainly acted as a kind of Star Chamber when airlines tried to steal a march on their competitors by offering any kind of extra in-flight luxury. Regulation even extended to the kind of sandwich they were allowed to serve. This led to a ludicrous row, in which the Scandinavians were accused of offering a smorgasbord as a way of getting around the rules.

Given this international climate of suspicious regulation, it was hardly surprising that individual governments were anxious not to

40

divert business from their state airlines, which were seen as providing vital mail and passenger transport services. Under the British Civil Aviation Act of 1946 (amended in 1949), privately owned carriers were limited to ad hoc operations. Bamberg, a charismatic entrepreneur who swept staff along with his enthusiasm but found it difficult to delegate decisions, wanted to run 'systematic' charters, back-to-back flights which would make for more efficient utilization of aircraft. But only state carriers were allowed to run such regular schedules.

This straitjacket had so frustrated Bamberg that he decided to quit the business. 'I thought the whole problem with British civil aviation was too complicated, or too difficult, and that any businessman who tried to tangle with the Government or a state airline should have his brains tested.' He was far from the last independent airline boss to suffer such pessimistic thoughts.

Bamberg did drop out for a while, after selling his fleet of Avro Yorks to rival Skyways, but two contemporaries (one of them John Sauvage who went on to head the Thomson charter airline, Britannia and later became chairman and chief executive officer of the entire Thomson Travel Group) persuaded him to get involved again. He bought ten Vickers Viking short haul airliners from BEA and took an option on fifteen more. The Viking was a descendant of the Wellington bomber. It had two engines, carried 36 passengers and had a maximum range of about 1200 miles. The next question was what to do with them. Package holiday flights looked like a good idea. So he went to battle with the Ministry of Aviation.

In order to overcome the rooted opposition of the state carriers, Bamberg came up with a system which he nicknamed 'the jockey and the horse'. The horse was the airline, the jockey the travel agent who decided on the destination. Together they would make joint applications for route licences to operate low cost packages. 'We had to create a virtually new class of traveller and persuade the authorities that this was genuine low cost travel for the masses – and we had to link the aircraft seat with a hotel bed.' After a long exchange of paperwork, the Ministry gave permission for a limited number of flights. The next task was to strike up a relationship with a travel agent. In 1954 he went to James Maxwell, the energetic general manager of Thomas Cook, to enquire whether Cook's might team up with him.

But Maxwell was 'not really interested in low cost air travel'. It was the first of several such rebuffs. Bamberg was staring defeat in the face. But during a visit to London he met Peter Cadbury, who had just bought Sir Henry Lunn Ltd.[1] The outcome was that Bamberg purchased the operation in turn. At last he had his jockey.

THE PACKAGE TOURS

There were two tours, one branded Treasures of Italy, the other Castles in Spain. They were not conventional packages as we now know them, Bamberg recalls, but exactly what the name implied — tours on which customers were dropped off in cities from which they could take in historic sights by road. Customers on the Italian tour flew into Pisa, a choice of airport deliberately calculated not to upset the state airlines, and were then taken on a 1700 kilometre bus tour. 'The tours were very tiring but the clients loved it.' He had his revenge over Cook's, recruiting two of its executives. These were Duncan Haws, who looked after Cook's agency branches in the UK and Ray Barker, a holiday tours specialist.

The next destination was Majorca. 'It was a lovely, countrified island then. The Vikings we used were noisy brutes which flew at 200 mph. The flight took about four hours. They were unpressurized too, so you couldn't get above the weather.'

Tour operating remained a business plagued by headaches. Every year the airline and travel firm would seek a certain number of route licences from the then Air Transport Licensing Board, only to see two-thirds of the application rejected. At every turn they would meet resistance from BEA, which would plead 'material diversion of traffic from its scheduled services'. And official decisions were made so late that they had to distribute their holiday programmes to other travel agents and customers before finding out how many holidays they would be able to offer.

'Generally speaking, the British public was early in its booking arrangements. People would sometimes book ahead for the coming season in December of the previous year and 90 per cent of bookings were taken by the end of March. But we did not actually get answers from the ATLB until February', recalls Bamberg.

Figure 3.3 Passengers enjoying a civilized drink at Palma Airport, Marjorca, while awaiting their flight home to the UK, 1954.

There were irritations for customers, too. Not only was their spending curbed by the Government, they still needed visas to travel to Spain. It was the only western European country which insisted visitors hold them. They cost 22s 6d, a considerable sum against the then average annual wage of around £150.

THE AIRPORTS

Gatwick

But there were already signs of the tidal wave of demand which, eventually, would wash away much of this restrictive regulation and bureaucracy. In July 1953, a government report said Gatwick was suitable for expansion as an alternative to London Airport – a £10million project which meant diverting a large stretch of the London–Brighton road. Much later, Gatwick was to become Britain's biggest jumping off point for charter flights.

Heathrow

In 1955 a new, permanent, short haul terminal opened at Heathrow, forerunner of today's Terminal 2. The airport owed its choice as successor to Croydon to the exigencies of the Second World War, and the need for an aerodrome capable of handling the latest, long-range military transport aircraft which had been designed to supply allied troops fighting the Japanese. In 1944 the Air Ministry used emergency wartime powers to acquire 2800 acres, embracing the hamlet of Heath Row and the former Great West Aerodrome, where aircraft manufacturer Fairey had tested the Swordfish, the Fleet Air Arm's celebrated 'stringbag', in the late 1920s. It was ideally suited because the land, once the haunt of highwayman Dick Turpin, sloped only five feet in two miles. One early plan for civil operations looks bizarre today. It was proposed that a circular passenger terminal should be built, with runways spraying off it, like sparks from a Catherine Wheel. The idea, based on the design of JFK's New York predecessor Idlewild, was that aircraft could land and take off no matter which way the wind blew. But the development of more sophisticated undercarriages made such considerations less important. Heathrow wound up with pattern roughly mirroring a Star of David, with terminal buildings at its centre, a layout which created a road traffic bottleneck and proved ill suited to cope with the huge, imminent growth in air travel.

In the airport's infancy, the arrival of a weekly flight by Douglas DC-4 from Spain caused an occasional flap. The pilot did not speak English, so a translator had to be summoned from the operator's Regent Street office. If he was held up on the road, the aircraft had to circle. At first, customs and immigration formalities were handled in tents. Passengers, whether they were Hollywood stars or diplomats, queued on duckboards to protect their shoes from the mud. When it rained, fire buckets were deployed to catch the drips. Nevertheless, it was an improvement on Hurn, near Bournemouth, where most long distance flights had operated previously, and which was over 100 miles from London. By the time Heathrow's traffic had jumped to 60,000 passengers a year, canvas had given way to pre-fabricated ex-RAF huts which, astonishingly, continued to serve long haul passengers until 1961, when Terminal Three, then called the Oceanic Terminal, opened at a cost of £3million.

FOUNDATIONS OF THE TOURIST TRADE

The British were still unable to buy dollars for holidays in America, though the travel trade was convinced that as restrictions elsewhere were loosened, the announcement of an allowance could not be far away. Agents were beginning to lay foundations for the day when they would send clients to the USA.

The Government announced the resumption of no passport trips to France after sixteen years, though its decision applied only to the summer peak. Tourists were allowed to take £10 spending money. In yet another indication of pent-up demand, 600 tourists sailed on the *Royal Daffodil* from Gravesend and Southend in late June, paying 35s (£1.75) each for the opportunity to spend three hours in Boulogne.

The Midland Bank published a booklet entitled *The Joys of Travel or How the Midland Bank Helps the Innocents Abroad*. Amongst other helpful hints, it contained information on foreign currency and exchange control regulations.

In July, Edward Westropp wrote in the *Sunday Express*: 'You won't catch me going abroad this year. Continental travel no longer holds any glamour for me.' His scatter-gun attack took in 'the boring scenery of northern France, dingy hotels the travel agent had extolled with an eye to his rake-off; weather; garlicky restaurants; plumbing'. Such xenophobic ranting was a sure sign that holidays abroad were no longer the preserve of the sophisticated few.

Hire purchase

And as the decade reached its mid-point, travel firms and airlines began to offer hire purchase. HP, as it was commonly called, was a moral issue. There was strong opposition to it from those who feared it would bury the poor and imprudent under mountains of debt. Some travel agents were wary of it, too. Those who offered credit conceded that it posed difficulties, not least that of getting their money back if customers defaulted. But so many other traders relied on HP for the bulk of their turnover that they swallowed their doubts.

Among the firms which jumped aboard the bandwagon was Sir Henry Lunn Ltd. From 1 January 1954, it offered credit facilities across its continental programme. There were two schemes: one demanding ten monthly payments, the other requiring advance payment of one third of the holiday price and six subsequent payments, which could be made after the customer got home. However, clients had to take out compulsory insurance to cover instalment payments in case they were prevented from travelling by illness, unemployment or death. Lunn's chairman, Harold Bamberg, said this should make buying travel 'as easy as buying a radio set on credit'.

Airlines soon followed suit. In November 1954, BEA and BOAC launched deferred payment arrangements for tickets worth more than £20, with deposits of 10 per cent and the balance payable over 6–21 months. Pan American joined them two months later, then SAS, Belgium's Sabena and Air France, though it whined 'with regret' that it had done so only because its hand had been forced by competitors.

Hire purchase was not the only issue which raised the eyebrows and hackles of moralists. Teenagers were also under scrutiny. Suddenly they had a new and defiant music of their own. In 1954, 'Rock Around the Clock', shot to the top of an otherwise bland hit parade. By 1956 the Memphis-born former truck driver Elvis Presley was gyrating his pelvis and, as one critic wrote 'sneering with his legs'. The *New York Times* described his appearance on the Ed Sullivan TV show in the USA as 'singularly distasteful' and there were suggestions that in future he should be screened only from the waist up, but the moral outrage served only to increase his popularity with young fans. In Britain, Teddy Boys with their suede, thick-soled brothel-creeper shoes, bootlace ties, velvet lapels and Brylcreemed hair sleeked back in a style known as the DA ('duck's arse') stalked the night streets. Scandalous though the disciplinarians may have found their behaviour, this demonstration of independence among those born just before, or during the war, and which was to burst into full bloom during the following decade, was another early indicator of the travel explosion to come. For it was that generation, more than any other, which was to fuel the boom.

TV advertising

Meanwhile, on 22 September 1955, advertising had come to British television. The BBC greeted the birth of its rival ITV, with a spoiler of which today's package holiday marketing executives would have been proud. As the first commercial transmission went on air, events in Ambridge reached an irresistible climax with Grace Archer, of the radio soap *The Archers*, trapped fatally in a blazing building. Pure coincidence, claimed the BBC.

The travel business was ill prepared for the new commercial television channel. Some companies had prepared travelogue-style advertisements but they were too long for the slots available. Global Tours said it had considered the potential very carefully but had concluded that 'it was not a suitable medium for advertising travel'. Costs were a deterrent. For example, one of the principal broadcasting companies, Associated Rediffusion, set a basic rate of £650 a minute, rising and falling by 50 per cent respectively at times of high and low viewing figures. The company announced it was making a programme linked with a competition. Viewers were invited to 'Film Your Holiday for the New TV'. But some travel firms were clearly disappointed that they would be unable to support such broadcasts with advertisements for the holidays or destinations covered.

Concerns

Presaging much later concerns about air rage, US airlines were asked by their now defunct regulatory body, the Civil Aeronautics Bureau, to consider proposals to curb drinking in the air. Suggestions from the airlines' own trade association, the Air Transport Association of America included limiting the hours at which alcohol could be served and banning already intoxicated passengers from boarding. British carriers were thought unlikely to follow suit. BOAC said haughtily: 'We find that the vast majority of our passengers are extremely sober'.

In Britain there were other concerns. Newspapers debated the growing worry that the bikini, that potent symbol of post-war sexual liberation, might be distracting the attention of motorists at seaside resorts and causing road accidents. At Folkestone, 500 members of the

Association of British Travel Agents and the Institute of Travel Agents got together for the first joint convention of what was to become a powerful trade lobbying organization. ABTA's president, the same James Maxwell who had rebuffed Harold Bamberg, grumbled about Britain's 'unadventurous' stay-at-homes.

'They are the reluctant eleven million. They are in a position to take an annual holiday away from home yet do not do so. What on earth's the matter with them? Are they afraid of leaving their homes behind them for a fortnight or so? Are they completely devoid of interest in what goes on outside their daily ken? Do they not realize that a holiday, in these hard working days, is virtually an essential? Whatever the reason for their shyness, something must be done about them.' He called for a joint campaign by the relevant government Ministries – such as those of Health, Labour and Transport, together with leisure organizations such as the Association of Health and Pleasure Resorts, to 'get them on the move'.

The further growth of air travel

Such exhortations hardly seemed necessary. The Government upped the 1955–6 foreign travel allowance to £100. The Board of Trade reported that air travel rose 18 per cent in 1956. Flying was also becoming relatively more popular as a means of travel, accounting for 36 per cent of trips, compared with 32 per cent the previous year. The writing was well and truly on the wall for the passenger shipping companies, which had begun to hedge their bets by buying into airlines. It was already three years since Clan Line Steamers and Hunting Group of Companies had formed a new airline, to be called Hunting-Clan Air Holdings Ltd, bringing together the two old shipping families of Cayzer and Hunting. Two years had passed since P&O's subsidiary the General Steam Navigation Company, had bought a majority shareholding in Britavia, which owned Aquila and Silver City, and since Blue Star Line had acquired an interest in Airwork, which had been established in 1928 and operated scheduled and charter flights around the world. It was a trend which would continue. And in 1955, Bibby Line had agreed to take a stake in Skyways.

The list of inclusive tours approved in 1956 contained some

unfamiliar names, such as Wenger Airtours, Travel Planning and Roberts Tours, but also included some which were to become major brands: Wings, Arrowsmith — which was to become part of Sir Freddie Laker's stable — Sky Tours, and of course, Vladimir's Horizon. The airports they flew from included Lydd in Kent, Blackbushe, Southend and Gatwick.

New destinations

As foreign travel grew, so airlines and holiday companies cast around increasingly for new destinations. In 1957, the Costa Blanca was born. Previously the Spanish, if they had called it anything, had known it as the Costa Azul. The new name was the brainchild of BEA, which had launched an air link between London and its principal city, Valencia, at a return fare of £38 16s. There were some 30 hotels along this 120 mile stretch of Mediterranean coast, whose emergence would reduce pressure on accommodation in the Balearic Islands and along the Costa Brava. They included the Victoria at Benidorm — a once quiet fishing village with two magnificent beaches, which would soon become a resort catering for more visitors than most countries. There was not enough fresh water to cope with this growth. Some guests turned on their taps and got salt water.

However, while Benidorm was setting off on the road to mass tourism, other destinations lay fallow. Though they may have attracted the odd adventurer, there was no significant tourism to the Portuguese Algarve or the Canary Islands. The Balearic island of Ibiza would also have to wait a little longer for its day in the commercial sun. The Spanish civil air authority rejected a bid by Aquila Airways to operate a scheduled flying boat service there from Southampton. Aquila was baffled. Britain's Ministry of Transport and Civil Aviation had approved the plan and there was undoubted demand for holidays on the island which had been frustrated by poor sea connections between there, Majorca and the mainland. Aquila had even offered to provide handling facilities for its aircraft, at its own expense. Whatever the underlying reason for the rejection, it was far from the only time that the hopes of the holiday industry were to be crushed by politicians.

Elsewhere, however, growth went on apace. Harold Bamberg's

Figure 3.4   A page on Benidorm from Horizon's 1963 brochure.

Eagle Aviation announced summer flights to Perpignan with coach connections to the Costa Brava at fares of £32 10s on Mondays or £36 at weekends. His King Flight inclusive holiday programme advertised a fifteen day package to Majorca for 38 guineas with 'all the magic of swift, comfortable travel in gleaming Viking planes'.

Figure 3.5 An early holidaymaker submits to a local sunburn treatment.

That April, Great Universal Stores took a substantial stake in Global Tours, though it soothed travel agents' fears by insisting it had no intention of setting up agencies in its shops. Milbanke Tours announced in October that it was to launch Flair Holidays. Hunting-Clan would carry its customers on Viscounts to Palma, Majorca for 39 guineas all in. Other promised destinations included the Costa Brava resorts of Lloret and Tossa de Mar, Benidorm, and Viarreggio in Italy.

And Doug Ellis, an old friend of Vladimir's, launched a tour operation called Sunflight from Manchester. Ellis, who was born in the

Wirral and left school at 15 to become a railway clerk, had joined
Frames Tours as a booking clerk after being demobilized from the Navy
in 1946, and had risen to become an agency manager in Birmingham
two years later. Initially aghast at the offer of the job, thinking he could
not possibly bring himself to live in Birmingham, he then reflected that
it was perhaps the ideal place in which to run a travel agency, 'because
it was so grim that people would be bound to want to travel, just to
escape occasionally'. By 1955, having saved £2500, he was ready to
open an agency of his own and soon decided to start tours to the Costa
Brava and Majorca. He opened negotiations with Derby Aviation, but
the airline wanted £28,000 to fly his planned route. He invited four
friends to join him, each putting up 20 per cent of the necessary
capital. Midland Air Tour Operators was born. By the end of 1956, it
had made a profit of £1200. The experience had convinced him that
among the factory workers of Britain's industrial cities was a huge,
untapped market for inclusive holidays. Manchester was just such a
city. In 1957, his grand plan was to offer holidays to the sun at 'prices
everyone could afford'. The travel business helped Doug Ellis to fulfil
his life's ambition: he became a majority shareholder and Chairman of
Aston Villa Football Club, known throughout the football world as
'Deadly Doug'.

The summer of that year (1957) saw the long awaited
announcement that currency allowances would be extended to the
USA and other countries in the Dollar Area, which included Canada,
Mexico and a clutch of other Central and South American countries.
Travellers were to be allowed £100. Thomas Cook immediately
advertised North American trips in six national newspapers and
reported a 'substantial volume' of enquiries. The Polytechnic Touring
Association unveiled plans for 28 day tours there. Trans World
Airlines, which, like Pan American, was preparing to launch flights
over the Pole to London, mounted a big promotional campaign aimed
at luring 25,000 Britons across the Atlantic the following year.

In less than a decade, it had become obvious that the package
holiday industry was poised for enormous expansion. The scheduled
airlines may have had trouble adjusting to the new phenomenon, but
they clearly recognized its existence. As John Brancker, IATA's traffic
director observed, what had been, ten years earlier, 'almost a custom
made business is now a mass production affair'. Anyone in any doubt

Figure 3.6 The interior of a BEA 'Elizabethan' turbo-prop aircraft.

need only have noted the objections of BEA, which railed that approvals of inclusive tour applications in 1956 had been far too liberal. Passenger capacity on such tours had more than doubled – a number which the airline regarded as too great and over too long a season. It was expected to go up another 25 per cent in 1957. Approvals on anything like the scale being requested could have grievous effects on BEA's traffic that summer, it complained.

Nonsense, retorted the independent airlines. Most people flying on those tours would not have used scheduled services in any case. They were creating new traffic. It was easy to see why BEA was worried, however. In 1956–7, it carried 2,461,000 passengers, 10.6 per cent more than in the previous year, but its profit fell by almost two-thirds. It had already commissioned a survey to find out why people went on holiday, perhaps the first piece of major market research undertaken by the industry. It found people were becoming more confident in their ability to get by in foreign languages and to cope with alien food. A large section of the public still tended to overestimate the cost of flying, believing it to be 'too much a millionaire's form of travel to be within the bounds of practical thought'.

However, almost half of those who had taken a holiday in Britain in 1956 – or were planning one in 1957 – said they would prefer a Continental break, and that held true across the social spectrum. While the middle and upper classes, white rather than blue collar workers, still predominated among those who went abroad, one in four were from the 'artisan class'. Doug Ellis was clearly on the right track. The face of foreign travel was changing dramatically and irrevocably.

NOTE

1. For a brief history of Sir Henry Lunn Ltd, see *Wintersports: How Skiing Lost its Exclusivity*. (See Chapter 6, 'Skiing and Cruising'.)

Growth of Horizon

VLADIMIR RAITZ

I had been able to add one new destination to our flying programme of 1953. A friend of mine, Father McDonald (known to all as Father Mac) was curate to Father de Zulueta (known to all as Father Zulu) of the Church of the Holy Redeemer in Chelsea. He had followed the see-saw fortunes of Horizon with mounting interest.

'You seem to be doing alright, Vlad,' he told me one morning. 'I have a destination in mind which might appeal to you. Have you considered flying pilgrims to Lourdes?'

I must say that I hadn't given this any thought at all.

'Thousands of Catholics make the pilgrimage to Lourdes every year,' he continued. 'Some by train and boat, others by coach and boat. It takes ages, and it's particularly tiring for the elderly and the handicapped who go in hope of a miracle cure. A comparatively short flight would be much appreciated by them all. I'll even be happy to take a party or two myself, as Spiritual Leader.'

I was always receptive to new ideas and new destinations, and this sounded like an excellent idea. I had recently met an airline man who had just graduated to Dakotas (having been operating the much smaller Doves and Rapides), which he used mostly to carry freight. He had a contract to fly national newspapers to Paris every night, returning with French papers and magazines as well as English language papers published in Paris — such as the Continental edition of the *New York Herald Tribune*. This man was Gerry Freeman, and his airline was called Transair. It was the beginning of an association that was to last many years, and our personal friendship is still going strong.

Lourdes–Tarbes airport served both of these Pyrenees townships and was roughly equidistant from each, in beautiful mountain country. Gerry Freeman and I formed a joint company, Pilgrim Tours, owned 50 per cent by Horizon and 50 per cent by Transair. The ATAC quickly granted us a licence, and I was immediately off to Lourdes to make hotel contracts for one DC3 load per week in a range of hotels, from the luxurious to modest *pensions*.

Father Mac had recommended one of his parishioners at the Church of the Holy Redeemer, Miss Elizabeth Molyneux, to manage Pilgrim Tours. She soon moved into our offices at 146 Fleet Street. Adverts were placed in the *Universe* and the *Catholic Herald* to publicize the flights and also to recruit 'spiritual leaders' to escort each plane-load as well as to stay with their party throughout the week. We were hoping that these spiritual leaders – invariably Catholic priests – would bring their parishioners with them. The response was overwhelming. We had more than twice the number of leaders applying for jobs than we needed, and every one of them was promising to recruit large numbers of their followers.

Pilgrim Tours was an instant success. The planes were almost invariably full. Although some sections of the Roman Catholic hierarchy didn't approve of our 'easy' way to make the pilgrimage, we scored a great prestige victory when the Archbishop of Westminster, Cardinal Griffin, went on our flights accompanied by his principal secretary Monsignor Worlock, later Archbishop of Liverpool. The Transair stewardess on that flight, and on many others, was the beautiful Joyce Ambler – sister of Eric Ambler, one of the great thriller writers of his generation.

I used to go to Lourdes several times a year to renew hotel contracts, and I made many lasting friendships in that extraordinary town – a curious mixture of the sacred and the profane. Nearly 150 years earlier, a peasant girl had had a vision of the Virgin Mary in a grotto just outside what was then a small village. The news spread like wildfire and curious sceptics and believers from all over France (and later from every Catholic country on earth) started travelling to Lourdes. By the time Pilgrim Tours was born, Lourdes consisted of, on the one hand, the 'domaine' with its austere and pious atmosphere which included the famous grotto, its entrance hung with hundreds of crutches discarded by pilgrims who had been cured. On the other hand there was the sprawling township with its huge number of hotels, hostels and *pensions* and innumerable tawdry souvenir shops.

The hoteliers, innkeepers, restaurateurs and shopkeepers of Lourdes were a race apart. They were cynics to a man (although their womenfolk were rather more upstanding and religious), and they cared little for the ideals of the pilgrims. Their interests centred on good food – which was quite magnificent in that part of France – good wine, shooting game, the pursuit of local and imported talent, and above everything the success of the local rugby team, Lourdes RC. At the height of its triumphs, the team had supplied as many as four members to the French national side. The most prominent business-men in Lourdes were on the committee of the rugby club and invested large sums of money in providing the players with a luxurious lifestyle (even though the game was then, of course, officially amateur). They regularly gathered in a bar called 'Le Winger', pronounced by all to

Figure 4.1 A Pilgrim Tours departure from Gatwick to Lourdes. From left to right: Cardinal Griffin, Vladimir Raitz, Elizabeth Molyneux, Monsignor Derek Worlock (later Archbishop of Liverpool).

rhyme with ginger. It was among these men that I formed my Lourdes friendships, although I must say I never accompanied them on their deer and wild boar shooting expeditions.

We tried to expand Pilgrim Tours in the years that followed, by arranging flights to other Catholic shrines such as Fatima near Lisbon, and Santiago de Compostela near the northern Spanish port of Vigo, but these never caught on. Lourdes, however, went from strength to strength. We doubled the number of flights and one year even tripled them.

CROYDON

Gerry Freeman's air company Transair flew, in its early days, from Croydon airport's grass runways and soon Horizon was able to give it additional work. Croydon had become London's main civil airport just after the First World War. Before that it was a military airfield – acres of corn and lavender having been dug over to make a home for the Royal Flying Corps. A squadron training to hunt down Zeppelins was based there, and Winston Churchill used it as a jumping off point when he flew to France as Minister of Munitions. In its infancy, before concrete runways were laid, a policeman had to stop traffic along a line which divided it – to allow arriving aircraft to reach their hangars. In a wonderfully evocative 1924 advertisement for an early operator there, Air Union, which flew 'thrice daily' to Paris, the copy ran thus:

'Come to France with me' – said he.
'But I can't sail the sea' – said she.
'Then fly above the sea' – said he.
'Avoid the pangs of sailing sea,
Arrive in half the time' – said he.
'And tell your friends you've flown with me.'
'Mais oui' – said she.

Even between the wars, passengers were flying from Croydon to Majorca, but the airport eventually gave way to Heathrow. BEA made its last scheduled flight from the airport in 1947 but it lingered on until

1959, finally closing on 30 September, just over a year after a young Queen Elizabeth II had cut the tape to open the newly developed Gatwick.

BKS was still carrying our Calvi and Palma traffic and was also operating a two-centre holiday for us with one week in Calvi at the Kallisté Hotel followed by the second week in Palma, at the Principe Alfonso. I had my eye on two new destinations that I had earmarked for Transair.

The first was Alghero on the island of Sardinia, and the second was Perpignan which would serve the Costa Brava of Spain, specifically resorts like Tossa de Mar and San Feliu de Guixolls which were much more easily accessible from Perpigan than from Barcelona. (The airport at Gerona, which carries this traffic nowadays, didn't exist back then.) I was also planning a coach tour out of Perpignan, through south-west France to Andorra then on to Barcelona with a week at a Costa Brava resort to recuperate.

ALGHERO

But let us turn in greater detail to Alghero. It was then, as is still is today, a picturesque fishing town on the north-west coast of Sardinia, with an airport halfway between it and Sassari, the island's second largest town. Sardinia did indeed look ripe for a tourist programme. The north-west coast especially looked ideal, as it had a reputation among meteorologists as the area with the most translucent light in the whole of the Mediterranean. I flew to Rome, from there to Sassari and made my way to Alghero. I saw a delightful port with many ancient buildings, a beautiful sandy beach and hardly any tourist facilities whatsoever. There was, in fact, only one hotel – and that was still under construction, called La Margherita. There was also La Lepanto, an inn of sorts that had an excellent restaurant and was used mostly by businessmen and commercial travellers. Third, there was a charming and ancient ancestral home type of villa, the Las Tronas. This was owned by the Conte di Sant'Elia, former Chamberlain to King Victor Emmanuel of Italy. The Count (who was married to an Englishwoman who spent most of her time in England, racing her horses) was taking a

59

maximum of eight paying guests. The Count himself stayed in Alghero but he left the running of the hotel part of Las Tronas to his butler, Rossi – with whom I signed a contract for 1954 there and then.

I also signed contracts with the Masia family who owned the Hotel Margherita. This involved convincing each family member in turn (uncles, aunts, cousins and in-laws) and most importantly Mama Masia, a quite formidable matriarch. I do not know how many times I had to explain the concept of back-to-back groups to them. 'You see, one group leaves, and another immediately takes its place.' Although I may have been bilingual in French, my grasp of Italian left much to be desired. Eventually, thank goodness, the lira dropped (so to speak): the deal was signed and it was grappas all round.

Next up was Signor Lepanto Cecchini of the Hotel La Lepanto – both named after the famous sea battle of 1571 in which the Italian fleet, under Andrea Doria, defeated a huge Turkish fleet and 'saved Christendom from the infidels'. Cecchini was easy to convince. He was more interested in running his restaurant than his hotel – which before Horizon's arrival catered mainly for commercial travellers. Not surprisingly, La Lepanto had the worst rooms of my Alghero hotels, but by far the best food. Signor Lepanto spoilt his clients with his generosity. His superb seafood and pasta dishes were legendary throughout the region. Complaints about the hotel's rooms and bathrooms were quickly forgotten when guests entered the dining room.

FRANCE AND SPAIN

Horizon had thus tied up all of Alghero's tourist accommodation in one fell swoop. After these Sardinian arrangements had been completed, it was the turn of the Spanish holidays on the Costa Brava, and the coach tours of France and Spain. Our London air broker, Gaston Levi-Tilley, had recommended a respected French coach operator with branch offices in most French towns – including Perpignan. It was called SGTD (Société Générale de Transports Départementaux), and in Perpignan it had a large fleet of reasonably modern coaches, and ran a scheduled service between Perpignan and Barcelona. SGTD were to transfer my clients to the Costa Brava resorts – as yet unchosen – and also to run the tours – as yet unplanned.

Perpignan

Their local general manager, Monsieur Gourbault and his second-in-command, Monsieur Padrixe, met me off the night train from Paris. Our first job was to visit the airport at Perpignan, at that time the least busy airport in France and quite possibly in the entire world. There was one flight a week (to Algiers), and the occasional plane stopped by to refuel. That was it. It was not surprising, therefore, when the airport commandant greeted us with open arms when he heard of our plans for holiday flights from the UK which might boost his airport's movements enormously. Within ten years of my first visit to this airport, new runways were laid, and large terminal buildings were constructed. It was not unusual to see a dozen planes lined up in front of the terminal, with two or three more preparing for take off.

Messieurs Gourbault and Padrixe made suggestions about possible staging posts for the coach tours I had planned. One of these was Prades in France, where Pablo Casals, the famous Spanish cellist, lived in exile and where he held an annual music festival. Another suggestion was a French ski resort named Font Romeu at an altitude of 10,000 feet, training ground for the French Winter Olympics team. Arrangements had to be made there and in Barcelona. The coach tours (or 'Leisure Tours' as we called them) were to last one week, with a second week included at a Costa Brava resort to recover. In addition, we were going to have a regular fortnight's sun and sea holiday, along the models of Corsica and Majorca.

The Costa Brava

I drove along the projected route of the coach tour and signed up various stop-over hotels. Then I began a thorough exploration of the entire Spanish coastline from the French border as far down as Blanes, the official end of the Costa Brava. One resort in particular struck me as being eminently suitable for our clients. Looking back now, it seems hardly credible that Tossa de Mar, with its huge numbers of high-rise hotels and apartment blocks, with its profusion of shops, bars, discos and beauty parlours, could ever have been a fishing village with only half a dozen tiny hotels, a couple of bars and nothing else. There was no bank in the village and one of the innkeepers, Señor Ros, had the sole concession to change travellers cheques and foreign currency. There were, however, two excellent beaches and a picturesque old town – the Vila Vella, a fortress-like agglomeration which rose high above the port. It was a perfect picture postcard setting. Tossa de Mar was to be the first Horizon resort on the Costa Brava.

Within the next ten to fifteen years, most of the villages along this stretch of coast were to undergo astounding transformations into tourism-oriented developments. Some of them were to grow into major holiday cities, and the number of tourist thronging their beaches was to increase almost a hundredfold between the mid-1950s and the late 1960s.

The Catalans, who inhabit this region, are probably the most enterprising people in Spain. They were quick to realize, at the onset of the tourist boom, that they were sitting on a goldmine. Land in Catalonia is measured in 'palmos' (palms of the hand) and by the early 1970s, a 'palmo' in a prime coastal position would have increased in value from roughly one peseta to well over two hundred. The Catalans are a people who do like to see a quick return on their invested capital and they tend, on the whole, to take a short-term view in their business operations. The result, as far as the Costa Brava was concerned, was not too happy.

Many tawdry hotels and apartment blocks were put up in a hurry without much thought to overall town planning, and many beautiful sites along the rugged coast were spoiled forever. The worst culprits were Tossa de Mar, Lloret de Mar and Calella de la Costa – the eyesore *par excellence*. Contracted almost entirely to German tour operators, it was known to the locals as Calella de los Alemanos – Calella of the Germans. Some places did escape overdevelopment, however. Calella de Palafrugell remains almost as charming as it was in the 1950s and the northern part of the coast, around Rosas and Cadaqués (home of the late Salvador Dali) has fared far better than the southern part.

While Tossa de Mar was chosen for the 14 day stay-put holiday I was planning, there were not sufficient beds in the tiny resort to accommodate the clients of the coach tour as well – another resort had to be found, where they could relax in their second week. I finally decided upon San Feliu de Guixols, the unofficial capital of the Costa

Brava, its largest town in those days, and not strictly a holiday resort in the conventional use of the term. Still, it featured two or three decent hotels and the beach of S'Agaro was nearby. S'Agaro itself also boasted a wonderful old hotel (one of the most luxurious and expensive in all of Spain), which was of course out of reach for even the most upmarket package tours. It was called the Hostal de la Gavina and its billionaire owner, Señor Encesa, played host to several British cabinet ministers – including the then Foreign Secretary, Selwyn Lloyd – much to the annoyance of sections of the British press, who felt that British politicians should not be holidaying in Franco's Spain.

HOLIDAY REPS

By 1955, Horizon was operating six different holidays, each with its own codename. Corsica was C1, Majorca was M2, Sardinia was S3, and so on. Each of these holidays had to have an individual whose job was to look after the welfare of our clients. On the face of it, this job is straightforward: arranging excursions and car hire, and doing the occasional piece of interpreting. In reality, however, it is never that simple. Aeroplanes can run late; coaches will break down; employees can go on strike; rooms can be changed at the last minute, and clients either fall ill, get horribly drunk, or drown. Crises are a part and parcel of a holiday rep's life – and the efficient way in which he or she deals with them is the measure of the man or woman concerned.

Horizon's policy (expressed in strict instructions to them all, from the very early days until the time when we employed several hundred reps) was to be as unobtrusive as possible. Reps were not to use hard sell techniques to push excursions, or to steer clients deliberately into certain shops (in case it might be thought they had an 'understanding' with that shop's proprietor). They were to be around only if wanted by the client, and they were to be helpful, cheerful and amusing at all times. A tall order? Certainly, but a very careful selection process, with long interviews carried out by myself in the early years and later by our Representatives Manager, assured that we managed to get a high proportion of the right people for these exacting jobs.

One interviewee in particular stands out in my memory. He was an Oxford undergraduate looking for a summer job. He was personable, highly intelligent and good-looking, and I was prepared to offer him the position there and then. Unfortunately, it transpired that he had prior commitments for the month of June, so I had to turn him down. His name was Alan Clark[1] – and I wonder, with hindsight, whether he was attracted to the job by the lure of our many female clients.

CLOSED GROUPS

By the fifth year of Horizon's existence, the 'big boys' of travel (Thomas Cook, Sir Henry Lunn, and so on) were still continuing to sell holidays in the traditional manner – by rail and coach, and on the services of the scheduled airlines. There were, however, one or two small outfits that had entered the periphery of our field. The first was a firm called Whitehall Travel, which organized holidays for the Association of Civil Servants, the National Union of Bank Employees, the National Association of Local Government Officers, and other, similar 'closed groups'.

The advantages of 'closed group' air charter were twofold. First, no licences were required, and second, the price charged for an inclusive holiday could be as low as the tour organizer wished to make it. This was not the case for air charter holidays sold to the general public, like Horizon's. The minimum inclusive price we were obliged to charge and advertise had to be no less than the air fare to the destination concerned, as set by IATA, the International Air Transport Association. For example, if the fare to Palma by BEA or Iberia was £60 return, that then was as low as we could go with our pricing on an all-inclusive holiday to that area – even though we could have made a perfectly satisfactory profit by charging £50 or even less.

Obviously, we still had a considerable price advantage over scheduled service holidays, but firms like Whitehall Travel could (and did) undercut our prices at will. Their problem was that the general public was not allowed to use their services. Whitehall themselves stuck to the rules, but other organizations bent them as far as they could go. Strange 'closed groups' and 'common interest societies' sprang up, formed with the sole purpose of circumventing the rules. My co-author mentions some of his favourites on pp. 177 and 178, but two that I recall are The West Hartlepool Bird Fanciers' Circle and The Society for Wine Appreciation in the Home Counties.

At this stage of Horizon's development, the company operated very much as a lone wolf in the travel industry. We were more or less ignored by the orthodox companies, who looked on charter holidays as a flash in the pan – in the same way that film studios had dismissed the arrival of television a few years earlier. We, in turn, paid little attention to the big operators, with whom we felt we had little in common. As long as they kept out of our particular line of business, that was fine. We did not sell our holidays through travel agents, as we could easily dispose of our products by selling directly to the public through our advertising, which was by this point becoming widespread. We were able to afford a half page in the *Daily Express* – costing £500 at the time – and featuring a holidaymaker on a flying carpet, drawn by the famous cartoonist Emet.

Our mailing list, too, was growing steadily, and we had an excellent word-of-mouth reputation and steady repeat business. Some of our original Calvi clients of 1950 would enquire which new resort was going to appear next in our portfolio, and would make provisional bookings for the new destination, long before the relevant brochure was even published. Travel agents were getting a 7.5 per cent commission in those days and although we were getting numerous requests from the trade to represent us, I saw no point in adding this extra charge to our costs when it seemed so easy to sell our holidays directly to the consumer, with demand so far outstripping supply. Neither did we belong to ABTA. Under their rules at that time, Horizon (operating air charter holidays only, with no IATA licence to sell scheduled air tickets, or indeed rail, steamship or coach tickets) was barred from ABTA membership.

This didn't worry me in the slightest. But in 1955, the quasi-monopoly we enjoyed was to be challenged by two colourful characters making their entrance on to the charter holiday stage.

CAPTAIN TED LANGTON

The first of these was Captain Ted Langton. He was, even then, nearing the age of sixty, and had spent all his working life in the travel business. Having started his career with Thomas Cook and Son, he left to form his own coach touring company called Blue Cars. Langton built it up into a major force in coach travel throughout Europe. After the war, Blue Cars grew even larger, and Langton sold it for a considerable sum to BET – British Electric Traction. Langton owned racehorses, nightclubs and restaurants, and even bought an ocean-going yacht which he kept in the Mediterranean and on which he hardly ever sailed. Despite his lifestyle, the lure of the travel trade was too strong. Even though he had signed a contract with BET that prohibited him from forming a tour company for the next two years, Langton (whose title of Captain was entirely spurious unless it derived from his ownership of a yacht) decided to ignore such a petty sanction. Six months after the sale of Blue Cars, and having recognized that air charter was the way forward, he formed his new company: Sky Tours. (Ted later told me that Horizon had been his inspiration.) BET promptly sued Ted for breach of contract, and won. He had to hand over a sum of money which was a fraction of the original purchase price, and which Ted could dismiss as a 'fleabite'.

Sky Tours started out with a mixed programme of stay-put holidays, mainly in Majorca and the Costa Brava, as well as few air-coach holidays similar to our own tour that I described previously. The holidays that Sky Tours offered were rather downmarket affairs. The emphasis was on mass travel at the lowest possible prices, within the framework of the regulations. Although Ted's operation was pretty large in its first year, it did not worry us too much. Esoteric destinations like Corsica and Sardinia were not his style – and in fact his marketing policy was so differently pitched from ours that there could only have been the most marginal overlap between our clientele. In any case, in a market that seemed to be growing at a phenomenal rate, there was certainly room for more tour organizers.

HAROLD BAMBERG

The second newcomer in 1955 was a totally different type of individual. In his early thirties at the time, he was the owner and chief executive of the air charter company Eagle Aviation (later known as British Eagle), and his name was Harold Bamberg. He had recently acquired Sir Henry Lunn Ltd, with the express intention of using it as a vehicle for launching holiday flights, giving employment to his planes.

Bamberg's main interest, Eagle Aviation, had been formed shortly after the war as had many similar private air companies, operating war surplus cargo- and troop-carrying aircraft. Eagle's great moment came in 1948, when everything that could fly was used in the highly lucrative Berlin airlift. Bamberg made a great deal of money out of that particular exercise, as did many other 'freebooters', including Freddie Laker.

Bamberg's initial programme at Lunn's was a substantial one, but, much as with Sky Tours, it did not worry me unduly. Their emphasis was on the bread and butter destinations like Majorca and the Costa Brava and their approach was certainly more downmarket than ours. I recall one hotel used by Lunn's in the little town of Soller in the north of Majorca. They had contracted it for a price that – even in those early days – was astonishingly cheap: £1 per day per person, for bed and full board. The hotel was called the Ferrocarril, which probably sounded imposing and romantic to readers of the Lunn brochure in Britain, but which was of course Spanish for the Railway Hotel. It was situated right next to the railway line that linked Palma to Soller, and by no stretch of the imagination could it be considered conducive to an agreeable fortnight on a sunny beach.

Horizon began to realize that, at least where our Spanish destinations were concerned, we were going to have a fight on our hands. Not only were Lunn's and Sky Tours looking for new hotels for their clients, but the Germans were beginning to shake off their post-war traumas, with friendly Spain as their first choice of holiday location. The French were also taking a new attitude to holidays abroad. Before the war, the average Frenchman rarely ventured beyond his own frontiers for his vacation. Now, he hopped into his car and Spain (so much cheaper than the Côte d'Azur) beckoned irresistibly.

Spaniards realized quickly that there was a golden opportunity to be seized. A moderate hotel, somewhat superior to the Ferrocarril, could be had for £1 10s all inclusive. Drink and entertainment were half the price of their equivalents in Britain, Germany and France, and Spain could also offer unique features like flamenco dancing and bullfights for the less squeamish.

It was no wonder, therefore, that before long a hotel building boom was getting under way in Majorca and on the Costa Brava. It was greatly encouraged by the Spanish government, which was not slow to realize that tourism could easily become the country's major industry, bringing in desperately needed foreign hard currency and providing employment for the building trade, the hotel and catering industry, and a wide variety of ancillary trades and occupations. The government's help mostly took the form of bank credits granted by the 'Credito Hotelero', which underwrote loans of up to 60 per cent of the total building cost of any hotel. The loan would then be extended by commercial banks at favourable rates of interest. The government also undertook improvements of Spain's roads, airports and other aspects of its infrastructure – but it was not until the late sixties that this programme got into its stride. In the 1950s, Spain's funds were still severely limited.

NEW COMPETITORS

The arrival of Sky Tours heralded an innovation that was to become enormously important in the years to come – an innovation in which most holiday organizers would be forced to take part, often against their will. This was the advancing of large deposits to hotels in order to secure block allocations of rooms. It was Captain Langton who must be credited with the first practice of this method – which was warmly welcomed by Spanish hoteliers but which effectively tied up large sums of tour operators' capital. Before long, British operators were competing for scarce rooms not only against each other but increasingly against their German and Scandinavian counterparts.

Before the holiday slump of the early 1970s, the rate of deposit for a bed in a popular hotel in Majorca was to rise to around 60,000 pesetas (about £400). If 200 beds were required in that hotel, this would represent an outlay of £80,000 to one hotel alone – a sum which might be tied down for several years before repayment, usually free of interest, was due. If you multiply this by several hotels in a number of resorts in a number of countries, it comes as no surprise that the major tour operators had several million pounds tied up in hotel deposits. The hoteliers themselves were now in the driving seat. For them, it was a seller's market *par excellence*. Armed with government loans from the 'Credito', top-up finance from the private sector, and now interest-free advances from tour operators, they entered into a blizzard of hotel construction the like of which had never been seen before. If any tour company refused to participate in the scramble (or was financially unable to do so), it was deprived of choice beds in the top resorts and had to either withdraw from those resorts entirely or take rooms in second-rate hotels that were difficult to sell.

But I am anticipating events. The second half of the 1950s was a time of new competitors for Horizon, and we had to position ourselves in the market. Horizon had begun by catering for a public that was looking for a holiday that was slightly different. Although the original arrangements for the Corsican holiday camp had been inexpensive, the intellectual level of the clientele we attracted was decidedly higher than that of your average package tour holidaymaker (at least that was what we liked to think!). Our policy had therefore been to provide a rather unusual holiday. Our resorts in Corsica and Sardinia remained in that category. In Calvi, the Chalets Tamaris, under the ownership of the Zemettes, were proving extremely successful. They were so popular that demand considerably outstripped supply and we had to add allocations at most Calvi hotels to our programme, just to satisfy the growing demand for holidays in Corsica.

Majorca and the Costa Brava, though they had been in the same category as Corsica and Sardinia just a few years previously, were now being exploited on a vast scale. By the late 1950s, there was no way that we could pass off these destinations as being 'esoteric' to our customers. Horizon would have to find new destinations to satisfy our particular end of the market, in order to make a sharp distinction between ourselves and the new mass travel operators. We were in a curious position. We did not wish to be seen as 'upmarket', but in a way we had to be so, in order to preserve our reputation as pioneers. We had to search out 'off the beaten track' destinations, we had to give our clients the opportunity of visiting resorts where few tourists had been before, and certainly where no inclusive charter firm had ventured.

The brief of the licensing authority at that time was to refuse licences to capital cities and other major commercial centres of Europe, as this might cause what was termed 'material diversion and wasteful duplication', harming the interests of BEA. Cities like Paris, Rome, Madrid, Lisbon, Barcelona and Athens were out of bounds to operators like Horizon – at least for the time being. There were attractive seaside resorts that were easily accessible from some of those cities, but there was little we could do about it. What we had to do instead was to find 'secondary' airports, to which licences could be more readily granted.

IBIZA AND MINORCA

One of the first possibilities I looked into were the other Balearic Islands apart from Majorca. Ibiza, which would have been a natural choice, did not at that time possess an airport. It was a longish sea journey away from Majorca, and I didn't believe our clients would be too keen on the trip. There were, at that time, two theories (never quite substantiated) as to why Ibiza was airportless. The first was that the Bishop of Ibiza was so firmly set against tourism that he would strenuously oppose any move to have an airport constructed. (With the benefit of hindsight, you can sympathize now with his point of view.) The second theory was that the Transmediterranea line, which controlled the sea route from Majorca, was doing everything in its power to stop the air services which would threaten its monopoly. Perhaps both of these theories were true, but the result was that it would not be possible to get holidaymakers to Ibiza quickly and easily for a few more years to come.

There was, however, a third Balearic island, Minorca, famous for having been British for a number of years during the Napoleonic wars, for having served as a base for Nelson's fleet, and for the fact that Admiral Byng had failed to defend it against the French during the Seven Year war and had been executed for this failure. 'Pour encourager les autres', according to Voltaire. Minorca also possessed in its capital, Port Mahon, the finest natural harbour in the Mediterranean.

The island was completely unspoilt. Though perhaps not as grandiosely beautiful as Majorca with her high mountains and lush plains, Minorca nevertheless possessed considerable attractions – above all, the many totally deserted sandy coves, or 'calas', many of which were only accessible on foot or from the sea and were ideal places for swimming and picnicking. And not only did Minorca have an airport that was able to take Transair's Dakotas, but the first 'real' hotel was just nearing completion on the island, in Port Mahon.

Figure 4.2 A page on Ibiza from Horizon's 1963 brochure. 'It has the individual charm of a very small island where nothing exciting is expected to happen.'

I got to hear about the hotel in a most fortuitous manner. Towards the end of 1955, when our brochure for the next summer season was about to go to the printers, I received a letter in Spanish from a gentleman named Señor Juan Victory, enclosing a leaflet that was short on text but with many artist's impressions of a hotel on the island of

Minorca, called the Hotel Port Mahon. It was owned by him, Señor Victory – a man who also happened to be the mayor of the town. His letter stated that he had heard about Horizon's success in Majorca, the sister island, and wondered if I could do the same for him?

There was no time to waste: the brochure deadline was looming. I did what I had never done before or since. I put Minorca, the Hotel Port Mahon, and descriptions of the fabulous 'calas' and other Minorcan delights into our programme without having seen any of it.

The very next week, I flew out to Minorca via Barcelona. Señor Victory welcomed me with open arms. It was his first contact with a tour operator, and the prospect of 32 clients arriving every week from May to early October filled him with considerable joy. He promised that there would be no difficulty in laying on customs and passport control; he was the mayor of the capital, after all, and if he couldn't arrange it then nobody else could. The hotel prices were reasonable, and the place itself was well constructed. Every bedroom had a private bathroom. Horizon had another new destination, exclusive to ourselves. It was an island that was to become a major tourist area within the next fifteen years but at the time it was only known (even in Spain) as a producer of gin, shoes and cheese. (Legend has it that mayonnaise takes its name from Mahon. Apparently, at a time when Minorca was besieged by the British fleet, the chef of the French governor of the island – one Richelieu, but not the Cardinal of that name – had run out of ingredients for his special sauce. All he had left was olive oil and eggs, which he proceeded to make into a sauce: Salsa Mahonesa. The natives swear that this story is 100 per cent true.)

Señor Juan Victory and I became very good friends. He didn't speak a word of English, and my Spanish was not too hot, but I was learning furiously. Juan was portly with a ruddy complexion and light brown hair, and could easily have passed for a commuter on the Clapham omnibus. One day I asked him where his Anglo-Saxon surname came from.

'Oh,' he replied, 'one of my ancestors was an English naval officer.'

Later, I discovered that Admiral Nelson's flagship had anchored in Mahon's famous harbour in 1803 and that many of the sailors had been warmly welcomed by the local maidens. The resulting offspring were named after their fathers' vessel, HMS *Victory*.

PORTUGAL

In the same year that we 'opened up' Minorca, I began to look seriously at the tourist potential of Portugal. Lisbon was excluded as a point of entry by the licensing embargo, and so the nearby resorts of Estoril and Cascais could not, at that stage, form part of our programme. Faro, the gateway to the Algarve, was not even a gleam in the eye of the Portuguese equivalent of an Airport Authority in those days. Oporto, in the north of the country, was the most promising airport town. Oporto (or plain 'Porto' in Portuguese) was a delightful town on the river Douro. It had strong ties with Britain and a considerable Anglo-Portuguese community that had lived there for centuries and had often intermarried. This community was largely engaged in the port wine trade and various related activities.

We decided to explore what northern Portugal had to offer. As a preliminary step, we sent out a man who had been our resident representative in Corsica for the past two years. He had shown that he knew how to deal with hoteliers and furthermore, his legal training came in handy when negotiating contracts. His name was Jan Adamowski, a former Polish Air Force officer who had come to the UK in the early years of the war and had qualified as a barrister in London. He was a valuable member of the Horizon staff for a number of years until, to my regret, he left to join a competitor – a common occurrence in our trade.

Jan returned from Portugal with an encouraging report. First of all, he had contacted a well-established firm of shipping and travel agents in Oporto – Tait and Company, members of that Anglo-Portuguese community so prominent in the commercial life of Portugal's second city. Alan Tait, the young scion of the family business, had proved a bundle of energy, and quickly got to work.

Two good hotels were available, about 60 and 80 miles respectively north of Oporto. The first was right on the beautiful, sandy Atlantic beach, and was called the Ofir. It stood in splendid isolation, surrounded by a pine forest and far removed from any commercial activity – ideal for the sort of peaceful holiday that many of our clients would appreciate. The second hotel, the Santa Luzia, was a few miles inland near a small town called Viana do Castelo. It was a delightful and very comfortable establishment that dominated the countryside from a commanding, fortress-like position on the top of a hill. It had its very own funicular railway and a shuttle service by a small bus to convey clients to the beaches.

Alan Tait had put together a series of excursions, including a railway day trip from Oporto to Lisbon. He had also arranged trips to many of Oporto's port wine lodges, where our clients not only sampled (most assiduously) the chief product on the spot but were given a liberal supply of souvenir bottles to take home. The port wine trade was, at that time, suffering a decline and the shippers and producers were doing everything in their power to revive it. Our clients enthusiastically aided them in their endeavours to popularize once more what had once been one of Britain's favourite tipples.

Northern Portugal thus became a natural choice for our holiday-makers. We made it clear in the brochure that this was a holiday for connoisseurs of peace and quiet, that nightclubs were non-existent, and that only the port wine tastings might introduce an air of bacchanalia. BKS were entrusted with the flying programme to Oporto. The licence was applied for and granted without difficulty, and a weekly 36-seater Viking was earmarked for Horizon's first venture to the Atlantic coast. The service was upgraded the following year to a 52-seater Elizabethan (the popular name for the De Havilland Airspeed Ambassador), three of which BKS was buying from BEA, as a replacement for some of its Dakotas and Vikings.

TORREMOLINOS

There were other parts of Spain for Horizon to explore. I remembered having spent a brief holiday there in 1948, before the Horizon days, travelling round the country by car with a few friends. I recalled a sleepy fishing village on the south coast, named Torremolinos. It had impressed all of us with its unspoilt charm and it was only a few miles away from the town of Malaga, which boasted an airport.

One of our Majorca reps, Mike Edmonds, had also visited Torremolinos after the end of a season in Palma – and he too was impressed by its potential as a Horizon resort. By this time I was married, and my wife Toni and I decided to combine a holiday with a prospecting trip to the Costa del Sol. It was, then, virtually a tourist-free coastline all the way from Malaga to Gibraltar. We met Mike Edmonds in Malaga, hired a car, and drove our way along the coast. As we drove, he regaled us with some stories from his two seasons as a Horizon rep.

There was the time when John Spencer-Churchill, nephew of Winston, had gone to Palma with his wife, on my recommendation. On arriving, John insisted on signing up for the bullfight excursion. According to Mike, he must have been a horse lover, for when the picador appeared on his heavily protected old nag and was repeatedly charged by the enraged bull, John lost his temper, started shouting imprecations and then throwing anything that came to hand at the horseman. After bombarding the poor man with bottles and cushions, John finally succeeded in unseating the picador. The Civil Guard promptly appeared, incensed at this slight to the *corrida* decorum, and tried to drag John off to the nearest jail. It was a nasty situation for Mike, as a rep, and he tried all kinds of explanations on the police. None of them worked, however, until he mentioned the magic name of Winston Churchill – at which point the mood changed entirely and John was released.

Another story from Majorca involved the weekly boat excursion that Mike had arranged, setting out from Palma harbour in the morning and returning in the afternoon. The trip was complete with swimming off the boat, and a refreshingly alcoholic lunch. Errol Flynn, the film star, was at that time living on his yacht at Cala Mayor. Mike had met Flynn in a Palma bar, and the two had formed a boisterous drinking friendship. He had managed to persuade Flynn to wave at the excursion boat as it passed by his yacht, and to shout greetings to the holidaymakers on board. Our clients were mightily impressed by this.

A final story from Majorca that Mike told us as we drove along the Costa del Sol is one that I remember well, as I was on the island when it happened. It took place at a hotel named the Dux, in the Terreno section of Palma. It was departure time for one of our groups, and the coach for the airport was waiting outside the hotel for the clients. Eventually, all were on board with the exception of one man. Mike phoned his room: there was no reply. Time was getting short to get to the airport. Mike and the hotel manager went up to the man's room. The door was locked, and they could get no answer from within. They broke down the door, to discover the wretched man sitting in a chair with his throat cut from end to end. He was not quite dead, however. In the ensuing panic (involving calls for doctors, ambulances and the police), the man somehow managed to throw himself from his balcony on to the pavement below. As the room was on the fifth floor, he achieved his suicide after all. Later, I got the facts of this sad story. The client was a Scotsman, employed by a whisky distillery in the Highlands. He had recently been dismissed for persistent drunkenness. He had then decided to go on a Horizon holiday to Palma without telling his wife or anyone else he knew. According to the hotel staff, he had not drawn a sober breath during his entire fortnight's stay. Clearly, he had wanted to take his life after one last alcoholic binge. One member of our staff remarked at the time that at least he had chosen the best tour operator for his grand exit.

When Mike, Toni and I arrived in Torremolinos we found that it now boasted two hotels and one *pension* run by a Dane – the Pension Escandinava. One of the two hotels was a series of converted farmhouses and stables called the Santa Clara. It was owned and run by a retired English ship's steward called Fred Saunders and his Swedish wife Edith. The accommodation they provided was unpretentious to the point of being austere, but the food was excellent and Fred was a genial host, especially when presiding over his well-stocked bar. It was also a very cheap hotel. We signed up the Santa Clara for our first Torremolinos programme.

We contracted the other hotel in town, too: the brand new Hotel Lloyd. This had been built by a recently retired British consul in Malaga, Mr Lloyd – who bore an uncanny resemblance to the Duke of Windsor and was the subject of persistent rumours. The hotel was run by his energetic Spanish wife, with minimal assistance from Mr Lloyd himself.

Just outside Torremolinos was the Club El Remo: a collection of bungalows built around a large swimming pool. It was owned by a Spanish marquis, who spent most of his time, as far as I could tell, playing golf on various courses around Europe. It was run by a woman named Maria-Luisa Rein, and it was with her that I signed a contract for the coming season. Club El Remo's poolside and bar provided a meeting point for the smart set of the region – expatriate villa owners from Britain and America. Film stars could occasionally be seen lunching by the pool.

Once again, we had no problems obtaining a licence to fly to

Malaga. It was so unknown at the time that Captain Stevens, the 'S' in BKS and its Managing Director, pronounced it as 'Malagna' for the first two years he flew there. I did not dare to correct him, but he finally got it right himself.

QUO VADIS TRAVEL

We had now reached 1957, and there was to be a significant development in the affairs of Horizon. In the past, we had stayed somewhat removed from the rest of the travel industry. We had been selling directly to our clients and we were not members of ABTA. But now, a regular travel agency (complete with all the necessary licences) was offered to us for sale. It was a company called Quo Vadis Travel and was owned by Charles Forte of the Forte catering organization. Some years previously, Mr Forte had gone into partnership with a leading Italian travel agent called Pier Buseti, to set up a travel operation in London. Originally situated on an impressive site at the corner of Regent Street and Hanover Street, the agency had not fulfilled the high hopes of its owners. Tourism to Italy was to have been its main activity, but additionally it operated as a general agent, selling travel to firms and individual clients as well as tours and holidays throughout the world. Fairly considerable losses had been incurred. Buseti had left the firm, later to commit suicide owing (it was said) to enormous gambling losses accrued in continental casinos. The business had moved to more modest premises in Maddox Street, but even with the considerable saving in rent and overheads it had failed to make a profit.

Charles Forte was used to turning everything he touched into gold, and he was determined to get shot of Quo Vadis. As for Horizon, I had decided that a diversification into the 'orthodox' travel industry was of considerable interest, primarily because it would provide us with an IATA licence, with the right to hold ticket stocks from all the world's leading airlines – and we could receive commission for selling them.

Another attraction of gaining an IATA licence was that each member airline would provide the travel agency with two tickets per year, at 25 per cent of the full price for members of staff. In theory, this meant over 200 cheap tickets every year. In practice, only the

Figure 4.3   Vladimir (right) with Honor Blackman and Bernard Braden on the occasion of Horizon's 10th anniversary. Braden is on the left.

major carriers' tickets were ever used (BOAC, BEA, Air France, Alitalia, KLM, Swissair and so on) but this was not to be sneezed at. Sixty pounds for a first class return to New York was a definite bargain, as was a £15 return trip to Rome. Other perks would include so-called 'educationals' and 'fam trips' – familiarization trips for senior members of the agency – as well as trips for clerks and consultants. There were also 'inaugurals', for when an airline started a new service. These were completely free, and included hotel accommodation, cocktail parties, lunches, dinners and banquets. They were sought-after trips, especially when the destination was somewhere like Tokyo, Hong Kong or Bangkok.

Ownership of Quo Vadis would also give us membership of ABTA, and although Horizon Holidays itself would still be excluded, we would have the chance to observe the workings of ABTA from the inside.

The negotiations with Charles Forte were brief. The price was quickly agreed, and Mr Forte (the knighthood was yet to come) and I signed the necessary papers in his office above the Café Royal. A new chapter of Horizon's history was about to begin.

NOTE

1. Alan Clark, the late Tory MP who sat most recently for Kensington and Chelsea from 1997 until his death in 1999. A maverick who held several ministerial posts outside the cabinet, he blew the whistle on British arms sales to Iraq and was also a distinguished military historian and a superb political diarist. Clark was a self-confessed philanderer, who sang the praises of Margaret Thatcher's ankles and once said he ought to be 'horse whipped' for his extra-marital affairs.

5

The 1960s: how the Wild West was tamed

ROGER BRAY

For the travel industry and its customers, the decade of the Beatles and the Rolling Stones was not unlike that brief period when the American West hovered between lawlessness and the arrival of the US Marshal. The difference was that along the Spanish Costas the cowboys were more real than mythological. These were years of such explosive growth in package holiday sales that consumers inevitably fell victim to over-optimism and risky enterprises. Just as inevitably, as consumers began to fight back, the holiday industry was forced to start putting its house in order.

The sense that mass travel had reached awkward adolescence, that it was on the cusp between childhood and maturity, manifested itself in other ways, too. The reins of regulation on airlines were loosened, but never removed. The rule that package holidays should not be sold for less than the normal return air fare was abused and eroded, but not completely abolished. The Government insisted that the growing number of travel clubs called 'affinity groups', which were often formed purely to skirt international airline rules and enable members to get cheap flights to North America, should be genuine associations, but it did little or nothing to channel the obvious demand elsewhere. Cunard Eagle attempted to inject new competition on the North Atlantic, applying for permission to start scheduled services to the USA, but was rejected.

And while the sexual revolution was boosting a sharp increase in package holiday sales to young people, whose sense of liberation was fuelled by hot nights and cheap Spanish alcohol, the resorts upon which they descended took time to adjust to the new promiscuity. In a vivid example, Italian Tourism and Entertainment Minister Umbero Tupini warned that 'overlong or exaggerated' kissing could get tourists fined.

'The fifties are gone', said *Travel Trade Gazette* in an editorial to mark the arrival of the new decade. 'Whatever history may decide on the first ten years of the second half of the twentieth century, it must surely be marked as the decade when mankind really got on the move. We flew into the jet age. For pleasure purposes, more people from more countries visited each other, by more ways and more routes than ever before. The jungle of red tape which hinders the easy freedom to travel has begun to be cleared away.'

The prospect of new hotels in resorts with guaranteed sunshine seducing ever more people away from Britain's tired seaside resorts was enough to provoke a bitter reaction from Eric Croft, director and secretary of the British Hotels and Restaurants Association. Much of the urge to holiday abroad, he said, stemmed from a strange form of snobbery and 'the fashionable habit of keeping up with the Jones's. It is much more impressive to be able to talk of the *pension* we found at some Mediterranean resort with an unpronounceable name, where sanitation does not exist, and where a visit to the chemist is almost a daily necessity, than to admit to having had a grand holiday at a boarding house, with good English food, at one of our seaside resorts.'

If he protested too much, his anxiety was well founded. In the ensuing ten years, the number of Britons taking holidays in the UK rose by 20 per cent while the number going abroad soared by 230 per cent. A 1966 survey by the British Travel Association (forerunner of the British Tourist Authority), revealed that over 20 per cent of those on foreign holidays were under 25, against only 17 per cent of those staying in Britain.

FURTHER EXPANSION

The last year of the 1950s had seen some 2.25 million Britons making foreign trips, about one in eight of the total, though as yet only 76,769 of them went to Spain. Thomas Cook believed that at least 10 per cent of the population could now afford foreign travel and that a growing number of people had enough disposable income to pay double the average holiday price. By 1967, the total going abroad had more than doubled, to around 5 million. Such rapid growth assisted the emergence of new destinations. Though Greece had always attracted culture seekers, it was not until 1960 that the Greek government opened its first tourist office in London. BEA and Olympic Airways advertised that Greece was 'becoming increasingly popular with tourists today', noting that hotel rates started at about £1 a day at A class properties – and the Comet 4B jetliner began flying from London to Athens in 3 hours 55 minutes.

That year, too, Harry Chandler, whose Travel Club of Upminster was by now chartering flights to Basle, Nice, the Italian Riviera and Perpignan (for the Costa Brava) was introduced to the Algarve. Although plans were already afoot to build an international airport at Faro, this corner of south-west Europe was then barely discovered by holiday travellers. The only way to get there by public transport was by air to Lisbon and then by train. There was only one real hotel in the Algarve, the 35 room Aliancia in Faro. Yet a businessman friend, who had bought some land there, was so enthusiastic about the area that he persuaded Chandler's wife, the redoubtable Rene Chandler, to buy a hilltop plot there for £5000, even though she had never been and had no idea what it was like. The friend would build a villa on it. Rene went to look and was delighted, returning convinced that she and Harry should operate packages there. Her conviction was supported by one travel writer, who wrote of the Algarve in 1962: 'I find it difficult to believe that with the post-war thirst for new travel areas, such a coast had remained unsullied and unsung for so long'. In the event, the Chandlers did not start a programme there until 1965, when the new Faro airport opened and they shared a chartered BAC 1-11 there with Lord Brothers, but Rene's somewhat risky purchase was to play a significant part in the development of a major new holiday area.

FURTHER REGULATION

While such new ideas were fermenting, however, pell mell growth was beginning to create serious problems. The new decade saw the travel industry's first significant failure, a debacle which fuelled calls for a safety net to ensure that in future, consumers were not left stranded abroad and led to the vetting of tour operators' finances. By its close, those calls had been partially answered.

Ominously, in 1960 clients were already beginning to complain about dirty rooms and shoddy service from overseas representatives, and travel agents were starting to question why there were no ABTA rules to protect them from the actions of unscrupulous tour firms. That year a County Court ruled in favour of an agent when a couple on honeymoon complained they had been booked into a filthy room in Spain. The judge ruled that the agent's duty was to make the reservation and nothing else. Otherwise, it would be a 'highly hazardous occupation'. But the writing was on the wall. The Appeal Court overturned the ruling, deciding the agency had failed to fulfil its contract. Some agents were already being accused by their peers of paying up too readily in out of court settlements. One critic described this as submitting to 'legal blackmail', rather than facing adverse press publicity. What was needed, he said, was a body of case law, which would enable the industry to 'carry on in the knowledge that if we do our jobs conscientiously we shall not be at the mercy of every client who looks for any opportunity to claim breach of contract'. Some factors were beyond the agent's control, he went on, such as a 'hotel which oversells its accommodation and offers our clients instead better rooms in a new building 200 yards away'.

The Government upset travel entrepreneurs on the industry's respectable wing by announcing that the newly established Air Transport Licensing Board would not be required to consider tour operators' standards when they granted licences. Opinion in the trade was beginning to favour the introduction of safeguards to protect the package holiday client, though there was no clear consensus on what these should be. Battle lines were drawn between those who wanted *laissez-faire* and those, including ABTA, who felt competence should be vetted. Many foreign hoteliers wanted the reassurance of a licence which doubled as a guarantee of reliability.

A new tours committee was set up by ABTA (its members included Vladimir) to consider all aspects of holiday marketing. Why license air travel alone, some industry leaders wondered, raising an issue which was still unresolved as the millennium drew to a close. What about companies using surface transport? The furore caused the Government to step back, saying there was now nothing to prevent the ATLB from making any enquiries it thought fit.

Already there were doubts that the rush to attract as many bookings as possible in January was providing sufficient returns to justify the cost of the huge accompanying sales drive. Perhaps, said critics, the public would prefer subtler persuasion than being stampeded with warnings that they should 'book now to get bargains'. If there was any merit in their argument, the industry, which still tries to provoke the same stampede every January, would seem not to have spotted it. Tour operators who imagine this was some golden age, when customers invariably committed themselves far in advance, might consider a survey published by BEA in 1961, which found that half of all holidaymakers booked within three months of travelling, and a quarter did so within one month of departure. Indeed, that year saw one firm, Sir Henry Lunn Ltd, set a precedent which was to become familiar by launching a programme of 15,000 late deals aimed specifically at people who had been unable to book the holiday they wanted. No matter how fervently operators wished they could manipulate the market, observing a tacit agreement to hold down capacity so that consumers were forced to pay deposits six months or more before travelling, one of them would always break ranks to take advantage of unsatisfied demand.

THE ABTA CODE OF PRACTICE

ABTA published a code of practice for its members. At the association's convention aboard P&O's flagship *Oriana*, chairman Cecil Garstang condemned firms which published misleading information about holiday destinations and hotels, knowingly provided services at levels lower than those they advertised, or imposed harsh and disproportionate cancellation fees. But self-regulation, he said, was better than that imposed by government licensing to rid the trade of unethical practices.

Rational voices in the industry issued early warnings that adverse publicity might become an uncontrollable avalanche. Ray Barker, then

Sir Henry Lunn Ltd's general manager, predicted that 1961 would go down as a year of disaster for the charter business. Not a week had passed without reports of stranded passengers and poor hotel accommodation. There should be talks between independent airlines and IATA to stop the operations of 'shady firms', he urged. The following year, a new tour operator called Spain International Travel, perhaps recognizing the danger signals, began offering its customers their money back if they were not completely satisfied with their holidays. It emerged that some travel companies were taking bookings before they were sure of getting licences from the ATLB. The Board said that if it caught them at it, they might not get those licences after all. Its warning does not appear to have been very effective. In 1962, Leroy Tours admitted taking 200 bookings despite not having received authority to operate them, provoking an angry attack from BEA.

By the following year, the Consumer Advisory Council was describing the purchase of a package holiday as 'buying a pig in a poke'. At every stage, it lamented, there was an opportunity for unscrupulous or careless arrangements which may leave passengers stranded or – though bookings and payments might have been made – with no holidays at all. 'In general, the more you pay, the more you get.'

Two operators, the Sir Henry Lunn and Poly Group – later to be called Lunn-Poly – and the Co-Operative Travel Service, put forward plans to ABTA for guarantee schemes. Other countries were ahead of Britain. Australia had a bonding system for agents, while those in France were already licensed. French agents had to subscribe by law to a 'default compensation fund' from which creditors could be paid out.

Fears were now growing that firms getting into financial hot water could too easily shake it off and emerge in another form. The Association of National Tourist Office Representatives (ANTOR) urged ABTA to re-vamp its code of ethics to ensure travellers were not left stranded abroad and, more to the point, that local suppliers such as hoteliers and coach operators were not left out of pocket. It demanded that the association should set up a special committee to which companies merging, going into liquidation, receivership or bankruptcy would have to submit any proposals for reorganizing their business. ANTOR suggested a voluntary guarantee to be provided by banks or insurance companies or a mutual or collective fund underwritten by a major insurance organization – or as a last resort, registration of travel agents with the Board of Trade and a requirement that they should deposit bonds – which could be used to pay bills if firms defaulted – with 'appropriate institutions'. ABTA agreed to look at the problem of members who failed to meet their financial obligations. It claimed it had often discussed a guarantee system but that it would cost over £100 for every £200,000 of its membership's turnover.

In February that year, Labour MP Edward Milne, who was fast becoming the package holiday consumer's most dogged champion, introduced a Private Member's Bill enforcing the official registration of travel agents. It called for a safety net which would ensure payments to customers and principal contractors when firms went under and proposed heavy fines or imprisonment for those who broke the law. Legislation was badly needed to deal with unscrupulous, get-rich-quick tour operators, he told the Commons. Holidaymakers were at the mercy of those whose methods were a menace to the travelling public and a threat to the best interests of reliable firms in the trade. Hidden extras lurked. 'Glossy brochures and advertisements offering package all-in holidays at little less than £45, when closely examined, and indeed experienced, by holidaymakers, turn out to cost them £60 or over', he said.

Meanwhile ABTA tightened its rules, suspending for up to three months member firms which changed ownership while its council decided whether to kick them out or reinstate them, but it objected to Milne's Bill, which failed to pass its second reading. But the flood tide of bad publicity was now so high that it would take only one more surge to breach the trade's resistance to reform. That surge was provided by the collapse, in the summer of 1964, of Fiesta Tours.

FIESTA TOURS

Fiesta had been bought from Dutch owners only weeks before the crash by Henry Whitfield, who already owned Travel and Holiday Clubs Ltd, which operated tours for the under-30s. It was immediately plunged into crisis when coach companies refused to transfer a group of its customers from Perpignan airport to hotels across the frontier in Spain. Despite Whitfield's pledge that the firm's summer programme would be completed, it quickly foundered, with some 2000 clients, who had either paid deposits or the full amount for their packages, still to travel. Television news showed a hostile crowd, angry that they might lose their money and their holidays, haranguing Whitfield in the street. 'This is the first time I have booked through a travel agent', said one, 'and it will be the last.' Reactions such as this, a reminder that consumers still failed to discriminate between operators and retail agents, stung ABTA into action. After a group of agents had taken matters into their own hands, rearranging holidays for Fiesta clients who had booked through their shops, the association's officers began thrashing out a solution with legal advisers and sixteen tour operators at Thomas Cook's Mayfair headquarters. Next day, with Whitfield promising to put up enough of his own cash to guarantee hoteliers would be paid, the operators agreed to provide £30,000 worth of aircraft seats. Most, if not quite all, of Fiesta's disappointed customers, went on holiday after all. It is impossible to overestimate the importance of that collective decision. The industry's establishment had acted at last to repair its tarnished reputation and in doing so had laid the foundations on which would be built, brick by brick, a remarkably successful financial protection system for consumers.

The prime mover behind the agreement was ABTA's chairman since early 1963, Ernest Garner, the fast-car-loving head of Hickie Borman, whose sobriquet 'Tubby' owed more to a friendly personality than to stature. He had declared himself against the registration of travel firms, arguing 'This is a free society and we believe in freedom to run our own businesses'. Now he conceded: 'If registration is the only way in which the public can be saved from similar occurrences, then I think the trade should seriously consider it.'

The Government remained lukewarm towards regulating the industry. In April 1965, Roy Mason, Minister of State at the Board of Trade, said registration would be 'too mammoth a task'. But it was clear that another debacle of Fiesta proportions would leave ministers little option, so when a compromise emerged from the association, it was in a mood to be receptive. The compromise was called Operation Stabilizer, brainchild of Garner's successor, C. D. 'Hoppy' Hopkinson. To some it looked suspiciously like a closed shop. From the start of 1966, ABTA retail agents would be allowed to sell only packages organized by member operators. And ABTA operators would be permitted to sell only through retailers belonging to the association. This would not stop companies going bust but members would have to observe accounting rules and a common fund would ensure customers did not lose their money. The plan received a qualified approval from Roy Mason, minister responsible for tourism, who told the Commons: 'If this problem can be solved within the trade itself this will be all to the good'. But his thinly veiled rider was that if the stabilizer proved anti-competitive, it could be referred to the Monopolies Commission or replaced with regulation.

THE MID-SIXTIES

Crucial though the Fiesta affair proved, it had not been the only significant development in travel. In 1963, the Boeing 727 had made its first flight. Mrs Reginald Maudling, wife of the Chancellor of the Exchequer, had opened the £8million Hilton on Park Lane, the biggest hotel built in Europe since the war. There was much admiring of American modernity. This was said to be the first hotel in western Europe with a moveable wall, designed to split the ballroom. A double room without breakfast was £7 10s. Pan American had ordered six Anglo-French supersonics, a project still referred to as Concord without the 'e'. Harold Bamberg had resigned as a director of Cunard in 1963, following the shipping line's tie up with BOAC. Three years earlier Cunard had acquired the airline he had founded, Eagle Airways. Bamberg had long been unhappy with the marriage, complaining that Cunard had no money to spend on expanding the airline. Later that year he had bought back control of what would now become British Eagle. Nor was it only ABTA which had to set about restoring public confidence. Bizarre though it seems today, Zermatt was hit by typhoid. The Swiss National Tourist Office offered victims three-week holidays as compensation with free air or rail travel. And while the industry's difficulties may have put off some customers, it did not appear to deter new players, such as the washing machine tycoon John Bloom, from breaking into the market. In 1963, aiming to sell cheap coach and air holidays and planning to use the direct sell techniques he had developed for his household appliance business, Bloom had formed Rolls Tours.

Describing existing methods of selling as 'Victorian', he promised a free washing machine to every fourth person booking a package to Bulgaria. Though his core Rolls Razor business went bust in 1964, its travel subsidiary, for the time being at least, kept going.

Meanwhile, sex had reared its head as a selling tool. Brochures

Figure 5.1   Leading the way, Horizon were offering holidays behind the Iron Curtain in 1963.

were beginning to sport bikini clad models on their front covers. BEA advertisements featured an alluring model in a jaunty hat and very brief shorts. Thomas Cook, however, decided to model its brochure on the lines of a women's magazine. The firm's publicity chief, Bill Cormack, explained that post-war research showed women were the prime movers when it came to holiday choice. Surprisingly, however, women were not yet the predominant sex in travel reservations departments. BEA, which had launched a drive to recruit new sales representatives, was castigated for failing to take on a single woman. *Travel Trade Gazette* correspondent Ben Wingate Wiggett may have had his tongue in his cheek when he wrote on this issue in January 1963 but his article seems to come from another age. 'Nobody can be more persuasive than a woman with her heart set on a certain course', he wrote, 'for she will employ every wile in her ample quiver to win the day. She is a good talker and a resourceful thinker.' But he counselled travel bosses against seeking '*chefs d'oeuvre*' of loveliness. 'Perfection of physical appeal will not alone send up the sales figures.'

The mid-point of the decade brought a development which was to prove enormously significant for the package holiday business. In 1965, Thomson Organisation acquired Universal Sky Tours and its airline, Britannia Airways, and Riviera Holidays (Gay Tours and Luxitours were added the following year). Between them, the three operators were operating around 100,000 packages a year. That year Britannia disposed of its fleet of Lockheed Constellations and took delivery of four Bristol Britannias – the aircraft from which it took its name – in addition to the one which it had received the previous November. In summer it carried 184,630 passengers. Today it carries some eight million. Originally called Euravia, it had been launched by Universal Sky Tours' founder Captain Ted Langton in 1962. Langton did not want to risk seeing his holiday customers left high and dry by some unreliable private operator – but neither was he prepared to pay the kind of seat rates being demanded by BEA. So he decided to start an airline of his own, buying three 82-seat Constellations from the Israeli carrier El Al for £90,000. Euravia made its first flight, from Manchester to Perpignan, on 5 May 1962.

Gordon Brunton, managing director of Thomson Industrial Holdings, noted how little travel companies knew about their potential customers. Later, the group unveiled what it claimed would be the

Figure 5.2 A very helpful-looking air hostess, starring in a British Eagle flight information leaflet from the 1960s.

most extensive market research project every conducted by the trade. 'It needs modern methods of research if we are to develop the industry to the full', he told a press conference, 'and my company is not going to stand still in this respect.' Meanwhile, a survey by the *Economist* showed Spain's income from tourism had almost doubled in two years and that the country had overtaken Italy to become Europe's most popular destination, with 14 million visitors a year.

Provision One, the rule setting minimum tour prices, was coming under increasing pressure. There was rising irritation among tour operators at the absurdity that short stay winter holidays in Majorca cost more than 15 day breaks in the same resort in summer, because of the high scheduled winter fare structure. If the restriction were axed, they claimed, the typical price of a winter week could fall from £48 to £30. BEA bent with the prevailing wind by introducing a night tourist winter fare of £36 18s to Palma, a cut of over £12. But the ATLB refused a proposal from British Eagle and Lunn-Poly-Rickards for an even lower package price of £25.

BEA's move was symptomatic of the way the major airlines were being stirred into action by the booming charter industry and the threat of independent scheduled carriers desperate to get a bite at their heavily protected routes. BOAC also bowed to the inevitable, announcing it would press IATA to agree a special inclusive tour fare on the North Atlantic. This would be £20 below its cheapest published price and could allow operators to offer two week packages to the USA for £115. The airline's chairman, Sir Giles Guthrie said: 'I believe the time is right to take this big step which is expected to tap a new market in conjunction with travel agents.' Caledonian Airways had been granted a permit to run UK–US charters in the summer of 1963. President John F. Kennedy had signed the authorization. Now the Scottish-based airline wanted to carry package tourists to America. At the end of 1965, the first ever programme of Transatlantic inclusive tours was unveiled. Operators selling the holidays were Hickie Borman, Lord Brothers and Wings. For just under £121, their customers were offered flights to Boston and an itinerary including Niagara Falls, Washington and New York. But not one tour was operated. Caledonian said the US authorities had approved it too late to allow proper marketing. Cynics pointed to BOAC and the new low fares which IATA was persuaded to accept. Whatever the reason, a sharp blow had been struck for the consumer.

The mid-1960s were heavy with other portents for the established carriers. Early in 1966 Freddie Laker, who had resigned as £3500 a year managing director of British United Airways, announced he would form his own airline. With his plan for a cut-price, walk-on Skytrain service to America he would quickly become a constant thorn in the sides of the major players. And in 1967, Pan Am ordered 25 of the new Boeing 747 jumbo jets. Its chairman, Juan Trippe said they would have operating costs 35 per cent below those of earlier aircraft and predicted that fares would tumble.

THE 1966 STERLING CRISIS

For the UK travel trade, as for all British industries at the time, the main preoccupations of the period were economic. In the summer of 1966 Harold Wilson's Labour Government, which had come to power two years earlier with a wafer thin majority, was hit by its first serious sterling crisis. In July it imposed a £50 limit on the amount of foreign currencies holidaymakers were permitted to buy.

The decision created an unholy mess. While credit or charge cards were still relatively few, nobody appeared to have worked out how to control their use abroad. Travel agents immediately claimed plastic would be a way of circumventing the limit. Executives of Diner's Club, American Express and Eurocard met officials at the Bank of England in an attempt to work out a solution. Travellers were to be allowed to take £15 in sterling on the grounds that they could hardly be expected to return to Britain penniless. They were not supposed to add this amount to the £50 allowance, turning it into £65. But how could anyone stop them using it as holiday spending money? 'We don't want people to go buying things with it', said the Treasury, lamely. From the initial confusion it emerged that while air fares would not be affected, hotel and other ground costs abroad would have to come out of the £50. And what about cruising? Treasury civil servants scratched their heads again. A spokesman said: 'If there is a content in the cruise which will mean the payment of sterling to overseas countries for such things as food and port dues, this will probably have to come out of the £50.'

The V-form undoubtedly cost the Government votes. It suggested strongly that some cabinet members had lost touch with social change. To many Britons it must have appeared as a sorry retreat from the modernizing crusade trumpeted by Wilson when he urged the country towards the 'white heat of technology', for it seemed to betray a belief that Labour supporters represented an insignificant proportion of foreign holiday takers and that the likes of Majorca and Corfu were still mainly preserves of the Tory voting middle classes. It was certainly hard to accept the economic justification for a limit so low that travellers needed to watch every peseta and Austrian schilling in their beach and ski resorts. Some travellers, that is, not all. Others found ways of avoiding the restriction. Anyone with a non-British friend who was resident, or who regularly visited the UK, could easily arrange a swapping of funds which was arguably not illegal and in any case virtually impossible to detect (they would pay for you abroad – and you would reciprocate in Britain). Thus it was the ordinary holidaymaker, unable to resort to such sophistry, who suffered most.

The moustachioed MP Gerald Nabarro (Tory, Worcestershire South) railed against the V-form in the Commons, saying how much he loathed being regarded as 'lower than the Albanian tourist' because of the paltry sum of money 'which my government will allow me for my peregrinations around Europe'.

It is arguable, however, that by opening the eyes of hitherto independent travellers to the value which packages represented, the restriction did tour operators more good than harm. But it is hard to ascertain whether a significant shift to inclusive tours took place, however. In the summer of 1967, the first full year affected by the measure, operators sold only two-thirds of the 1.74 million holidays for which charters had been licensed. Yet for summer 1968, the overall number of charter seats authorized rocketed to almost 2 million. Overall spending abroad by the British in 1967 fell by £20 million to £300 million. The average cost of a foreign holiday was £57, down from £59 in 1966 while the amount spent on a holiday at home stayed the same at £19.

The following year, Wilson went to the country in a bid to strengthen his position. The government won an overall majority of 97 seats over Edward Heath's Conservatives. But its economic woes were deepening. Israel attacked Egypt on 5 June 1967 and its leader, President Nasser, closed the Suez canal. Countries including Iraq, Kuwait and Syria, cut off oil to Britain in anger at its support for the Israelis. Arab governments threatened to withdraw their sterling balances. Not long afterwards the Nigerian Civil War, sparked by the secession of Biafra, cut off oil supplies from there, too.

The impact of the Middle East war on Britain's balance of payments was worsened by industrial strife at home. There were dock strikes in London and Liverpool. Following attempts to bolster sterling with a loan from the International Monetary Fund, the Government was forced into what was seen as an even greater humiliation. The pound, whose value had fluctuated little in previous decades, was devalued from US$2.80 to $2.40.

Wilson drew howls of derision when he appeared on television to reassure the nation that devaluation would not affect 'the pound in your pocket'. If it was possible to see what he was driving at in terms of the impact on domestic consumers, it drew a hollow laugh from regular travellers abroad, for it was the start of a long slide in the value of the pound, which was commuted only by rampant inflation and high, resultant pay increases to British workers. Outside the USA, this slide was most noticeable in what came to be known as the 'hard currency' European countries – Germany, Austria and Switzerland. Even after devaluation, the pound was then still worth 62.50 Austrian schillings, for example. The Chancellor, James Callaghan, told the Commons he recognized that travellers to many countries would now get less for their £50 allowances but added: 'I do not think this is the right moment, when people in this country are being asked to forgo an increase in their standard of living, to allow foreign exchange for an additional amount to be spent on foreign travel.' The immediate pain was soothed by the fact that Spain followed suit, devaluing the peseta by the same amount. But the longer term implications for the travel trade and its customers were immense, for devaluation heralded a long and painful period of struggle against the problem of currency fluctuations. Eventually, operators would become adept at hedging – buying all or some of their currency requirements on the forward markets. At that time, few, if any, did. The result, for years thereafter, was the imposition of surcharges every time sterling took an unforeseen nosedive.

CONSUMER PROTECTION

As if there were not troubles enough, and despite the advent of the stabilizer, the issue of consumer protection had not gone away. The

MP Edward Milne had repeatedly but unsuccessfully attempted to push his registration bill through parliament. The Consumer Council was on the warpath against hotel overbooking and unfinished hotels were emerging as a problem. In 1969, some 160 Cosmos customers arrived at Arenal's Metropolitan Beach hotel for Easter to find that the swimming pool, terraces and the top two floors had not been completed – including some guest rooms. The firm blamed bad weather for the failure to finish. In September, Global had been fined under the Trade Descriptions Act after sending clients to a Spanish hotel described as having a pool surrounded by a large sun terrace. The pool, complained one customer, was nothing more than a hole in the ground with one tile in the bottom.

None of this could halt the long term revolution, a fact recognized by the BBC with the launch in 1969 of its first series of the 'Holiday' programme, produced by Tom Savage and starring the great Cliff Michelmore whose job was to sniff out the best value deals. Savage grumbled that it would be seen by 10 million viewers but travel industry chiefs 'don't seem all that interested'. He had attended ABTA's convention in Dublin but had not been invited 'to one reception or cocktail party'. The industry quickly became very interested, for the series would often ruffle its feathers. It was only two weeks old when P&O attacked its report of a cruise on the *Chusan* as 'biased' and 'deliberately hostile'. In a memorable clip, a women passenger had complained that 'when you pay £322 each for your cabin you don't expect to have a pound whip round to pay a pianist to entertain you of an evening'.

THE END OF THE DECADE

But as the 1960s drew to a close, it was airlines and the long, slow death of protectionism which dominated the travel horizon. British Eagle collapsed in November, 1968. Though some had foreseen that increasing competition in the skies would inevitably force casualties, the speed and timing of its demise took the industry by surprise. A later report said it had been under strain for some time and was severely under-capitalized. It turned out that Eagle owed £7 million. Soon afterwards, a second charter airline, Transglobe, also went under.

Provision One was slowly withering on the vine. In November 1967, a slump in the value of sterling forced a 6 per cent jump in scheduled fares. ABTA lobbied Ray Colegate, an aviation official who would later wield huge influence as economic director of the Civil Aviation Authority, complaining that this would make a nonsense of their winter prices, which had been long published. Colegate went to his Ministers and told them it was unreasonable that operators should be expected to increase those prices at such late notice. His view was accepted.

There was still some way to go before the industry would get the freedom it craved, however. The following year (1968) the Air Transport Licensing Board confirmed that prices agreed when operators applied for licences need no longer be raised at short notice if IATA airlines subsequently increased scheduled fares. But tour firms' hopes for more dramatic changes were frustrated. In a 20 page judgment, the Board said lack of minimum price control would lead to discounting, which might encourage less scrupulous operators to enter the travel business, would put pressure on profit margins and could cause companies to collapse, could cause financial headaches for airlines which could jeopardize safety and – the old chestnut – would deprive the scheduled carriers of so much traffic that they would no longer find it viable to serve popular holiday destinations.

By now the Edwards Committee was looking into the entire future of British civil aviation, but as an interim measure, ABTA urged that air package tours should be allowed at not less than half the price of two single, tourist class scheduled tickets. This would allow operators to sell holidays in Majorca from £30 7s instead of £35 3s – which may not sound much now but was a significant reduction at the time, when £30 a week was considered a very healthy salary. The problem was that the rule still made no allowances for the duration of the package. As the association's memo to the Board of Trade, which was investigating the issue, noted, most people still took two-week holidays but shorter holidays were becoming more popular, particularly in low season. Operators also wanted to encourage midweek departures with lower prices, a key to getting more efficient use of aircraft and creating huge increases in the number of customers they carried. ABTA's initiative came to nothing, but the industry had an ally in Colegate. His desire to experiment removed another brick from the wall of protectionism when he persuaded the Department that 1969–70 winter holiday prices could be held at the previous winter's levels, regardless of whether the scheduled carriers upped their fares – and whether they did so before or after operators had applied for their licences.

The Edwards report was published in May 1969. Most of its recommendations, such as the formation of a 'second force' airline to compete with BEA and BOAC, which would be brought under a single holding board, had no direct implications for the package holiday trade, save that they created a climate in which innovation could thrive. Two of them did, however. One urged the creation of the CAA; the other that minimum pricing, at least on some routes, should be scrapped. The stage was set for another great leap forward.

6

Skiing and Cruising

ROGER BRAY

SKIING

For those who bought early packages to the still quiet ski slopes of Europe, travel could be anything but seamless. At the end of the 1950s, Eagle was running night flights, using Viking propeller engined aircraft, from Blackbushe in Surrey to Basle in Switzerland – where passengers would catch trains to their resorts. One night, shortly after 11 p.m., the coach laid on to ferry a group of skiers to the airport from the airline's terminal at London's Marble Arch stubbornly refused to start. The passengers were asked to step down and push the reluctant vehicle along the road until it could be jump-started.

A vivid snapshot of skiing around that time comes from Roy Dawson, then working with Erna Low, who helped pioneer wintersports holidays to the Alps.

'I took a group to the Austrian resort of Hochsölden in 1956. It was the first time I had ever been to the Oetztal. When we got there it was a filthy night. Erna was buying bulk seats at the time on Ingham's "Snow Train" and I had to trust that they had made all the right arrangements. We got to Sölden in heavy snow and there was just a single seat chairlift to take us on to the resort, which is higher up the mountain. The coach couldn't make it up the hill to the foot of the lift so we had to manhandle the baggage up.

'A single lamp was swinging, as if in a ghost film. The cases were loaded on the lift and disappeared into the darkness. I didn't know whether to go up first or last but I was assured there was someone waiting at the top, so I let the customers go ahead. They were pretty terrified by this time. When they got on the lift there were big black hooded capes to protect them against the storm. The chairs whacked them on the calves and they went off, swinging wildly in the night. At the top we had to haul the cases another 150 yards across the snow to the Hotel Sonnblick.

'But not a single one complained. They had survived – and it was an experience to remember and talk about. And next morning there was a wonderful winter mountain view, and sun and snow such as they had never seen before'.

Organized wintersports trips had existed since long before the war. Four Englishmen are credited with taking the first wintersports holiday, in the winter of 1864–5. During a visit to St Moritz the previous September, the owner of the Kulm Hotel, Johannes Badrutt, offered them free accommodation if they came back when snow was on the ground, promising that it was sometimes so warm then that 'we go about in shirtsleeves'. It was an early example of what came to be called a loss leader, for he knew they would bring others. Indeed, one of them subsequently wrote in the visitors' book: 'Far from finding it cold, the heat of the sun is so intense at times that sunshades were indispensable. The brilliance of the sun, the blueness of the sky and the clearness of the atmosphere quite surprised us.'

Henry Lunn and wintersports

In the winter of 1892, Dr (later Sir) Henry Lunn organized his first wintersports package to Grindelwald in Switzerland. The holiday cost around ten guineas, which included a second class return rail ticket to the resort via Dover and Calais (first class was £2 5s extra), meals on the outward journey, and ten days in a hotel with breakfast, lunch, dinner, 'lights and attendance', and free use of toboggans and the ice rink.

Lunn was the son of a Leicestershire grocer. His entrepreneurial instincts surfaced early when, as a boy, he was gulled out of his money by three card tricksters on a train. Not wanting to admit this folly to his father he began breeding bantams and mice, and advertising them for sale in *Exchange and Mart*. Later he graduated to sports goods, and in particular equipment for *sphairistika*, which was to become lawn tennis. His Methodist upbringing persuaded him he ought to be in something more uplifting than trade, so he went to India as a missionary. After an illness he returned to Britain, soon organizing an ecumenical meeting beneath the Jungfrau, in the Swiss village of Grindelwald. He found he made a fair amount of money out of this gathering. The idea of ski trips was born.

Skiing was still in its infancy. In the first year of his new enterprise, Lunn sent out pairs of the newfangled skis to customers more familiar with skates and toboggans.

While it is perhaps an overstatement to claim that the British invented downhill skiing, those with the money to indulge embraced it with particular enthusiasm. By 1902 Henry had discovered Adelboden in Switzerland, which was yet to become popular with skiers and whose hotels were idle in winter. He founded the Public Schools Sports Club, whose membership was limited to those with a public school or university education (lending it a certain snob appeal) and persuaded the owner of the Grand Hotel to open during the ski season. The owner was dubious – but his hotel and another in the village were filled. In the first year they had 440 visitors, the following year 660, the next more than 1000. The new sport was beginning to catch on. Around 1903, new bindings, designed for Alpine rather than Nordic skiing, were introduced and skiers were starting to use two sticks instead of the single long, braking pole carried by the pioneers. That winter in St Moritz saw what may have been the first preparation of a slope reserved for skiing. Lunn expanded into other Swiss resorts such as Mürren and Wengen, villages already served by mountain railways, which doubled as ski lifts. Eventually he was arranging holidays for more than 5000 visitors a year in some 30 hotels. His son, Sir Arnold Lunn, described downhill racing as 'the Cinderella' of competitive skiing until the British persuaded the International Ski Federation to accept it in 1930. And it was the British who organized the first downhill and slalom championship the following year.

Figure 6.1 The first winter sports inclusive tour, organized by Sir Henry Lunn (front, centre, sitting on sledge) in Grindelwald, Switzerland, 1892. Photo: Ray Barker.

Inghams

Three years later, the operation which became known as Inghams Travel was born. Walter Ingham had become intoxicated with the outdoor life – including skiing – when his father's work took the family to live in Vienna in the 1920s. Walter returned to England to work for Remington Typewriters but the mountains proved an irresistible lure. He left his job, advertised for skiers in the personal columns of national newspapers, and took his first private party to Austria at Christmas, 1934. That same winter, he organized five more trips. The business diversified to include mountaineering and walking. Soon, Ingham had expanded into the French Alps.

The war brought a nine year interlude. It was not until 1948 that Ingham resumed his business, but over the following fourteen years the company grew steadily, eventually employing 80 full-time staff and 30 overseas representatives, and carrying some 14,000 people abroad each year. They were still, by and large, the educated middle classes. By

1962, when Walter Ingham sold out to Hotelplan, part of the Swiss grocery wholesaling and retail organization Migros, skiing had begun to attract a new kind of customer.

Erna Low

When Roy Dawson went to work for the redoubtable Erna Low in the early 1950s, the clientele making bookings at her headquarters in South Kensington consisted largely of well-bred young ladies, many of whom had never been abroad before. Dawson, who was given a job on the front desk, reassured them that skiing was nothing to fret about – and ensured that in each group he took to the Alps the ration of females to males was about two to one. 'And most of the men were my friends.'

Erna Low, like Harry Chandler, is a character whose impact on the package holiday story has been disproportionate to the size of her business. She was born Erna Löwe in Vienna in 1909 and threw the javelin for Austria. She had come to London between the wars to work on a doctorate on the Victorian English poet Lord de Tabley. Then in her twenties, she was looking for a way to fund trips home to Austria and thus it was that in 1932, an advertisement appeared in the personal columns of a London newspaper: 'Young Viennese graduate invites other young people to join her Christmas skiing'. A keen sportswoman, she would teach them how to ski and throw in a bit of conversational German. Five men and her chaperone went with her to Sölden, in Tyrol. They paid £15 each for full board at the only inn. Sölden (now a straggling resort with access to over 80 miles of prepared pistes) had no ski lifts. One customer, a Mr Sassoon, recalled: 'Our days were spent climbing on skis and doing every variation of the christiania and snow plough [ski techniques]. Our evenings were spent dancing in ski boots and playing "Where are you, Moriarty?" and other games in which one spends a long time on the floor.' The trip was a huge success.

Erna left Vienna permanently in 1937, eventually joining the BBC to monitor German radio broadcasts for British intelligence from a centre in Evesham and – on such odd occasion as snow fell in Worcestershire – practising her ski turns on Bredon Hill. In March that year, Hitler's troops marched into Austria. The fledgling ski tour operator began sending customers to neutral Switzerland instead.

With the war over, she was back in the ski business. 'Wintersports are on the map again', ran the copy in her 1948 programme. Post-war currency restrictions increased her usefulness to skiers seeking to make the most of their allowances. Erna offered fully inclusive deals to Mürren for 38 guineas, with enough of it paid in sterling that customers had £17 spending money left.

She never married but was wedded to her business. Associates described her as a perfectionist who insisted on signing every outgoing letter herself – and opening every item of incoming post – and as a hard taskmistress, happier to sell holidays than to allow staff to take them. She was also keen to save pennies. One former employee recalls how she sent staff next door to a coffee shop when a health and safety inspector came to check her South Kensington premises. 'She was worried she might have too many of us for the space available. But when the coast was clear she managed to call us all back without even paying for the coffee.' Such stories are invariably told with affection, however. To her legion of friends, Erna displayed and continues to attract fierce loyalty.

Her subsequent business was built largely on the snow trains, which she sometimes shared with Inghams. Inghams was credited with organizing the first dancing bar on board in the winter of 1960–1. The trains, which carried up to 400 skiers via Calais or Dieppe to the Austrian Arlberg and on to Zell am See, became the stuff of folk legend. Carriages rocked through the night with dancing and drinking.

As in all sectors of the travel industry, the gathering speed of growth brought the odd administrative problem. Hubert Schwarzler, now director of the tourist office in the Austrian resort of Lech, worked for Erna Low at the start of the 1960s. 'One year, hoteliers suddenly began contacting us to say we had exceeded our room allocations. There was chaos. I persuaded Erna that I should look at the contracts, which she kept locked up in a safe. It turned out that nobody had checked the group business we were taking that winter against the number of individual customers who were booking.' Erna sold her original tour operation in 1972. The buyers went bust in September 1975 with around 200 clients abroad and she bought back her name.

Figure 6.2 The front of Inghams' 1975/6 winter brochure.

Four years later she sold out for a second time but quickly set up a new business as a consultant representing, among other interests, the French ski resort of La Plagne.

Expansion

As early as 1953, travel companies had recognized the importance of attracting first time skiers. Sir Henry Lunn Ltd, which was offering inclusive holidays from £23 10s 6d in a 72 page catalogue, advertised 'special introductory arrangements for beginners' in the Swiss resort of Engelberg. Poly Tours and Thomas Cook were doing much the same. Austria had begun promoting its ski slopes to travel agents.

But they cannot have anticipated the enormous growth to come. How did it come about that skiing, a sport associated with the privileged, spread its appeal so rapidly throughout the social spectrum that, by the mid- to late 1960s, office workers of modest means and groups of student nurses were taking their first, teetering turns on the slopes? As dustmen and duchesses danced to the music of the Beatles, social barriers became less insuperable – but that was only part of it. Another powerful driving force was that fact that some of the funds paid to Austria under the Marshall Plan, to enable the country to reconstruct after the war, had been spent on building ski lifts, providing the springboard for resorts hungry for business and offering relatively cheap prices. It took some years for Austria to establish itself as the most popular package destination. Switzerland was still the most popular destination in the 1955–6 season. Ingham's was selling sixteen-day rail holidays there with fourteen nights' accommodation for £23 15s. Fully inclusive party arrangements with tuition and 'an ample supply of lift tickets' were offered at 27 guineas. Norway (now a minority destination because of the limited range of its skiing and a period during which prices were too high to attract the mainstream market) was also providing stiff competition. Skiers travelled there by sea. Bergen Line trumpeted that 'for a gay, friendly and inexpensive winter holiday there's no place like Norway, where the snow lies thicker and the £ goes further'. In 1955, there were only five ski lifts or tows in the whole country. Six years later there were

52 but even that was a tiny total compared with Austria's tally. By 1963, St Anton and neighbouring St Christoph alone had seventeen, for example.

But while supply undoubtedly created demand, the key reasons for the skiing revolution were much more prosaic. As tour operators expanded their summer package programmes to the sun, so the industry looked increasingly for ways of squeezing more productive work from charter aircraft in winter. Minimum price regulations (discussed elsewhere in this book) prevented operators from organizing holidays cheap enough to attract the mass market to winter sunshine destinations but seemed not to deter skiers. Improvements in equipment and clothing helped, too. In 1966, when I took my first trip, to the Tyrolean village of Ellmau, I hired leather, lace-up boots which needed regular tightening with cold, wet fingers. Skis still had bindings with cables, which stretched around the heel of the boot. To gauge the length you needed, rental shops made customers stand with an arm raised straight above their head. Where the fingers stretched, there the skis, stood on end, also reached. As a result, beginners were rented skis which were very difficult to turn. Only later, with the advent of *ski evolutif* in the French resort of Les Arcs, was it judged better for them to start on very short skis and progress to longer ones as their technique improved.

There was some advantage to package tour operators in this adversity, however. Many of those who endured it became hooked on skiing for life and returned time and time again. And while learning may have been an often uncomfortable process, the many small resorts were sufficiently unused to large scale tourism that clients struck up friendships with local people.

The skiing take off was given afterburn by the development of a new generation of purpose-built resorts, high in the French mountains. They lacked the soul of those small Austrian villages but the snow was more reliable and the lifts were linked, so that guests could ski for many kilometres without walking, catching buses or covering the same piste twice. When the first complex opened at La Plagne in 1961, many people thought it had been designed deliberately to look like the liner *France*. This was nonsense, though the Compagnie Generale Transatlantique, which owned the ocean greyhound, had invested in a hotel, Le France, which was incorporated in the building.

Figure 6.3 An 18–30 age-group skiing holiday, from Hotel Plan's 1962/3 brochure. 'Impromptu parties seem to spring up like daisies on the lawn'.

Tignes was created in the 1950s when a village was flooded by the building of a dam, forcing the authorities to move its residents up the mountain to a snow bowl with great skiing potential. In 1960 it had

20,000 beds. Two decades later it had 200,000. Another modern resort, built in the Bauhaus style, was Flaine, which opened in 1968. Its central plaza boasted sculptures by Picasso and Dubuffet.

Meanwhile, the resorts of the now vast Trois Vallées lift network in Savoie had been drawing more and more Britons. They included Méribel, which was developed by a syndicate brought together in the late 1930s by a British Colonel, Peter Lindsay, who was driven to look for an alternative to Austria when it was annexed by Hitler. A road was built up the valley in 1938 and buildings were constructed a year later, but it was not until after the war that the first lift was installed. In 1950 it was linked by lift with Courchevel, where farmers had objected to development for fear that discarded cigarette butts would be eaten by the cattle which grazed the slopes during the summer, spoiling the flavour of their milk. Méribel remained small until 1972. Brigitte Bardot used it as a bolt-hole. But it was forced to expand in order to keep pace with neighbouring resorts such as Val Thorens, which opened in 1973, and in 1975 a satellite, Méribel-Mottaret, was opened.

Until the start of the 1960s, Inghams' air tours had been based on scheduled services but for the 1960–1 season the firm announced it was to run charters, using Cunard Eagle to Innsbruck, BUA Viscounts to Zurich and Dan-Air Elizabethans to Geneva. Poly Travel also used charters for the first time, including aircraft of Tradair from Southend, at night, to Basle and to Innsbruck. Thomas Cook said it expected wintersports bookings to jump 11 per cent that season and, significantly for the future, schools travel to the Alps was beginning to increase.

Erna Low took a roadshow around Britain with Norwegians, Austrians and Swiss wearing ski clothes. Sir Henry Lunn Ltd offered first timers the chance to 'ski in a week' on special beginner packages to Chateaux d'Oex in Switzerland. They cost £45 and the brochure carried a short story recounting the experiences of two girls who took a ski holiday. In time for that winter, Austrian Airlines began a new London service to Innsbruck via Stuttgart. Transalp was offering two week Italian ski holidays in Sauze d'Oulx (later to become such a honeypot for young, party loving skiers that it became known as 'Benidorm on Snow') from 45 guineas. Another travel firm, Wayfarers, was flying customers by Cunard Eagle to Innsbruck and

Zurich, offering holidays at resorts in Austria, Italy and Switzerland with names which now look obscure – such as Partenen, Obsteig and St Cergue.

Because of the time needed to reach the Alps by rail, most people had taken two week ski holidays. But for that winter Poly Travel advertised eight days in Igls for £24 18s and Seefeld for slightly less. And Thomas Cook launched packages of similar duration to Austria, proudly advertising that the Hochgurgl Hotel (eight days from £33 9s), had 'a private bath and toilet for every room'.

In October 1962, Sir Henry Lunn Ltd took over Poly Travel and its subsidiaries to form what was the third biggest holiday organization in Britain – behind Thomas Cook and American Express. Poly Tours had a pedigree stretching back to 1888, the date of the founding of its forerunner, the Polytechnic Touring Association. The rationale for the association, soon to be known simply as the PTA, was to provide holidays abroad at reasonable cost for the students and staff at London's famous Regent Street Polytechnic. It was a success from the start and grew steadily, appealing to an ever widening public. That winter, it advertised fifteen-day ski holidays by air to Switzerland with 'daylight flights' by Elizabethan aircraft from Gatwick to Basle. Prices were 44 guineas to Wengen, for example, or 50 guineas to Engelberg. The ads featured a model wearing tuck-in ski pants.

Clarksons

Anyone still sceptical that skiing had reached an entirely new market must have been disabused in the second half of the decade when the cut-price tour operator Clarksons Holidays broke into the wintersports business with Snowjet. Former director Mike Hooper recalls: 'We recruited an entire management team from Inghams. One advantage we had was that we were already running lakes and mountains holidays to Austria in summer, so we could offer hoteliers business all year round.'

The arrival of the mass tour operators forced a major upheaval in the way operators such as Erna Low did business. Previously she had never needed to make down payments to hoteliers. Now it became the only way to secure beds. When Clarksons ran its first skiing programme in the winter of 1966–7, one of its reservations team was a 17-year-old Peter Dyer, who went on to found Crystal, which, much later, became Britain's biggest wintersports operator. He recalls the atmosphere at Clarksons, whose rise and demise is discussed in detail in another chapter, as 'dynamic' and brimming with new ideas. 'It was just more aggressive than the rest. We were undercutting other ski operators and attracting a new kind of clientele.'

Currency restrictions

The economic storm which buffeted Harold Wilson's Labour Government in the mid-1960s did not leave the ski holiday business unscathed. In July, 1966, with England still aglow over its triumph in the football World Cup, the Government slapped a £50 currency limit on Britons holidaying abroad. Fares to and from destination countries were not included, but the cost of hotels and meals had to come out of the allowance. It was a fortnight before the Bank of England announced it would allow an additional £15 to pay for transfers from airports to hotels, though it was quick to emphasize that this concession was intended to cover genuine costs and should not simply be added to the £50. There was more gloom to come. The Bank was soon hinting that ski lift ticket purchases would also have to come out of the allowance, provoking a protest from the Swiss Tourist Office. Its Austrian counterpart estimated that would cost independent travellers about £7 and those on packages – with tour firms which had secured bulk discounts for their clients – an average of £5.

The result was the notorious V-form, on which travel firms had to show how much had been taken out of the allowance to pay for hotel and other local costs. For example, on one operator's eight-day packages to Norway costing from £44 8s to £77 1s, the V-form amounts were £19 and £27 respectively. On a £48 2s holiday at the Villa Rosenegg in Grindelwald, it was £23.

The currency restriction and its impact is dealt with in greater detail in our chapter on the 1960s. It may have deterred those who regarded skiing as less important than a summer holiday. But it seems equally likely that a number of otherwise independent holidaymakers may have been persuaded to take packages by the reassurance of knowing what all the essentials would cost before departure. British guests had to watch the drinks bill in Alpine hotels, however, and the currency limit, coupled with the following year's sterling devaluation, heralded a period in which they were regarded as the poor relations of Europe. This had a marked effect in some resorts, such as Austria's Saalbach-Hinterglemm, where it was decided that, for the time being at least, it would be better to concentrate on attracting business from countries with healthier economies such as Germany and the Netherlands.

In Austria, hoteliers and others were sometimes their own worst enemies when it came to preserving relationships with British visitors, who had played a key role in the development of the country's wintersports business. The weak pound fuelled popular sentiment throughout the 1970s that Austria was becoming very expensive. This feeling was exacerbated during that decade by minor local action which registered loud in the minds of skiers who already felt victimized by economic circumstance: a night club in the small resort of Gerlos, for example, which refused to sell wine in glasses of one eighth of a litre, insisting customers bought at least a quarter. And a hotel in Niederau charged British guests for tap water with their dinners. Restaurant staff, it was later reported, earned a percentage on drinks and preferred to push mineral water. The incident made the front page of the tabloid press. The main effect of such shortsightedness was a remarkable rise in the fortunes of Italy, where the pound went further. Between 1970 and 1978 its market share increased from 5 per cent to over 30 per cent. Italy's success, however would always be tied to the exchange rate. When sterling was healthy, Austria bounced back.

Swans

In 1974, Clarksons went under when its owners, the airline and shipbuilding conglomerate Court Line, collapsed. Among those who picked up its ski customers was Swans. The following year it also picked up Peter Dyer. He was shocked at what he found.

'I had worked for what I considered to be the best tour operator in the country. Swans was unbelievable. The difference was enormous. For one thing they called customers ''punters''. We would never have dreamed of calling them that at Clarksons – even when we changed their hotels four times after they had booked. Then I discovered that letters of complaint were simply being thrown away. I was told the customers would always write in repeating their complaints. I couldn't believe how sloppy it all was.'

The company had acquired a tarnished public reputation. There were reports of heavy overbooking and of customers being asked to pay surcharges when they got to their airport. The company's performance, not least through the urgings of Dyer, began to improve, but when it was sold to Inghams in the late 1970s, its new owners were faced with a dilemma. Swans was a strong brand, well marketed but it did not sit easily with the old established Inghams image. Though the clientele carried by its new owners were no longer just the well-heeled middle classes, there was an attitude of superiority among its managers which is vividly illustrated by a remark Dyer claims he overheard one of them make about him: 'That wretched Dyer – he's so common'. On the other hand, to absorb Swans' brand into its own would be to risk losing many of the customers acquired with it.

Dyer thought this latter course 'stupid' and fought it tooth and nail but he lost the argument. The Swans name disappeared – and with it many of its clients. 'The result was that they went to Thomson, who had been number two behind Swans in the wintersports market and now quickly jumped to number one.' The decision had another, even more significant outcome. Dyer went off to start his own ski operation.

More expansion

Even as late as the early 1970s, ski holiday operating was still an unsophisticated business. One regular customer recalls telephoning the reservations department of a tour firm and asking what kind of lifts there were on his chosen resort. 'Well', came the reply, 'ski lifts'. In the winter of 1971–2, Lunn-Poly sent a representative with no experience of skiing to a small resort in the Austrian Tyrol. One Saturday a client, whose boots had failed to arrive on the luggage carousel at Munich Airport, asked where he could hire some for the following day – until his own could be delivered to his hotel. 'Surely', asked the rep, with all the bewilderment of a Scots non-comformist, 'You'll not want to be going skiing on a *Sunday*?'

There is little doubt that in the decade that followed, mainstream package holiday firms failed to keep pace with the growing knowledge and widening experience of leisure skiers. John Neilson, who launched the eponymous tour operation with a group of like-minded colleagues in 1979, recalls that too many of the men and women running their ski operations 'were not skiers themselves and had no real affinity with the sport'. As a travel agent he had visited popular resorts on 'educationals' – fact finding trips for retailers and their agency counter staff. 'The people who took them often preferred to stay in the bar than get out on the slopes'. The subsequent, soaring success of the company he founded tends to prove his point. In just four seasons, before Neilson Ski was sold for £2.7 million, it came from nowhere to be the country's second largest wintersports operation.

How? Partly by thinking laterally. Neilson invested in ski guides. 'When we started, people who had skied for maybe four seasons were joining because they didn't want to ski alone, but John Sheddon (the ski coach) said he had studied these classes and concluded that in a two hour lesson, they only actually skied for an average of two minutes. We knew, because we were skiers ourselves, that what they needed at that stage was mileage.

'We also invented the snow guarantee and we took goodies to resorts such as sweatshirts and baseball caps with our logo on them and told the reps to give them to the girl at the supermarket checkout and the guy who worked on the lifts so people would see them all season. One of our staff even suggested we should cut our name into the tyres of our local vehicles so it would be left in the snow every time it was driven up a village street. We didn't take that one up – but we did instruct reps to surround the airport arrivals gate en masse so that, whoever the clients travelled with, they would only see Neilson people.'

Peter Dyer formed Crystal Holidays in 1980, with partner Darko Emersic. The Macedonian born Emersic had also worked at Swans and mused that it was a toss up between staying in tour operating and going off to become a long distance lorry driver. In its first season, Crystal carried a mere 1500 passengers. The company's representative at St Johann, in the Tirol, was Andy Perrin, a law student taking leave from his studies to do some skiing. He never went back to the law. Later he became marketing, then managing director.

Crystal quickly became a real competitive force. David Crossland, founder of the major mass market operator Airtours, offered to buy the company. Dyer was not happy with the deal. Emersic disagreed. 'We had a big row', says Dyer, 'and I said I would buy him out'. To do so, Dyer was obliged to arrange a huge loan. So when the Arizona-based Dial Corporation, best known for its soap, offered to buy Crystal for £5 million in 1984, he was far from reluctant to accept. It was an odd marriage, but Dial was already involved in airline catering and was looking to diversify in Europe. The relationship lasted until 1997.

North America

The American connection saw Crystal develop a major programme of ski holidays to the United States. Inghams were the first major operator to launch packages there in the late 1970s, sending customers to Colorado and California. Until then, American skiing had existed as a kind of parallel universe, unknown to all but a handful of British skiers despite the fact that the USA boasted superb resorts such as Aspen and Vail (which had influenced the design of post-war developments in Europe) and that Squaw Valley had hosted the 1960 Winter Olympics. For some seasons, it came and went from the brochures, depending on the strength of sterling against the dollar, before becoming firmly established during the following decade. Its position was cemented during the 1995–6 season, when Crystal announced that the Colorado resort of Breckenridge, a former mining town, had climbed into its top ten best sellers. By then Canada, which had been slower to attract the interest of British tour operators, had overtaken the USA in terms of market share. With the Canadian dollar weaker than its US counterpart and an estimated 8.8 per cent (in 1998–9) of package holiday skiers opting for resorts such as Whistler, Banff and Lake Louise, tour firms began operating charters. At first, with the over-optimism so typical of the industry, they offered more seats than business warranted. Nevertheless, charters to Canada have proved more enduring than those to the USA, which were quickly killed off by a rash of very cheap scheduled fares. The length of the journey and, despite a fall in real terms in fares, its cost, will ensure that North America remains a relatively minor player in the UK market, attracting about 14 per cent of the half million or so skiers booking through travel agents compared with the 28.8 per cent and 15.4 per cent respectively who went to France and Austria that season. But its rise has had a medicinal effect on European resorts, some of which have been jolted out of their arrogance by unflattering comparisons with the higher standards of customer care long evident across the Atlantic.

Airtours

Airtours, by now running its own ski operation, made a second approach to buy Crystal and was again told it was not for sale. Soon afterwards Dial was split into two, leaving the ski operator under a new parent, VIAD. Subsequently Dyer found himself dealing with new faces, too. In 1997 he successfully sought a management buy out, raising £14 million in venture capital and acquiring other tour operators, also owned by the US parent – notably Jetsave and Tropical Places.

Again Airtours came courting. This time Dyer and his colleagues decided to put the firm up for grabs. Swiss-owned Kuoni and Thomson joined the bidding. Thomson emerged the winner and in 1998, just eight years after its inception, Crystal was sold for £66.2 million.

It was an intriguing move. Only five years earlier Thomson Holidays' then managing director, Charles Newbold had stirred up furious controversy among wintersports operators in a newspaper interview. His contention? That skiing had acquired a new, fashion image among the upwardly mobile young of the get-rich-quick, Thatcherite 1980s but had somehow lost it in the 1990s. Some saw a grain of truth in this, though it was impossible to tell whether the market suffered as a result. Others disputed it angrily. Right or wrong, his company's subsequent acquisition illustrated vividly how rapidly the travel industry sands can shift.

CRUISING

Cruising as we know it today is a remarkably young business. It was not until the early 1960s that tour operators began selling fly–cruise packages to the Mediterranean and another decade was to pass before holidaymakers were flying in significant numbers to join ships in Miami or the Caribbean.

With hindsight, the fly–cruise seems an obvious solution to the problems of passenger shipping lines, which could no longer compete with comfortable, fast, long haul flights, and needed ways to use otherwise redundant capacity. There was also a certain irony in that their apparent executioners, the airlines, turned out to be their saviours.

Much of the credit for the industry's spectacular re-incarnation must go to three men: the Greek Chandris brothers, Dimitri (known to everyone in the trade as 'Mimi') and Anthony, whose cruise line was a major early force in the Mediterranean and who launched what were perhaps the first air–sea packages to the Caribbean, and the Norwegian Knut Kloster, who is credited with the idea of persuading Europeans to fly to Miami and set sail on the vessels he based there.

But it was closer to home that the mass market had its first taste of cruising. Before the 1960s, a cruise had seemed an indulgence of the idle rich, a way of whiling away time wrapped in plaid blankets, reclining in chairs on varnished wooden decks – something that ordinary people promised themselves if they won the pools. In too many instances, however, that first taste turned sour. As tour operators tried to get costs down they came under fire for cramming too many customers into converted cargo ships. Vessels of 4000 tons were too small for 400 passengers, Greek ship owners complained. To make matters worse, delays at shipyards where ships were being converted stirred up a storm of adverse publicity as cruises were cancelled and passengers were kept kicking their heels at the dockside.

Chandris Cruises

All that was in the future, however, when Chandris Cruises was launched in 1963. One of its first vessels was the former royal yacht *Mansour*, bought from the ruling family of Saudi Arabia. Built in Glasgow in 1936 she was converted, renamed the *Romantica* and carried some 190 passengers a week on cruises from Venice. Customers were supplied by Milbanke Travel, who acted as the company's general agent in Britain. By 1965, Chandris was operating five vessels from the Italian port and was also selling cruises through Global and Vladimir's Horizon. The Chandris ships were small and only good for summer coastal voyages around the Mediterranean. Ideally, the line needed winter business.

'We hit on a wonderful idea', recalls Eric Phippin, who had been taken on as passenger manager and set up the cruise line's London office. 'We discovered that there was airline capacity available on cabotage routes (routes on which airlines were allowed to pick up passengers in one foreign country and drop them in a third). KLM had a service to the Dutch Antilles via New York but they didn't have much traffic. The Friday night flight from New York to Curaçao was invariably empty. We based the *Romantica* in Curaçao and for the first time we had an airline which would sell cruises linked with the air ticket.' The ship operated two different, back-to-back itineraries. Then the line added a second vessel, the *Regina*, which carried about 600 passengers and alternated between the Mediterranean during the summer and the Caribbean in the winter. Once a fortnight she called at Antigua. Before long, Chandris was buying 80 seats a week from BOAC so that its customers could join the ship there.

The *Romantica* was to make another small piece of travel history. In 1970, under charter to Lindblad Voyages, she made the first cruise to the Galapagos Islands. When the trip was planned it emerged that the only hydrographic survey of the waters around the archipelago dated from 1816 and had been used by the crew of Charles Darwin's *Beagle*. Because of the *Romantica*'s draught, a new one had to be carried out by an American hydrographer from Panama before the cruise could proceed safely.

Cheap cruises

It was in the second half of the decade that the major tour operators began to take an interest in cruising. Just as on dry land, their aim was to keep prices as low as possible. Elderly, unsuitable ships were sailed into action. Profit margins, when they existed, were wafer thin. It was a recipe for disaster. Troubles came to a head in 1971, when the failure of package holiday companies to deliver the cruises they had promised was a staple diet for the press. In spring, late delivery of the 10,822 ton *Delphi*, due to be operated for Clarksons by the Greek Efthyamiades Line, forced the operator to scrap five cruises. Faults in its electricity generating equipment delayed the maiden voyage of the *Delos*, another vessel chartered by Clarksons, by four days. A postal strike prevented the firm from notifying passengers in time. When they turned up at Luton Airport, all the agreed to fly out and wait until the problems were solved. Later that spring, the ship broke down on a cruise around the Greek islands, and the customers had to be flown home. Clarksons' head, Tom Gullick, protested that cruise lines charging much higher prices had also run into difficulties with late delivery and breakdowns. They included Cunard, which had axed the first departure of its new vessel *Adventurer*. But it was the cut-price operators who felt the coldest blast of bad publicity.

A classic saga of the way these cheap cruises ran into choppy waters was that of Cosmos which chartered the 14,976 ton *Galaxy Queen* also in 1971. The ship had been built almost 30 years earlier as an aircraft carrier and had seen service with the Royal Navy as HMS *Fencer*. Italy's Lauro Lines bought her in 1950 and converted her into a liner to carry emigrants to Australia, renaming her the *Sydney*. By 1967, now called *Roma*, she was back in the Mediterranean with Lauro. She was then acquired by Cosmos and Sovereign Cruises, run by the same Captain Ted Langton who had been in at the beginnings of the package holiday.

The new owners discovered she was short of lifeboats. According to a report in the *Sunday Times*, a harbour official at the Italian port of La Spezia had 'claimed his usual perks' and promptly sold six of them off. The previous owners agreed to provide new ones. Four spring cruises were cancelled as the owners awaited seaworthiness certificates, including one from the Cypriot authorities. The ship made her maiden voyage in May but there were reports of chaos on board, with many facilities not functioning. In July it was announced that the *Galaxy Queen* would have to be withdrawn from service for eight weeks, causing cancellation of four more two week cruises and hitting over 2000 holidaymakers. Passengers who flew to Nice to join the ship for a fifteen-day cruise in September were shocked to be told that yet again there were problems. The vessel was not ready. Some flew straight home again. That cancellation alone cost Cosmos around £100,000 in revenue, and as a succession of technical problems refused to go away, her remaining programme for the year was cancelled in early October. Cosmos told clients they could switch to a vessel operated by Costa Line, but the two companies failed to agree terms and passengers were offered refunds. Eventually the joint owners lost patience, and sold the ship. Cosmos managing director Wilf Jones professed himself 'thoroughly fed up' with her.

Tour operators soon became disenchanted with ships. The oil crisis of 1973 had pushed up the cost of ships' bunker fuel as well that of aviation fuel. Suddenly it soared from around 8 per cent of operating expenditure to some 25 per cent. And while airlines were becoming increasingly fuel efficient, consuming less and less per passenger mile, the ageing vessels chartered by tour operators remained as thirsty as ever. One was so ancient it had served as a sort of floating holiday camp for the Hitler Youth in the 1930s. Staff were more productively used selling cheap air packages. Those operators still selling packages after the Court Line collapse hung on for a while but eventually gave up. Thomson pulled out in 1977 after a season of alarming losses in which it had filled only 4500 of 5500 berths on offer, and that only after heavy discounting.

The Russians

They remained uninterested until the 1990s, when Airtours, followed by rivals, began operating a new series of budget cruises. In the meantime – thanks to a scheme which helped Britons emigrate cheaply to Australia – their role was adopted by the Russians. The Soviet Union recognized, as early as the 1950s, that building passenger ships and selling capacity to westerners was a good way to rake in hard currency. Demand for capacity on the Australia run had soared following the introduction in 1947 of the assisted passage scheme. This was launched by the Australian Government, which wanted to increase the country's population, partly to boost the economy and partly because a sense of vulnerability to Japanese attack during the war had led to demand for more defensive manpower. Britons and other Europeans who were prepared to give life Down Under a reasonable shot could get there for £10, a fraction of the normal one way fare of around £200, provided they stayed for at least two years. Two local entrepreneurs set up a company called CTC Lines (it stood for Charter Travel Company), to handle this business. Unable to get the cabins they needed, they chartered from the USSR. At one time, up to six Soviet ships operated on the run. The need for traffic in both directions, and the fact that most Europe-bound Australians wanted to arrive at the start of summer, left these vessels looking for work between voyages. CTC, which had been set up in Australia to handle the immigrant business, began organizing local cruises to fill the gaps. Royal Mail Lines did the same at the London end. In the mid-1970s a company called Anglo-Soviet Shipping bought CTC lines, and turned it into a London-based, Soviet cruise agency.

Ships painted with the hammer and sickle sailed from Tilbury. The cruise business in Europe was boosted by Soviet intervention in Afghanistan. Russian ships, banned from US ports, were relocated there. Prices were up to one fifth lower than those on western vessels. Among them was the *Mikhail Lermontov*, which struck rocks and sank off New Zealand in 1986. In 1984, these ships were reckoned to have earned over US$2 billion in foreign currency. On some ships, passengers who did not want to pay for cabins could spend the entire cruise sleeping in reclining seats in cavernous deck areas which, many were convinced, were intended to be used for tank landing craft if war broke out. To supplement their home built fleet, the Russians even acquired foreign flagged ships, including *Carmonia* and *Franconia* from Cunard and the German *Hanseatic* – which became the *Maxim Gorky*.

Despite the sometimes indifferent food and patchy service, cruising, Russian style, proved surprisingly popular. A row had blown when Britain went to war against Argentina over the Falklands in 1982. UK lines accused CTC of filching their business after British liners had been requisitioned as troopships. It seems unlikely many stalwart customers of Cunard or P&O made the crossover, however. The Russians, after all, were offering a very different experience.

Crew members who had just served dinner popped up on stage singing and performing Cossack dances. Before the advent of *glasnost* and *perestroika*, when Moscow regimes were at their least compromising, they were often recruited to keep an eye on each other, lest they displayed unhealthy political tendencies or, worse, attempted to defect. An American who worked aboard the *Odessa* in the late 1970s, quoted by William H. Miller in *The Cruise Ships* (Conway Maritime

Press 1988), said they were allowed to discuss the US system of government but not their own. He described a typical dinner as 'boiled fish, boiled potatoes and white asparagus on a white plate – no colour whatsoever', and recalled the 'rubber duck' on Wednesday nights.

When the old order was toppled at the end of the 1980s and the Soviet Union became fragmented, its passenger fleet, once the largest in the world, was also scattered. The Soviet state had owned the ships, but the state no longer existed. Who should get them? Countries that had emerged from the Soviet bloc as independent nations began to squabble over who should get what. Ships were detained, some were sent for scrap. In 1997, CTC, which had kept afloat chartering the Belfast-built *Southern Cross*, was disbanded.

Norwegian Cruise Line

Seeds of a shift to the Caribbean had been sown in 1965, when Knut Kloster built a ferry, the 11,000-ton MS *Sunward*, to ply between Southampton and Algeciras in southern Spain. But the imposition of foreign currency restrictions the following year nipped the service in the bud. Not long afterwards, Kloster received an approach from Ted Arison, who went on to found Carnival Cruise Lines, the world's biggest cruise company. Born in 1924 in Palestine, Arison served in the British army during the Second World War, after which he assumed control of his father's small Tel Aviv shipping company. He later fought for Israel's independence in the Israeli-Arab War of 1948. He had been virtually penniless when he moved to the USA in the early 1950s, and his business ventures over the next two decades were not conspicuously successful. Arison suggested Kloster should relocate the *Sunward* to Miami, to operate a passenger and vehicle service between there and Nassau, in the Bahamas. Most of the passenger vessels then operating out of Miami were decrepit and their safety record was lamentable. Arison would act as agent for Kloster's ship, which was a roaring success. Norwegian Cruise Line was born.

In 1971 the partners fell out. Arison, who died in 1999 at the age of 75, bought his first ship, the *Empress of Canada*, which he operated as the *Mardi Gras*, and went on to become a billionaire, eventually buying a controlling stake in Israel's biggest bank, the Bank Hapaolim. Besides

Carnival itself, his corporation owned Holland America Line, Windstar Cruises and had majority interests in Cunard and Seabourn Cruise Line. Kloster, meanwhile, was enjoying such success with his Nassau operation that he commissioned the construction of two more ships, the *Starward*, whose vehicle deck could be quickly fitted with ten pre-fabricated cabins when demand justified it and which operated to Montego Bay in Jamaica, and the *Skyward*. The first pure cruise was operated by a fourth vessel, the *Southward*, which was launched with a programme of two week itineraries.

Within a short time, NCL faced competition from Royal Caribbean, which was set up by three Scandinavian shipping lines and operated smarter ships with long, raked bows, the first of which was *Song of Norway*. NCL suddenly needed a gimmick to ensure it did not lose market share. Until then it had packaged its fly–cruises with a fully inclusive price. Bob Duffett, who was working for NCL in London, came up with the idea of offering the cruise with a £99 return fare between London and Miami. When tour operators rang BOAC and demanded seats at the same price, the airline was incensed, threatening to withdraw its agreement with NCL. Duffett's opposite number at Royal Caribbean, Jennifer Brown, responded by offering customers 'free flights' to Florida. It was a spat which was to continue for some three years in the mid-1970s.

In 1979, Kloster had what Duffett still regards as 'a stroke of genius', when he was persuaded to take a look at the former ocean greyhound, the SS *France*. A symbol of Gallic pride, she had been built at a cost of £30 million for an earlier era and she had entered an already shrinking market when she began service in 1962, a 67,379-ton dinosaur with wooden fittings abandoned in favour of aluminium alloys, glass enclosed promenades and a jukebox, which, until recently at least, still worked. With a first class lounge which looked as though it could be the set for a dance routine by Fred Astaire and Ginger Rogers, she had taken five days to cross the Atlantic before being withdrawn from service in 1974.

An Arab businessman had bought her with the idea of using her as a floating casino on the St Lawrence Seaway, but the Canadian authorities had vetoed his plan. Now she lay, forlorn but still cared for by a team of cleaners, in the French port of St Nazaire. Duffett recalls: 'Armed with flashlights and torches – there was no power supply to the ship – we began to explore this monster. It was staggering. Apart from the artwork every chair on board had an individually tailored dust cover.'

Kloster pulled off a 'magnificent coup', buying the ship for a mere $18 million. After a brief tussle with the French unions he had her towed to Bremerhaven in Germany, where she underwent a complete refit, at a cost of $95 million, to become the *Norway*. In summer, she sailed to her new base in the Caribbean. One of her pools had been turned into a disco. On the deck where lady passengers had once left their poodles in a kennel area, complete with French lamp posts, there was now a 150 metre (480 foot) long replica of a boulevard, with pavement cafés.

THE *ORIANA* AND BEYOND

Despite such entrepreneurial brio, the withdrawal of the major tour operators becalmed the market. In 1974, around 150,000 Britons took cruises. At the start of the 1980s there were only 55,000 and it took another decade for the industry to claw its way back. Not until 1988 did bookings reach the level seen in the year Clarksons collapsed. And it was only in the 1990s that numbers began to grow by leaps and bounds – expansion which was seized upon and fuelled by cruise lines, which ordered ever larger ships, and major package tour companies, which decided the time was now ripe to tap the market again. But business was increasing at sufficient speed in 1988 to prompt the launch of Project Gemini, the code name for what would become P&O Cruises' new *Oriana*. The company, which includes the separate Princess and Swan Hellenic brands, needed her to complement the *Canberra*, then the most successful cruise ship in the UK market and accounting for one-fifth of cruises sold there. *Canberra* had been built as a two class passenger liner for the Australia run but in 1974 she had been converted into a single class ship operating Mediterranean and round the world cruises. P&O was early to spot a growing desire among British holidaymakers to sail from home ports. In the first three years of the 1990s, the number doing so rose by two-thirds to over 80,000. So *Oriana*, ordered from Germany's Meyer Werft shipyard in 1991 and built at a cost of £200 million was specifically designed for them. Because they represented a small market compared with the vast catchment area that was North America, that meant ensuring there was something on board to suit all tastes. The 69,000 tonne *Oriana*, fast enough to sail to the eastern Mediterranean and back, visiting a half-dozen ports, during a typical sixteen-day cruise, was also built to provide a high standard of comfort at middle-of-the-road prices. She was launched by the Queen in Southampton in 1995.

That same year Britain's second largest tour operator, Airtours, started operating cruise holidays. Its decision to break into the market removed the lid from a bubbling well of demand. The previous year 270,000 Britons had gone to sea. In a single year the total soared to 340,000. Rival Thomson, caught flat footed, quickly joined in. Its entry into the market in 1996 helped boost the figure to 416,000. By 1998 it had swelled to 635,000 – an impressive jump even without the 40,000 or so cruises to Egypt and Israel, sold to holidaymakers in Cyprus, which the UK Passenger Shipping Association had not included previously in its statistics.

Clearly people wanted to go cruising if the price was right. Suddenly it was cheaper. In 1993 fewer than a quarter of all cruises booked had cost less than £1000. Four years later it was 44 per cent. The Mediterranean fly–cruise staged a huge comeback. In 1994 only 40,000 Britons cruised there but the return of the tour operators boosted that to 240,000 three years later.

Airtours decided to buy ships, rather than follow the pattern of the late 1960s, when operators had chartered them. This would enable the company to exercise much tighter control over quality than its predecessors had been able to command. It set up a separate division, Sun Cruises. By the end of the 1990s it had acquired four vessels. When it bought the fourth, the firm moved up market in an calculated effort to win repeat business from customers who had tasted cut-price, three star cruising and were now prepared to try something a little smarter. Thomson returned to the charter formula, however, operating four entire ships by 1998 and taking cabins on others. It decided to position a ship in the Caribbean year round and to turn another, the *Topaz*, into an all inclusive floating resort, where everything would be covered by the brochure price. To use that term – floating resort – was to sum up neatly the change which had swept over the industry. There would always be a demand for small, intimate vessels or for a more authentic seagoing experience, such as that offered by the sailing ships of Star Clippers, but, increasingly, the new giants were designed to provide distractions to rival those on land. Ships were beginning to be run more as hotels. Customers were no longer passengers but guests. Ships, ordered in batches rather than singly in order to cut costs through common specifications, had great, hotel-like atria and shopping malls. On *Voyager of the Seas*, the first of three enormous, 142,000 tonners ordered by Royal Caribbean International and capable of carrying over 3,800 holidaymakers, there are two such lobbies, each eleven decks high. There is a climbing wall, a skating track, a full size basketball court and a 1350 seat show lounge designed in the style of La Scala opera house in Milan.

No longer does a cruise imply a long, leisurely progress from continent to continent. In 1997, the number of one-week holidays bought by the British overtook the total of longer trips for the first time. The average age of those going cruising has dropped, too, though not as far and fast as the industry would have liked, for it is still around 55, and the proportion of under 35s taking fly cruises in 1998 was still only 14 per cent. Yet there is no doubt that cruising fulfils the same purpose as the all inclusive resort, which attracts a younger clientele. It is likely, therefore, that the averages may obscure an interesting detail – that the industry's extraordinary upsurge partly reflects a need among people in high pressure jobs to wrap themselves into a safe cocoon, protected from a ravening modern world.

Horizon at its Peak

VLADIMIR RAITZ

Horizon now had its own travel agency outlet in Central London (in Maddox Street, off Regent Street), and was, over the years, to establish fifteen branches across the UK in towns like Nottingham, Cardiff, Bristol, Manchester and Glasgow. Our offices at 146 Fleet Street had become far too small, and we set up new headquarters in Hanover Street in the West End – an area that was rapidly becoming the location for many airline offices and National Tourist shops, and was becoming what Harley Street was to doctors and Bond Street was to high-class jewellers.

Further expansion of our tour operating programme was the number one priority. Let me briefly review the Horizon Holidays brochure of 1970. It consisted of 196 pages of text and colour photographs, compared to our four page black and white mimeographed leaflet of the years 1950 and 1951. The cover showed a reproduction of a painting by Raoul Dufy of a south of France seascape (very different from our competitors' brochure covers, showing couples or families lying on deckchairs on the beach), and was supposed to underline Horizon's sophistication and exclusivity.

All of our flights were now entirely by jet aircraft. We used the BAC 1-11s of British United Airways, which had absorbed Gerry Freeman's Transair, as well as British United's VC10s for our long-haul holidays, and some of BOAC's 707s, BEA's Comets and Britannia's 737s. In addition to the traditional seaside holiday, Horizon was now offering holidays in villas, coach tours, Mediterranean cruises, and a 'Far Horizons' range of holidays to the Americas and the Far East. The brochure featured holidays to the south of France – Cannes, Menton and Nice. In Corsica, our old stalwart Calvi had been augmented by Algajola and Propriano. Long, exploratory car journeys by myself and colleagues throughout Italy had yielded many resorts on the Neapolitan Riviera such as Amalfi, Positano and Sorrento. The Venetian and Adriatic coasts were well represented, as were Sicily, Sardinia and other islands like Capri and Ischia. The Greek mainland and a multiplicity of her islands was well featured, and also Yugoslavia, which was making a powerful entrance on to the tourism market at that time. Portugal, Tunisia and Turkey were also featured, and the Soviet Union and the USA were included for the first time.

I had also created, in conjunction with two large travel agents (one in Birmingham and the other in Wolverhampton), a new tour operator, flying to the most popular Mediterranean resorts from Birmingham and East Midlands airports. This company was named Horizon Midlands and was, in 1972, to be floated as a public company – the first travel organization to do so.

An independently commissioned opinion poll had asked travel agents throughout the UK to rank all the major tour companies in order of preference on seven different counts:

Which company had the highest standard of accommodation?
Which company had the fewest complaints?
Which company had the most charter plane experience?
Which company had the best brochure?
Which company had the widest choice of resorts?
Which company would the agent recommend to his most discerning clients?
Which company would the agent choose for his own holiday?

Horizon came out as first choice in all seven categories. No wonder, then, that we featured this fact prominently in our literature, and also used it in a TV commercial in which travel agents appeared as cartoon characters, shouting 'Horizon!' as each of the questions was put to them by an announcer.

INCREASED COVERAGE OF RESORTS

Horizon's coverage of all the main resort areas had increased dramatically since the early 1950s. In Majorca, we now offered holidays to Palma, Cala d'Or, Camp de Mar, Paguera, Magaluf, Santa Ponsa, Calamayor, Palma Nova, Arenal, Cala San Vicente, Cala Millor, Cala Ratjada and Puerto Pollensa. We still offered holidays to our first port of call, Puerto de Soller, where Noreen Harbord's hotel was now supplemented by three others.

On the Costa Brava by 1970, we were featuring San Feliu, Lloret de Mar, Playa de Aro, Calella de Palafrugell, and above all, Estartit – where we had built our own chalet hotel, the Club el Catalan, after 'discovering' this wonderful and totally unspoilt village with its enormous sandy beach.

We have already seen how Torremolinos was 'discovered'. By 1970, Horizon had built its own hotel there, the Torremora, but we were using many others to supply the demand that now embraced both summer and winter sunshine holidays. The resorts of Marbella and Nerja had been added to our Costa del Sol arrangements.

We owed the addition of Tangier to our programme to Mike Edmonds, who had moved to Torremolinos from Majorca, to become our chief resident rep for the Costa del Sol. Mike organized weekly excursions from Malaga to Tangier, in northern Morocco, a half-hour flight away. It was an enjoyable day trip, and clients loved visiting another country (indeed, another continent) and loved to browse through the markets and visit the Casbah. These excursions were such a success that we decided to make Tangier (and later Agadir and Marrakesh) an integral part of the programme.

Tangier in those days was still an international Free Port, with all the attractions of duty-free shopping. Wonderful bargains could be had, especially in drinks, cigars and cigarettes. Leather goods, too, were sold at astonishingly low prices. Tangier in 1970 had all the charm of a provincial French town, with open air cafés and restaurants, as well as the mysteries of north Africa. There was even a splendid casino. All of this was to change a few years later. The Free Port was abolished, as was the casino. The French atmosphere, too, gradually disappeared. But until that happened, our clients were put up in excellent hotels along the seafront. My favourite was the Rif Hotel, run by a larger-than-life manager named Aimé Serfati who had acquired, as a result of his many trips to the UK to visit travel agents (as well as favoured lady clients) the nickname of Bullshit Harry.

GORDON BRUNTON

Horizon's 1970 programme marked the apogee of the company's success. It was compiled during the summer months of 1969 – the year that we achieved the highest net profit of our history (over £6 million in today's terms), which was not bad for a privately owned small firm with still only one shareholder: myself. I felt that I was on top of the world, blithely ignoring the fact that hubris is often followed by nemesis. In 1970, although one of the leading and largest tour operators in the UK, we were by no means in the kind of virtual monopoly position that we had enjoyed for the first years of our existence. An important newcomer was now in the field, and I felt very much responsible for putting him there.

It was late in 1964 when I received a call from Gordon Brunton asking if we could meet, and we did a few days later. Gordon and I had known each other since 1939, when we met at Cambridge as students at the London School of Economics which had been evacuated there, to Peterhouse College, at the beginning of the war. At Cambridge we had shared lodgings together and we had remained close friends ever since. In 1941, Gordon went off to war and I was recruited by United Press and then by Reuters to do reporting jobs where my three main foreign languages (Russian, French and German) were essential. By 1947 we were both back in 'civvy street' and resumed our friendship. We would meet regularly for a modest lunch in a small City luncheonette named Scott's. Gordon had joined a publishing company and was selling advertising for a group of trade papers, while I was nearing the end of my stint at Reuters. We were both 25 years old.

When, two years later, I started Horizon Holidays in Fleet Street, Gordon came to visit me and wished me the best of luck with my Corsican venture. Neither of us had any idea then of the significance that meeting was to have. Gordon had progressed rapidly and impressively in the publishing industry and was now the Chief Executive of Thomson Publications, the magazine and publishing division of Roy Thomson's rapidly growing Thomson Organisation Ltd. Over lunch, Gordon explained to me that, having carried through a large and quick diversification of Thomson's interests in magazine and book publishing, he was now in charge, as Group Development Director, of planning further diversification into new fields.

He told me that roughly half of Thomson's profits came from Scottish Television – famously (or infamously) described by Roy Thomson as a 'licence to print money'. That licence was under threat and was looking increasingly vulnerable as the Labour government was becoming more hostile towards cross-media ownership of television and newspapers. In addition, there was increasing public concern over the concentration of newspaper ownership in too few hands, and it was harder than ever for Thomson to grow and develop in their core business of newspaper publishing. Gordon's job was to find a major opportunity in an entirely new field – preferably one which might have some synergies with the firm's existing interests. To achieve this he had limited financial resources, since Thomson's were tightly stretched by their need to fund major capital investments in order to modernize a number of old newspaper operations.

Gordon explained that he needed to find:

1. A young growth industry with high potential.
2. An industry not requiring deep technical know-how, which Thomson's did not possess.
3. A business with a cash flow that worked on a different cycle to newspapers.
4. A business that might employ some of the resources Thomson's already had, and in an area where Thomson's management skills (particularly in marketing) could make a contribution.

After analysing dozens of industries and opportunities, Gordon Brunton concluded that the package holiday industry fulfilled many of these conditions. He reasoned that the tour industry, which was still at an early stage of its development, had the potential for massive growth. The British climate was unpredictable, particularly during the summer holiday season, and the British public could have a holiday in the Mediterranean sun in a decent hotel for the same price (and sometimes a lower price) that they would pay for the possibility of sitting in a Blackpool boarding house watching the rain pour down.

By dint of analysis, market research and applied economics, Gordon had reached the same conclusion that I had – the only difference being that I had proceeded by instinct, seat-of-the-pants reasoning and a gambler's opportunism. Gordon felt that the package tour business would dovetail perfectly with Thomson's other interests. Holidays were paid in advance at a time of year when newspaper revenues tended to be low, and conversely the holiday bills had to be paid when newspaper revenues were high.

Gordon asked me if I would sell Horizon Holidays to Thomson's and go there to run a newly formed Thomson travel division. He suggested that Horizon, being the premier up-market tour company, would fit in particularly well with such Thomson newspapers as *The Times*, the *Sunday Times*, the *Scotsman* and the *Western Mail*. It was part of Gordon's plan that the newspapers could deliver millions of messages each week at marginal cost to promote the company's travel interests and give them an enormous advantage over the competition.

I was greatly surprised by Gordon's proposal – as well as intrigued and even flattered. However, it didn't take me long to decide that I valued my independence too much to become part of a huge organization like Thomson's, however tempting the financial induce-ments. Gordon expressed his disappointment but told me that he understood and respected my decision. He did brighten somewhat when I said that I owed it to him, because of our long and close friendship, to assist him and Thomson's to implement their plan. Gordon immediately asked me to work for them as a consultant in this matter. Satisfactory arrangements were made and I set to work, using my wide knowledge of the trade to identify and negotiate with prospective sellers.

It was clear to me that the most important player in the industry (apart from myself!) was Captain Ted Langton, who had started Universal Sky Tours. Sky Tours also owned a controlling interest in an air charter line called Euravia – soon to be renamed Britannia Airways – that operated out of Luton airport with three Britannia aircraft, made by Bristol Aviation and nicknamed the 'Whispering Giants'. I met with Ted Langton and told him of Thomson's interest.

At that time, Ted was in his sixties and was not in the best of health. He chainsmoked continually, and had a trail of ash perpetually cascading down the front of his suit. Ted was immediately very interested in the offer. I arranged a meeting during which Ted met Gordon and they very quickly reached a tentative agreement – subject, of course, to accountants' reports and other vital investigations. Agreement would also have to be forthcoming from the Thomson Board, who had still to be sold on Gordon's plans. (The Thomson Board, it must be said, was really Roy Thomson himself. He and his family trusts owned 70 per cent of the company.)

I also advised Gordon that he should consider buying another tour company, much smaller than Sky Tours but growing fast, called Riviera Holidays. It was owned half by Aubrey Morris, a former taxi driver and half by Joe Morrison, an accountant. Aubrey and Joe, formerly close friends, were by this time at daggers drawn, and they could only resolve their differences by selling 50 per cent to each other (for which they lacked the cash) or by selling the whole company to a third party. Aubrey and Joe met with Gordon and myself, and a tentative deal was struck.

Price Waterhouse, Thomson's auditors, then undertook due diligence in both companies. The preliminary report that came to Gordon was hardly encouraging, particularly in the case of Universal Sky Tours. By the time the full report was completed, the conclusions were totally negative. According to this report, financial control was non-existent, the company was running at a loss, there was no coherent management structure whatsoever, and every single decision was taken by Captain Ted himself, who appeared to be a complete maverick. The only positive aspect was Euravia Air, which was professionally run by Jed Williams, an old aviation hand. But the airline at that time was a relatively small part of the whole.

The day came for the Thomson Board to meet, which they did in the boardroom in Elm House, off the Grays Inn Road. Gordon Brunton presented his project and explained that with the financial resources that had been put at his disposal, and with his brief to achieve rapid growth, any venture would be bound to contain a high degree of risk. (That was certainly true of this project.) Gordon said he was absolutely confident that the time was ripe to enter an industry that was poised for explosive growth.

The accountants then took over and damned the 'whole crazy project' with brutal efficiency. Many years later, Gordon read me an extract from Roy Thomson's autobiography, *After I was Sixty*.

The project was presented to us by Gordon Brunton in the boardroom of Elm House. He had called the accountants to examine the balance sheets and the projections, and to give their views of the proposal. We had found an opening in the travel business fairly early in its developing story; this can be judged by the fact that Sky Tours had not yet shown a profit. Nor were there any assets other than three or four Britannia aircraft. Only goodwill and shrewd faith. I don't think I have ever heard a less favourable report than what the accountants gave that day. In our three hours' discussion, a great deal was said about what could go wrong with Gordon's scheme. I did not say anything until all this had been aired, and then I said I wanted to go ahead with Gordon's proposal. 'I think he may be right', I said. Our marketing director raised some doubts about including an airline in the scheme. He had the idea that ordinary working people would not go for aircraft travel. We went into the travel business.

Having been given the all-clear, Gordon then had to line up the final details with Ted Langton. The price was agreed at £300,000, based largely on Langton's projection of the season's trading plus an additional payout based on performance. Gordon asked Ted if, in the event that the minimum profit projections were not met, he would be prepared to repay part of the £300,000 asking price? Ted was adamant that under no circumstances would any of that amount be repayable – that must be Thomson's risk. Gordon countered by saying that there should be a ceiling placed on the additional, performance-related payout. After much haggling, it was agreed that the additional payout would be limited to £700,000, giving a maximum total purchase price of £1 million. In its first year under Thomson's ownership, Universal Sky Tours and Britannia Airways made in excess of £1 million profit. Thomson's were delighted while Ted Langton was less than happy that he had sold his business too cheaply.

The Riviera Holidays acquisition was also completed, and so was my task in helping Gordon to achieve his aim. Thomson Holidays went on to become the market leader in the package holiday field, largely due to a brilliant managing director Gordon had installed, named Brian Llewellyn, a former marketing director of Thomson Regional

Newspapers. Within 40 years of Thomson's original investment of £1 million in buying Sky Tours, Thomson Travel was sold to a German conglomerate, Preussag, for £1.8 billion – a pretty decent return. Gordon Brunton had brought off a major coup. But by then he had left the organization. After Lord Thomson's death, the set-up there was no longer to his liking.

Should I have accepted Gordon Brunton's offer to sell Horizon to the Thomson Organisation? With hindsight, I certainly ought to have done. After the Thomson approach, I received numerous others, including from Cunard and from Sir Charles Forte, from whom I had earlier bought Quo Vadis. I turned them all down without even entering into preliminary discussions.

THE MEDITERRANEAN AND CLUB 18–30

The traditional fortnight's holiday by the sea, largely around the Mediterranean coastline and mostly by charter aircraft, is still the preferred vacation of the majority of holidaymakers. There is, nevertheless, a significant minority of clients (some of whom have had their fill of lazing around on beaches and some of whom have never been interested in doing that) who require holidays of a different nature. And this section of the market has existed for some time. To cater for its needs, a variety of travel operators came into being – some developed by large organizations like Thomson's, others established by independents with a good idea and a modicum of capital. These 'niche' operations include holidays for birdwatchers, music lovers, battlefield buffs, art students and amateur archaeologists.

Among the most successful of these operations (and one which has been popular for many years) is Swan's Hellenic Cruises. Swan Hellenic takes parties to Greece, led by a guest lecturer who is often a renowned historian or archaeologist of the calibre of the late Sir Mortimer Wheeler, who will guide their charges through the sites of Ancient Greece, explaining the historical background and enthusing in equal measure. Swan Hellenic was run for many years by Ken Swan, and was formed by Ken's father (W. F.) and uncle (R. K.) Swan. Ken eventually sold the company to the P&O Shipping Company which continues to run it with considerable flair and success. In the days when

Horizon was riding high, I attempted to buy Swan Hellenic but was repulsed. I have at last, after all these years, started up my own niche operation: tours for lovers of Havana cigars, to Cuba. A little more of this later.

At Horizon, we did start our own niche operation in 1970. It was

Figure 7.1 Vladimir suffering through one of the more mundane days in the Horizon office.

more of a 'superniche', in fact, and in the course of time it became a large-scale operation of its own accord, although by that time it was no longer under our own aegis. The name of this Frankenstein's monster was Club 18–30, and it came from the mind of a man named Paul Latcham.

Paul (bright, serious and about 6 foot 8) had joined our company at the age of 19, recommended by our advertising agency, and had rapidly risen through the ranks, having covered the various divisions of tour operating such as reservations, planning, hotel contracting and supervision of the resort representatives. His special love was the island of Minorca. I vividly recall taking him there on his first foreign journey with Horizon, to introduce him to a typical Mediterranean resort. I was driving with him in our hired SEAT on the deserted roads when Paul spotted a tree he didn't recognize. It was a fig tree and, having never eaten fresh figs before, we stopped so that he could sample the fruit. He fell in love with the taste, and made me stop at every fig tree we came across, eating more each time. By the end of our drive, he must have consumed over 40 figs. When we finally reached Señor Juan Victory's hotel, Paul retired to his room to 'lie down for a bit'. He did not leave his room (or, more accurately, his bathroom) for the next 36 hours. After this experience, he knew all about figs.

By the time Paul Latcham was 25, he was a highly valued member of staff. In early 1970, he came to see me in my office.

'I've had an idea which might interest you,' he said. 'I've been travelling around many of our destinations, and I've noticed that a lot of the younger clients – especially the single people – feel a bit out of place in many of our hotels. They feel constrained by the presence of the older crowd. They want to dance, they want to drink, and they want to pitch up at the hotel in the early hours of the morning without having to be deadly silent. There have been complaints to the reps about the rowdiness of some of our younger clients, and I think we should do something about it. Why don't we try to separate the young crowd from the mums and dads?'

I thought this over for a few moments. It was an excellent idea. Not only could we eliminate the friction caused by the generation gap, but we could attack an entirely separate segment of the market. A new division of Horizon Holidays would have to be created. What we needed most was a name that might catch the imagination of our target clients. The board of the company, and a few other key executives, sat in the boardroom and threw out over a hundred possible names. None of them were any good. At last, someone uttered the words 'Club 18–30' – I can't recall who it was, but it certainly wasn't me. In any case, the name was greeted with acclamation, and a new travel concept was born.

We seconded one of our bright young executives, David Heard, to manage Club 18–30. (He took to it swimmingly – so much so that he later claimed the whole thing had been his idea. Paul Latcham would have something to say about that!) We started advertising Club 18–30 in a fairly restrained way: they were simply holidays for young people in the 'bread and butter' destinations such as Majorca and Benidorm, anywhere that featured plenty of nightlife. We contracted small hotels and *pensions* that were cheap and in which we could take over the entire allocation of rooms. Spain was the ideal country for this. We put our 18–30 customers on charter flights that departed and arrived in the middle of the night, thus getting extra use out of our air companies and saving money. We reckoned that these customers wouldn't mind what time they flew, as long as the holidays fitted in with their budgets and left them with more money to spend in the resorts.

To begin with, bookings were satisfactory but not spectacular. In our advertising, there was absolutely no emphasis on drinking or on sex. One might even say that our ads at the time were prudish. The attitude at Horizon was very much one of not worrying about what these young clients got up to on their holidays, as long as they didn't frighten the more sedate clients in the same resorts. There was one genuinely frightening incident that I recall, however.

I was staying at the Club el Catalan in Estartit, which belonged to Horizon, when I was woken up at 4 a.m. by the Club 18–30 rep who was in a state of total panic. Apparently, a 19-year-old woman had arrived the evening before, checked into her hotel, and had immediately proceeded to a nightclub with a group of her friends. Having (presumably) consumed a fair amount of alcohol over the course of the evening, she had returned to her hotel room in the early hours, lit a cigarette and promptly fallen asleep. Her room caught fire but the hotel manager had succeeded in dragging her out, and she was now in the nearest hospital with severe burns. We quickly alerted her parents in Scotland and flew them to Gerona on the first available flight. I met them at the airport and escorted them to the hospital. For the next five days, I was with the parents constantly. On the sixth day, their daughter died. I would never wish to experience what those parents felt when the doctors told them the news.

After three years of only modest results, David Heard came to me and said that he had a buyer for Club 18–30, if I was interested. By that time, I must admit I was fed up with the whole concept and the disproportionate number of problems that came with it. David led a management buy-out with the capital of Maurice Harskin – with whom, incidentally, he soon started to quarrel. The pair sold the Club, which later found its way to ILG of Intersun fame, and finally found a home with Thomas Cook where it resides presently. In the meantime, the Club (and especially its advertising) has become notorious, with the emphasis on sex, sex and sex again. Several times the company was taken to the Advertising Standards Authority, and was condemned on a number of occasions. I was sincerely pleased not to be associated any more with a product that had to be sold in this manner.

8

The Rise and Fall of Clarksons

ROGER BRAY

Much as everyone can remember where they were when President Kennedy was shot in Dallas, so anyone working in the travel industry on the evening of Thursday, 15 August 1974 can recall how they heard that the Court Line holiday and shipbuilding empire had collapsed.

For those directly employed by the company, memories are particularly vivid. Christopher Kirker was at home, cooking dinner. His wife, who had been watching the BBC's 9 p.m. bulletin, came into the kitchen to deliver the grim news that he was out of a job. Only an hour and a half earlier he had been at the offices of Clarksons, Court Line's major package tour subsidiary, helping the operator's marketing director, Bill Robertson, to put together the brochure for summer 1975.

Espionage between the major tour firms was rampant. A 'mole' at the Italian print works used by Clarksons' bitter rival, Thomson, had managed to smuggle out a copy of that company's brochure. Robertson and his colleagues were desperate to learn whether they could push the price of some packages through the psychological £100 barrier. They combed the Thomson price panels to discover that their competitor had done just that. In an environment in which price comparisons were so sensitive that they could mean life or death for a tour firm, it seemed Clarksons was safe to follow suit.

Sadly Clarksons was far from safe. Its problems were much graver than Kirker, now the successful operator of a city breaks programme, had realized. 'I knew Court Line was in trouble, but I did not appreciate how bad things had become.'

Another who was taken by surprise was Ian Champness, who had also been working on the brochure. He left the office to go out to dinner, ignored several telephone messages when he got home, and was distraught to be woken by his radio alarm with the words '. . . following last night's collapse of Court Line . . .'.

Indeed, only a handful of people outside the Court Line board-room did appreciate the true gravity of the company's financial position. Among them was Tony Benn, then Secretary of State for Industry in Harold Wilson's Labour cabinet, which had just decided that the Government would bail Court Line out by taking over its shipyard and ship repair interests. After attending a meeting to discuss the deepening crisis a week earlier, he wrote in his diary: 'It appears that the company is in a much more serious position than when we decided to acquire the shipyards. The whole company will go into liquidation next week and we must be sure that the shipbuilding interests are safeguarded. The holding company which owns Court Line shipbuilders is just a shell and the whole thing is utterly rotten.'[1] Benn's role in the affair, as we shall describe later, was to spark a bitter political row.

Why should the rise and fall of Clarksons merit a whole chapter of this book? Because its impact on the history of the package travel industry was seismic. Because it was the first major operator to adopt the 'pile 'em high, sell 'em cheap' philosophy which was copied, despite its spectacular demise, by a clutch of other companies. And because the changes in consumer protection which were forced into being by its collapse are still felt today.

RISE

In just nine years to 1973, the firm expanded from a small operation carrying 4000 customers a year into a giant providing packages for 1.1 million. That expansion took place mainly in Spain, where the Franco government was subsidizing the growth of its tourism industry through a system of credits to hotel developers to enable them to build the accommodation needed to cope with ever-increasing demand. When this system ended towards the end of the 1960s, Clarksons kept hotel building ticking over with its own form of financing, advancing so called 'bed deposits' to developers in return for reduced bed prices when the hotel began to receive its customers. The company also bought shares in a variety of holiday projects on the Costas – not just in hotels but in land, beach barbecues, English-style pubs and a local travel agency.

The man driving it all was Tom Gullick. He and Vladimir never saw eye to eye. Between them was a fundamental difference in business philosophy. Vladimir blamed Gullick for dragging down prices and quality. Gullick thought Horizon Holidays were simply over-priced.

He was born at Westgate-on-Sea in Kent in 1931, was evacuated to North Wales during the war, entered the Royal Naval College at Dartmouth as a 13-year-old cadet, and in 1948, aged 17, joined the Navy as a midshipman. After a spell in submarines he became assistant operations officer with the reserve fleet on the Clyde, where his shooting and management skills on the Scottish grouse moors so impressed his superiors that he was appointed flag officer to the Commander in Chief of the home fleet. Later he said: 'I suppose this was the gilded period of my service career. I led a country gent's life in the Navy, wined and dined with heads of state and kept a watchful eye on the admiral.' The experience was to stand him in good stead.

After 14 years in the service he left in 1958, using his naval contacts to get a job running a small travel agency called H. Clarkson (Air and Shipping Service). It was a business call on the Petrofina oil company that set his mind racing about the possibility of day trips to the continent. The firm wanted to run an outing for its employees to the World's Fair in Brussels, where the symbolic construction of tubes and spheres known as the Atomium had become a huge attraction. In the event, that deal failed to materialize, but Gullick soon began to organize outings to the exhibition for other groups, charging clients £7 a head to travel from Charing Cross. Realizing that here was a market waiting to be tapped, he set up a group tours department at the agency. It was the first building block of an empire.

One of those trips to Brussels was arranged for the Walthamstow Chamber of Commerce. An official of the chamber suggested he should organize similar outings somewhere else. 'What about the tulips in Holland?' he wondered. 'I'm sure my people would like to go.' But it proved to be the Women's Institutes of Britain who really wanted to go. So extensive was this network of clubs, so great the demand to see the Dutch bulb fields, that in the second year of his operation there he chartered some 50 aircraft.

In 1959, Clarksons, as the firm was now known, was hived off as a separate operation. For the next three years it concentrated solely on short breaks, including slightly longer ones lasting three, four and even six days. By now it was offering trips to the Rhine, Copenhagen and the vineyards of Burgundy. In Holland, Gullick displayed an early symptom of the business flair which was to take Clarksons briefly to the stars. Couriers were always trying to divert tour buses to particular souvenir shops, where they could earn commission on the side, rather than get them straight to the bulb fields. He recalls: 'By the time they had taken them round all the places selling Blue Delft pottery, cheese, clogs and whatever, the time they had in which to see the tulips at the Keukenhof was very limited. So we banned shopping diversions and erected what could best be described as a sort of giant aircraft hanger, where we sold all these things ourselves. We limited customers to 20 minutes' shopping time. There was a chap with a stopwatch to ensure they didn't linger any longer. That's how we learned about charging people for a licence to sell souvenirs to people at our beach barbecues or on our donkey rides later, in Spain.'

Michael Hooper, then acting as public relations officer for a nuclear power station and who later became a director of the company, recalls how he was recruited by Gullick at the Antelope pub, near Sloane Square, where the two drank together socially. 'I told him I was interested in taking groups to Paris. We took a group of Americans and when we got there, Gullick and his girlfriend and a couple of other friends disappeared to Maxim's, leaving me to look after the customers. After that I moonlighted for Clarksons for a while before joining them full time. I left the day job half an hour early and went to the Columbia Club in Bayswater, to see if I could round up enough of the Americans who went there to fill a DC-3 to Paris. There were GIs, teachers and some embassy staff. They never had much luggage and I remember one of them buying a grandfather clock which we got into the hold of the aircraft.'

Clarksons broke into the Spanish summer holiday market in 1965. 'We realized we could do it more cheaply than anyone already in the market', says Gullick. The first brochure offered packages of eight, eleven, twelve or fifteen days – with prices from 26½ guineas. Hooper recalls that Gullick was doubtful many people would go for anything but the shortest of these tours, and that most would be previous short break customers. But the programme was a sell out.

'I think one reason for our success was that we had established tremendous contacts with the Women's Institutes', Gullick believes, 'and that they included the next generation of young holidaymakers. At that time we made very few sales through travel agents – virtually all holidays were sold direct following word of mouth recommendations. Our prices were probably around 20 to 30 per cent less than other people's, which was partly to do with negotiating better rates with suppliers such as hoteliers, partly down to the intelligent use of charter aircraft, and partly down to the fact that we were paying less commission than our competitors.'

The operation began with Vikings and moved on to Viscount turboprops. Soon afterwards Clarksons bought a Comet jet and leased it to the airline Dan-Air. The airline acquired two Comets of its own which were used to carry the firm's customers. Then another airline, Autair, offered to buy the new BAC 1-11s if Clarksons agreed to give them a 'bankable guarantee' on the hours they would fly carrying its charter business. By 1967, the firm was able to promise that its holidaymakers would travel by jet.

Within about four years of launching into the mainstream summer package business, Clarksons had shot to number one. Gullick's boast is that, while he ran the company, the aircraft it chartered never flew with an average of less than 95 per cent of their seats filled. Never content to sit on its laurels, the firm built on its success by offering potential customers free calls to its reservations centre after 6 p.m.

More than any other, the firm was responsible for the creation of Benidorm, which became Spain's most popular resort. Clarksons customers took up some 6000 of the total of 10,000 or so beds there in the late 1960s. It singled out hoteliers who had shown good management skills and lent them money over five years to build new properties to its own specifications. But even this system proved inadequate to keep up with its mushroom growth, so Clarksons formed its own development company in Spain and built eight giant hotels, each with 600–800 beds, in major resorts.

These were heady, exciting days, with the youth culture of the 1960s in full bloom and the prospect of unlimited horizons and vast

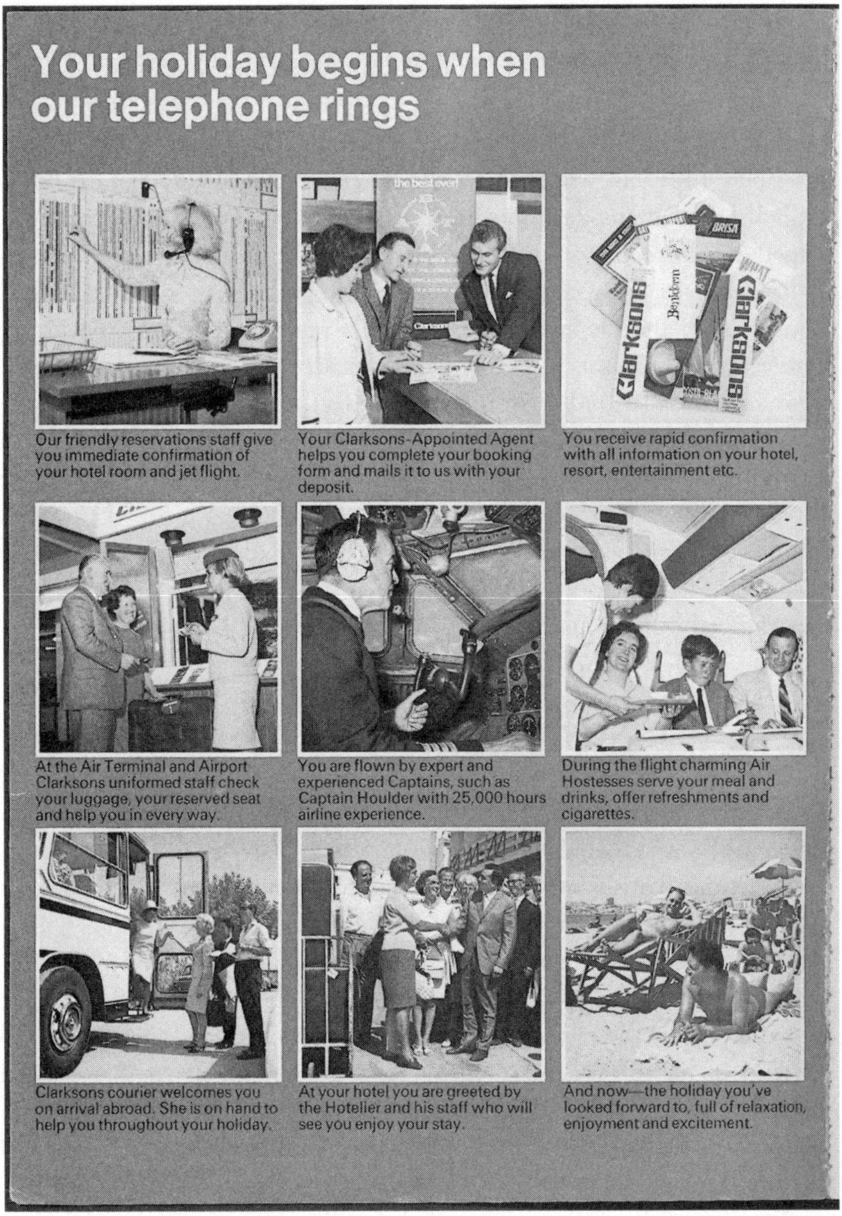

Figure 8.1 A page from the 1968 Clarksons brochure, explaining the whole package holiday process.

riches for the holiday industry. England's World Cup triumph at Wembley in the summer of 1966 had put a new spring in the nation's step which not even the economic woes which beset Harold Wilson's Labour Government – and whose impact on the holiday industry are described fully elsewhere in this account – could dampen. Indeed, Gullick felt that the re-imposition of foreign currency limits that year helped his business rather than hindering it. 'It made more people realize that for less than £50 you could get a two week holiday.' Figures from the Department of Trade's investigation into the Court Line collapse bear this out. They show that in 1966, Clarksons carried approximately 16,000 customers, and that in the following year the total had soared to 90,000. By 1968, it had multiplied more than tenfold in two years – to 175,000. But Gullick claims it was never just a cash machine. 'We always considered ourselves as more than just a commercial organization. We felt we were expanding horizons and making a lot of people very happy in a way they might never have experienced but for us.'

INNOVATION AND EXPANSION

Those who worked for Clarksons were intoxicated by the constant ferment of new ideas. A vivid example was the Clarksons chicken farm. At that time British holidaymakers were still not entirely happy with Spanish cooking, so the firm felt it necessary to provide them with a blander alternative, such as an omelette, on standard hotel dinner menus. But Gullick began to suspect that somebody was profiteering at his expense, for the egg dishes began to cost more than they should. So a friend of his offered to set up a farm at Benidorm, so that several thousand eggs a day could be supplied at a controlled price. 'We knew', says Gullick, 'that we could always pull down the farm and sell the land at a profit later.'

Such control was the key. Gullick and his colleagues knew that they could make a lot of money in resorts if they could channel customers' activities, so they set up a department with a self-explanatory label: Resort Development Activities. It acquired nightclubs and barbecues – including one in Benidorm which handled some 1000 holidaymakers every evening. It purchased donkeys in central Spain and imported them to resorts in Majorca and along the Costas, making money from tourists who had their picture taken in the saddle. Squeezing every last penny of revenue from the operation became an art form. Demand for single rooms outstripped the capacity available, so the firm offered lone customers twin bedded rooms with screens down the middle, even to shares of opposite sexes. Some of them didn't bother to have the partitions sent up from reception. Michael Hooper recalls the inception of the 'hot bed system' in which rooms were used twice in the same night by different clients. One group would leave at midnight and another, having arrived on a night flight, would take its place.

It was not only Spain which earned increasing amounts of revenue from Clarksons' growth. In Eastern Europe, the Romanians were quick to appreciate that the rapid returns which tourism produced would outweigh the potential social damage which might be caused by the infiltration of capitalist aspirations. Gullick went to dinner in Bucharest with Nicolae Ceausescu, who was the country's leader from 1965 until 1989. Ceausescu wanted Clarksons to come up with new ideas for holidays there. He and his guests spent much of the evening telling stories against the Russians. Clarksons subsequently launched tours of Transylvania and cruises on the Black Sea.

Gullick saw nothing wrong with using customers' deposits to finance the building of new hotels in Spain but it was perhaps inevitable that, in the stampede to create extra capacity, schedules for construction were cut to the bone and that the merest hiccup, such as a spell of severe weather, led to damaging delays. The reputation of package tour operators in the late 1960s and early 1970s was heavily tarnished by recurrent reports of unfinished hotels. Artists' impressions became commonplace in brochures. 'We had to show customers something', says Michael Hooper, 'but what horrified me was the way builders were putting up breeze block walls and just slapping plaster on them.' While he accepts that the headlong rush to build hotels created problems, Gullick insists that these problems were inflated by the press. 'We always guaranteed that if a hotel wasn't finished, we would put the customers who had booked to stay there in a higher class of hotel. The press, on the other hand, weren't above moving cement mixers from one place to another to create emotive pictures. As I recall, it happened in Ibiza.

'At the time we were taking a huge amount of flak with claims that we had too big a share of the business. I invested in a Tavistock Institute report into why people complained. We were running a complaint rate of about 5 per cent at the time. The report showed that the majority of those complaints were pretty spurious. I never believed that in order to placate a small minority of difficult people it was right to put up prices for everyone else.'

Publicity could be manipulated to positive effect too. Take the case of a hotel in Minorca which was still unfinished as the summer season opened. At first, most customers were happy to be offered more expensive holidays in Tenerife, but as the July peak approached, Clarksons knew there would be no more spare beds in the Canaries. Crisis loomed. By now the firm knew the hotel was ready, but the Spanish authorities were dragging their feet over the issue of a licence. Gullick handed the problem to his public relations department, which called officials in Madrid with the threat that UK newspapers might soon be reporting how they were wrecking the holidays of some 200 ordinary Britons. 'That night, we were asleep in a room next door to the tourist office in Mahon, when there was a knock on the door from the inspector who said he had just opened the hotel.'

The firm launched its first series of Mediterranean cruises in 1970, having chartered the 7000-tonne *Melina* from Efthymiadis Line of Piraeus. The ship was converted to cater for 480 passengers. Cruising, said Gullick, had for too long been the province of the 'high class market'. Announcing sailings from Ancona, he said: 'We want to offer a top class ship at rates which are within the means of many more people'. Top class meant air conditioning – but there were major problems installing it, recalls Hooper. 'People would get on board and open the portholes.'

As Clarksons expanded, much of Gullick's time was absorbed in trying to persuade the Government to abandon Provision One, the clause in the Civil Aviation Act which forbade tour operators to offer package holidays at a price lower than BEA's economy return fare, ostensibly as a way of preventing the diversion of passengers from the state airline. We deal in detail with the impact of this rule – and with the campaign to get it scrapped – in other chapters. Gullick realized very early that it undermined the efficient use of charter aircraft and hampered growth, notably by preventing the sale of very cheap winter breaks in the sun. Like all bad or superannuated law, the provision was gradually abused and eroded. In 1970, for example, when Clarksons doubled the size of its winter programme, Gullick tweaked the nose of the Board of Trade by undercutting the minimum prices allowed and including vouchers in some deals, for car hire, laundry, excursions and other entertainment.

By then the Edwards Committee, set up by the Government to look into the future of British civil aviation, had included among its sweeping recommendations a proposal that Provision One should be abolished. In return for that, announced Gullick, Clarksons would accept the Government bonding and licensing of tour operators. The rule, he claimed, was preventing some 10,000 Britons from buying £18 holidays in the sun. It was forcing Clarksons to operate flights at night, when the firm was allowed to charge a cheaper rate. As an example of the way customers were losing out, he quoted a six day package to Athens, which he wanted to sell for £39, but which Provision One obliged him to sell for £10 more.

News that the Government had decided to relax the rule, though only for short winter holidays of seven nights or less (and to a limited range of destinations) broke in February 1971. Gullick recalled later that he had anticipated the breakthrough. The day after it was announced he was due to fly to Bucharest. 'I arranged to meet my advertising man and an artist at Heathrow and we sat down there and designed a full page advertisement for the *Daily Express*. We offered long weekends in Benidorm, for example, for about £15. The following weekend we sold about 200,000 of them. We only made about 30s (£1.50) profit on those winter holidays but we could probably make another £5 from selling excursions in resorts. Relaxing the rule also allowed hotel owners in Spain to reduce their prices – because they were now able to offer their staff year-round jobs at lower overall wages.'

DECLINE

By now, however, Clarksons was running into trouble. Its problems were two pronged – the capital structure of its investments in Spain and the fact that passenger numbers were outstripping the ability of its administration to cope. Though its turnover continued to increase, its profits shrank inexorably. The structural problem was that funds for bed deposits to hoteliers and other investments in Spain were fed through a Lichtenstein company, Sunotel, to its Spanish associate, the hotel firm Cristaltour, which was owned equally by Sunotel and a Spanish bank, the Banco del Noroeste. The bank had advanced large amounts of money to enable Clarksons to expand, requiring its repayment in seven years. But it soon became clear that Clarksons was not making enough money to meet the deadline. So Cristaltour leased its hotels to its subsidiary, Servicios del Sol, at rates which were high enough to guarantee the bank repayment. Unfortunately they were also too high for the subsidiary to make an operating profit. Clarksons was stuck with the consequent losses. Administration headaches began to pile up after 1968, when the firm introduced a disastrous computer reservations system, which was not flexible enough to cope even with routine changes in holiday bookings. This developed into a dreadful mess, in which some customers simply did not pay anything for their holidays. Flights, for example, were checked by booking staff to see that all passengers had paid – but only after they had departed. So some people travelled without paying in full. They were sent standard demand letters but generally failed to cough up until they had received two or three reminders. This was just one of the problems to hit the firm's cash flow. Another arose when holidaymakers were switched to alternative resorts because of poor bookings in the ones they had chosen originally, a process known in the travel business as 'consolidation'. If this happened, a new invoice was raised by the administration department and fed into the computer but no check was made to see if the customer had paid, so he or she would be registered as a debtor. Travel agents, confronted with demands for money from clients who had already paid, began to hang on to those payments until their accounts could be properly reconciled.

Michael Hooper, who had argued for the retention of the early, manual system of booking charts until the gremlins could be exorcized, says: 'Nobody ever knew exactly how many bookings they had. They were having to issue invoices manually but they could never reconcile that with what the computer was doing. If we had kept a firm hand on the company as directors I don't think any of this would have happened, but in the end the whole thing was out of control.'

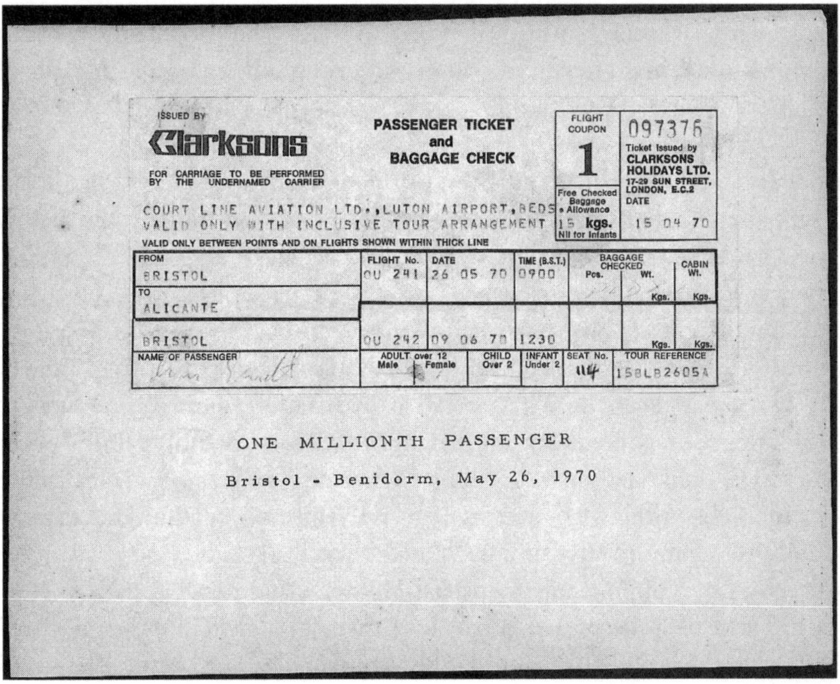
ISSUED BY
Clarksons
FOR CARRIAGE TO BE PERFORMED BY THE UNDERNAMED CARRIER

PASSENGER TICKET and BAGGAGE CHECK

FLIGHT COUPON 1

097376

Ticket issued by CLARKSONS HOLIDAYS LTD. 17-29 SUN STREET, LONDON, E.C.2

COURT LINE AVIATION LTD.,LUTON AIRPORT,BEDS
VALID ONLY WITH INCLUSIVE TOUR ARRANGEMENT

Free Checked Baggage Allowance 15 kgs. Nil for Infants

DATE 15 04 70

VALID ONLY BETWEEN POINTS AND ON FLIGHTS SHOWN WITHIN THICK LINE

FROM / TO	FLIGHT No.	DATE	TIME (B.S.T.)	BAGGAGE CHECKED Pcs.	Wt.	CABIN Wt.
BRISTOL	OU 241	26 05 70	0900		Kgs.	Kgs.
ALICANTE	OU 242	09 06 70	1230		Kgs.	Kgs.
BRISTOL						

NAME OF PASSENGER	ADULT over 12 Male / Female	CHILD Over 2	INFANT Under 2	SEAT No.	TOUR REFERENCE
				114	158LB2605A

ONE MILLIONTH PASSENGER

Bristol - Benidorm, May 26, 1970

Figure 8.2 The ticket of Clarksons' one millionth passenger, 1970.

FALL

Before its crisis became acute, Clarksons might have been sold several times over. In mid-1970, an American corporation, W. R. Grace, offered its parent company, Shipping and Industrial Holdings, £10 million but was rejected because Hambros Bank valued it at £14 million. Two years later American Express came close to taking a 19 per cent stake, but was frightened off by the firm's deepening losses. But the most intriguing of these potential deals involved the late Jimmy (later Sir James) Goldsmith and a plan to merge Thomson Holidays with Clarksons, again with participation by American Express. This scheme was not only the product of Clarksons' worsening plight. By 1972 the Thomson Organisation was also intensely nervous about the future of its package holiday offshoot. To stimulate demand and buy market share, the tour operator had slashed prices by an average of £5 a head – an immense amount at the time. The move banged yet another nail into Clarksons' coffin but it also pushed Thomson Holidays into serious loss. Anxious voices within the group advocated getting rid of it.

Goldsmith was among the most aggressive of the 1960s' takeover moguls, and a brilliant corporate manipulator. In 1971 his main company, Cavenham, made a successful contested bid for the Bovril food group. He then snapped up Unilever's stake in Allied Suppliers, the big food retailing group best known for its Liptons grocery chain. His involvement was not entirely fortuitous, for he was close to Gordon Brunton, the Thomson Organisation's chief executive. Indeed he had a part share in a racehorse with Brunton, Jim Slater (another headline-making financier of that period), John Sauvage of Britanna Airways – and Vladimir. A Thomson source recalls Goldsmith turning up for talks with two henchmen, in his Rolls-Royce. But the scheme came to nothing. By mid-1972, Gullick had fallen out with the directors of Shipping and Industrial Holdings and decided to bow out. 'I had lost overall control. I had told them they should either develop Clarksons or sell it to another big company who would. They had become frightened by the bad publicity over unfinished hotels and complaints about cruises and they weren't prepared to develop it themselves. If they had stayed in the game it would have been Clarksons heading the industry – not Thomson.' He departed for Spain, where he capitalized on the great love which had helped his extraordinary career off the ground, organizing shooting parties.

In April 1973 Court Line bought 85 per cent of Clarksons from SIH for a nominal £1, in a deal to protect its charter airline interests. SIH, which threw in £3,428,000 as a provision for the operator's expected losses, said that if Court Line did not take on the operation, it would be put into liquidation. Because Clarksons was by then providing 40 per cent of the turnover earned by Court Line's charter airline business the company felt it had little choice, though as things turned out it might have been wiser to have let the tour operator go, prune its airline business and limit the damage. That year, Clarksons lost an enormous £3,166,000.

Court Line had been founded in 1905 as a tramp steamer business, which is how it remained until the early 1960s, when it acquired a fleet of tankers and a shipbuilding yard in North Devon. In 1965 it had bought Autair, a scheduled and charter airline and at the end of the decade it was flirting more overtly with the holiday business, developing hotels on the Caribbean island of St Lucia. In January 1970, the name of its flying division was changed to Court Line Aviation Limited. It began to concentrate exclusively on charters and acquired a fleet of BAC 1-11 short haul jets. It was then that Court Line became closely linked with Clarksons. In 1972, after buying more shipyards, hotels in Antigua and the Bahamas, and a Caribbean airline, Leeward Island Air Transport, the company leased two TriStars, with options on three more. One of the new generation of wide-bodied Jumbos, the TriStar could carry up to 400 passengers. Clarksons agreed a five-year deal, promising their use over five years. Painted in candy stripe colours of pink and lime green, they were launched with lavish inaugural flights to Amsterdam and Palma. But no guarantees of utilization were obtained from Shipping and Industrial Holdings.

Soon after buying Clarksons, more problems emerged for Court Line. In May 1972 it agreed to buy the ATLAS group, which had set up an advance booking charter programme,[2] which it marketed as Airfair. This allowed passengers to buy any combination of outbound and homeward flights, exactly as if they were buying scheduled seats, provided they observed certain minimum-stay rules. When the programme was introduced in early 1973, it was massively over-subscribed. Instead of the 16,000 customers ATLAS had anticipated, 40,000 booked. Within four weeks, a backlog of 5000 bookings had built up. They had to be switched to scheduled flights at a total additional cost of some £35,000. When they discussed acquiring ATLAS, Court Line's directors expected it to make a profit of £60,000 for that year. Now, a loss of over £78,000 was projected.

The reasons why Court Line subsequently foundered are too complex to deal with in detail here but there is no doubt that it was tipped over the brink by the economic crisis into which Britain was plunged that year. The Arab–Israeli Yom Kippur war, which broke out in October, had the effect of pouring water on drowning men. In protest at US support for Israel – and as a warning to other Governments – Middle Eastern states upped oil prices by 70 per cent. Britain was faced with an increase of £409 millions a year in its oil import bill. At ABTA's convention in Palma, Majorca that November, the gloomy talk was of aviation fuel contracts, and how long-term price agreements were giving way to deals with break clauses, allowing suppliers to increase prices to airlines, and forcing tour operators who chartered their jets to pass those rises on to customers in the shape of surcharges.

Just before Christmas, Chancellor Anthony Barber had unveiled a crisis budget to counter what he described as 'the gravest crisis since the end of the war'. The aim was to limit the damage to the balance of payments by cutting the bill for non-oil imports. £1.2 billion was pruned from public spending. Hire purchase and credit controls were tightened and 10 per cent was added to the top rate of tax. Adding insult to the injury inflicted by the oil states, Britain's miners had imposed an overtime ban. With coal supplies to power stations down 40 per cent, industry and commerce were limited to five days electricity consumption in the fortnight to 30 December and three days a week from the beginning of 1974. Except during the Christmas and New Year breaks, even television stations were obliged to shut down at 10.30 p.m. Lights went off suddenly in restaurants and candles were lit.

By December, Austrian wintersports bookings had plunged by an estimated 66 per cent. Even the country's tourist office admitted to a 40 per cent drop. When the post-Christmas summer holiday booking season arrived, some tour operators, including Thomson, Lord Brothers and Sovereign were still weathering the storm in relative comfort but others had seen business slump by 30 per cent from its level a year earlier. Few were in robust enough shape not to feel deeply concerned. In January, the Tour Operators' Study group, which represented 20 companies handling the bulk of the inclusive tour business, reported that its members had suffered a collective loss of £6,700,000 in their most recently ended financial year. Within that figure, ten made a combined profit, the other ten losing almost £8,200,000. If the figures were not quite as bad as they looked at first glance, it was only because Clarksons alone had lost £4,800,000.

Everything seemed to be conspiring against the industry. Britain was in an intense state of nervousness about the threat of Arab terrorism. January was barely five days old when a large force of tanks, armoured vehicles and infantry was deployed around London's Heathrow Airport in a show of strength. It was concentrated on take-off and landing points, where guerrillas would be best able to hit a low flying airliner using a surface to air missile, fired from a shoulder launcher. Three days later, Home Secretary Robert Carr confirmed that dealing with such a threat was indeed the purpose of the exercise.

By February, Gabriel Escarrér, head of the Mallorquines hotel group in Majorca, was conceding that bookings from Britain were down by between 30 and 40 per cent. Industry realists were forecasting that 1,000,000 fewer Britons would take packages in 1974 and, with prescience which turned out to be thoroughly justified, that several tour operators would collapse. With their seemingly indefatigable optimism, many operators continued to hope for a flood of late bookings, choosing to avoid, in public at least, the awful truth that these grim statistics reflected a malaise which had been developing before the Middle East war and the three-day week and whose full impact was yet to be felt.

In February, swingeing new increases in fuel surcharges were agreed by ABTA's tour operators' council. There had been a furious argument between companies with access to the latest, most fuel efficient aircraft such as the DC-10 and the Lockheed L1011 TriStar, which came out for smaller increases, and those using older, thirstier jets, with higher costs to claw back. Within the travel industry, the fuel crisis continued to cause frayed tempers. Airlines were forced to live within strict fuel allocations, which sparked a diplomatic row between Britain and Italy. When the Italian charter airline SAM (Societa Aerea Mediterranea) used up its January allocation of 57,000 gallons (216,000 litres) with more than a week of the month left, following a leap in the number of flights it operated, it asked to be exempted. The British Government said no. Italy banned charters from Britain in retaliation. At Gatwick, almost 100 bewildered passengers on a Dan-Air flight were among the first to be told their trips were off. Clarksons customers in Naples had to be flown home via Malta. And it was in Malta that those still waiting to travel to Italy were offered alternative holidays.

Court Line agreed to take over the travel interests of the ailing Horizon on Thursday, 31 January (see Chapter 9). There followed predictable reports that foreign suppliers such as hoteliers were threatening problems for guests unless they were assured of payments. Horizon clients at a hotel in Brand in Austria, for example, were told they would be charged for their rooms, even though they had already paid through the operator. They were also informed they would have to pay for their coach transfers back to Zurich. Court Line sent representatives scurrying around resorts to sort out the problems.

By May, Clarksons' managing director Peter Drew was openly predicting that his firm would end the year with around 25 per cent fewer bookings than in 1973. The assumption that Clarksons would survive that long proved remarkably optimistic. The fall in bookings was no reason for dismay, Drew asserted, 'for Clarksons will be geared toward operating a smaller number of holidays, costed on a lower overall capacity and able to make money on all such targets'. The hoped-for late booking boom had indeed materialized, he claimed. In recent weeks, business had been running 47 per cent up on its level during the same period of 1973. Clarksons would be 'in a profit earning position by the end of the 1974 season'. A Thomson Holidays director, Francis Higgins, was also busy chastising the Jeremiahs, foreseeing currency refunds for customers as the pound regained health and reporting 'a massive upswing' in recent bookings. Among his targets was Wilf Jones, managing director of Cosmos, who described the year as 'the most critical' the travel business had faced and warned that some operators could see bookings fall by 50 per cent.

There were two quick slaps in the face for the optimists from Portugal and Cyprus. That April the right wing Portuguese dictator Dr Marcelo Caetano was deposed in an almost bloodless coup mounted by young officers who had grown weary of conflict in the country's African colonies. Airports were closed, although Faro reopened in time for many tourists to fly home as planned. In a telling observation, the late Harry Chandler, whose Travel Club of Upminster had been largely responsible for opening up the Algarve to package tourism, recalled that the revolution had been so peaceful there that many of his customers had no idea that it had taken place. In the event, while its longer term effect on hotel wages in Portugal and consumer confidence abroad was considerable, the political upheaval is thought to have had relatively little impact on that summer's bookings.

The Turkish invasion of Cyprus in mid-July, which led to the fall of the Greek colonels' junta and the island's long-term partition, sent a shiver through the industry. It happened not long before the holiday peak and the spectacle of British holidaymakers being evacuated from beaches by warships of the Royal Navy evoked dark thoughts of what might happen if Spain disintegrated into internecine warfare after the death of General Franco.

In June, Castle Holidays, which included Leroy Tours, Whitehall Holidays and Lyons Tours and was then one of the country's ten largest operators, announced that the dismal state of bookings had persuaded it not to run a programme for the following winter. It was a further blow for Court Line, from which Castle chartered airline seats. On 2 August, less than a week before Court Line collapsed, a senior director of one tour operator was predicting the end of 'wild optimism' in the industry and the dawning of a new age of conservatism. Many hapless holidaymakers might have wished the change had come about earlier.

The oil crisis had affected not just Court Line's package holiday and airline interests but its shipping business, too. The Department of Trade's report into its demise concluded that it was rendered vulnerable by inadequate management and flabby financial control. It could have been laid low by a setback in any of its three divisions – but the economic crisis hit all of them. And cash resources which might have been used to bail it out were locked up unprofitably in the Caribbean hotels, which were haemorrhaging money. By July 1974 it was forecast Clarksons would lose £5,847,000 in the year to 30 September, far more than the £3,428,000 provision made when it was bought from SIH. In June, Court Line's directors had approached the Labour government for help. The cabinet agreed to acquire all its shipbuilding, repairing and engineering interests. But it was to little avail. By August, hope that the company would survive was fading fast. By the 15th, the game was up. Early that morning at the offices of the London *Evening Standard*, I took a telephone call from an industry source who indicated obliquely that the company was on the brink. In its last edition, the newspaper ran a story that a massive rescue operation was about to swing into action, to bring home clients of Court Line's package tour operations who were on holiday abroad. The BBC's 9 p.m. news bulletin confirmed the worst. The group had collapsed.

Faced with the need to organize such a massive rescue operation, tour operators and airline executives negotiated through the night of 15–16 August. The crash could hardly have happened at a worse time.

This was bang in the middle of the summer peak. Even in a year when the economy had depressed bookings, more people went abroad in August than any other month. It was estimated that some 40,000 customers of Clarksons, Horizon and its offshoot 4S were abroad when the group ceased trading. Clarksons alone had clients scattered across 75 resorts in 26 different coastal areas.

There was fury among customers who had paid but were yet to travel. They besieged Clarksons' offices at Sun Street, not far from London's Liverpool Street station. Christopher Kirker recalls how staff were advised to move to the back of the building, in case the crowd decided to smash the front windows.

The Industry Secretary, Tony Benn, was quickly accused of having reassured Court Line customers, in the House of Commons on 25 June, that the Government's acquisition of the company's shipbuilding interests meant their holidays were safe. He insisted that his remarks then had been no different than a later statement to the House (on 1 July), that 'the board of Court Line accept that this should allow the holiday operations to continue'. However, the dispute set him at odds with his own civil servants and with his colleague Peter Shore, the Secretary of State for Trade. Shore was reluctant to deny that the Government had not given any guarantee or underwritten the company. The public would not buy that, he feared.

On 19 August, Benn wrote in his diary: 'I must admit I am beginning to wonder whether the public anger against me, based on the belief that I'm responsible for losing them their holidays through Court Line, won't actually lead to some incident'. *The Sunday Express* went so far as to wonder whether the crash was the result of a Labour plot, to discredit the notion that private enterprise was invariably more efficient and successful than state ownership.

Cliff Paice, former deputy economic director of the Civil Aviation Authority, is less critical of Benn's role. 'The Tories said it was all Benn's fault. He was supposed to have said that someone else acquiring the shipyards would assure the future of Court Line. In fact, he left that impression but had hadn't actually said anything of the sort. The Government said it was our [the CAA's] fault, claiming we had said bonds would ensure that everyone would get their money back. We had gone to great lengths to say exactly the opposite.'

He concedes that the Authority's attitude towards Court Line in the run up to the crash was 'deplorable'. But he defends it with the argument that it all happened too quickly after the establishment of the ATOL licensing system (for full details of the birth of the Air Tour Organizer's Licence, see Chapter 10), which required the monitoring of tour operator finances. 'One of my abiding memories is how bloody sure of themselves the people at Court Line were. We hadn't got our act together yet. They weren't providing financial information. We let them get away with it. The first thing you learn is that when financial information dries up, you have got problems. It appeared to me that they were so diversified that they didn't really know what was going on – but the Authority wasn't sufficiently sure of itself to do what was necessary. There was no way then that we could have acted as decisively as we did later, when Laker Airways and ILG (Harry Goodman's International Leisure Group) went down.'

Even if Court Line had survived, Paice insists, the problem would have arisen over some other firm. 'The critical thing that we grasped as a result of it was the timing of a failure. We did a lot of theoretical work trying to predict such failures but it all proved to be a chimera.' Despite that, collapses in the summer peak soon became rare.

On 30 July 1975, almost exactly a year after the Court Line collapse, two reports were published which pointed the finger of guilt squarely at Benn. The Ombudsman, Sir Alan Marre, said he found it difficult to agree with the Minister's claim that statements about the firm's future had included an appropriate degree of reservation. The Government, he concluded, could not be absolved of all responsibility for holidaymakers' losses when Clarksons and the other Court Line companies went down. Sir Alan said the Government had been anxious not to tip Court Line over the edge, but added that 'the statements were liable to leave a misleading impression with the public'. Among those who felt they had been misled were many of the 100,000 or so people hit by the collapse, who were estimated collectively to have lost anything up to £8,000,000.

The second report contained the interim conclusions of a an investigation into the crash by Department of Trade inspectors under the 1948 Companies Act. It found that the statements must be regarded as 'assuring summer holidaymakers on behalf of the Government that they *would* get their holidays. The words used and the context seem to us capable of no other meaning to ordinary listeners and readers. Neither the Government, nor the Department of Industry nor Mr Benn were in a position to assure the public without qualification. In our view the statements were not fair and reasonable in the circumstances: accidentally, no doubt, but nevertheless so.'

Benn came under withering fire from the opposition benches. Eldon Griffiths, Tory MP for Bury St Edmunds, said: 'Mr Benn has been found guilty of misrepresentation of House and country, against the advice of officials and in order to posture as saviour of holidays.' Benn assumed sole responsibility for the statements when he talked to Department of Trade inspectors – but the interim report said the Government must accept collective blame.

Apart from its impact on the way holidays were sold, Clarksons left a huge legacy of consumer protection. In 1975, in order to refund victims of the Court Line collapse and at least partly to cover its embarrassment over the Benn affair, the Government announced the establishment of the air travel reserve fund with a £15 million loan from public funds, which was to be repaid with a 1 per cent levy on packages, rising to 2 per cent the following year. This sparked a new row, with critics arguing that future holidaymakers should not be asked to foot the bill for past failures, but the dust soon settled. In fact, the Government could probably have got off the hook fairly cheaply. The £3.3 million Court Line bonds covered the rescue operation with £1 million to spare. The total estimated amount which was owed to customers yet to travel was somewhere between £6 million and £7 million. The liquidators estimated that at the time of the crash, High Street travel agents, anxious not to see client's cash disappear into a black hole, were sitting on payments of some £3.7 million. This suggests that the whole reimbursement problem could have been solved with less than £2 million from the Treasury without the need for a fund. Instead, a financial safety net was erected which ensured that, in the quarter century since then, hardly anyone hit by the collapse of a licensed tour operator has been left out of pocket.

NOTES

1. Tony Benn (1989): *Against the Tide. Diaries 1973–76* (Hutchinson).
2. For an explanation of advance booking charters, see Chapter 10.

9

The End of Horizon

VLADIMIR RAITZ

Despite Horizon's financial results for 1970 being our best ever, what happened in the following year completely wiped out the previous year's profit, replacing it with a loss of around £300,000 (or £4.5 million in today's money).

What had gone wrong? We were still selling holidays of the same quality that had gained us approval and a high degree of satisfactory responses from returning clients. Travel agents throughout the UK seemed to be as solidly behind us as our market research indicated. Our planning of aircraft utilization seemed to be as meticulous as ever – if anything, erring on the conservative side. In other words, instead of laying on 21 weekly flights to Palma de Mallorca, we stuck to the previous year's figure of fourteen. We were not overstaffed, and the directors were not paying themselves huge salaries or bonuses.

Crucially, the load factor on our aircraft was falling short of the number of bottoms on seats required. Let me explain the way that holidays on charter aircraft are costed. The price of the hotel and the coach transfer from the airport is allocated at a net price. Added to this is the cost of having reps at the resort, as well as a charge for head office overheads and ancillary expenses. At this stage, there is no element of profit in the equation. We take the total charter price for any given series of flights and divide it by the number of departures (allowing for the so-called 'empty legs' at the beginning and the end of the season). The profit (or loss) is determined by the number of clients on each plane. Let us imagine a notional aircraft with 100 seats. We have taken account of the divided charter price and the various net costs referred to above, and we have fixed what we feel is a reasonable selling price. For example, in 1971 the 'right' price for a fortnight's stay at a good hotel on Mallorca was £120. Let's say that the costs of the 'land portion' (hotel, transfers, etc.) plus overheads came to £70 per holiday. Allocating £50 for the 'flight portion' would result in a load factor of, say, 85 per cent of the plane. In other words, 85 of the 100 seats on each plane had to be filled before a penny of profit could be made. Every seat filled over the magic number of 85 would be worth £50 to us, every seat below that figure represented a loss of £50. If, as happened in our heyday, all 100 seats were filled, we would make a profit of £750 on one plane alone. But if only 75 passengers were carried on that flight, the loss would be £500. It's easy to see how a small number of aircraft seats can make the difference between triumph and disaster.

Horizon's decline continued throughout 1972 and 1973. This wasn't unique to Horizon, however (as Roger's account has illustrated). The decline affected the bulk of the package tour industry, especially the larger operators like Thomson Holidays. The main reason was that a vicious price war had broken out – fortunate for the customers, but very unfortunate for those of us who were providing the holidays. The culprit for this price war was easy to identify. It was a newcomer to the industry, and its name was Clarksons.

CLARKSONS

Clarksons had appeared on the scene in the late 1960s, offering cheap daytrips and one and two-day tours to the bulbfields of Holland. The company was managed, not owned, by Tom Gullick, a naval officer who had retired at a youngish age with the rank of Lieutenant Commander and had then opted for a career in travel. The owners of Clarksons were a prosperous City company called Shipping and Industrial Holdings (SIH) and Tom, a persuasive and hard-drinking gentleman, had talked the Board into putting up the money for a travel operation. The Dutch tours had gone well, and now Tom decided to break into the charter tour scene and beat Thomson and Horizon at their own game. In fact, he publicly declared that 'in a few years' time' he was going to be the biggest operator of all.

Beginning in 1970, Gullick (armed with naval discipline and the large funds put at his disposal by SIH) started upon his three-pronged attack. First, he set about securing large hotel allocations at the principal resorts in Mallorca, the Costa Brava and others by paying huge advances to hoteliers for block bookings and even having his own hotels constructed in places like Minorca. Second, he cut his prices to the bone by setting his break-even load factors at the impossibly high level of 95 per cent, in the hope of always achieving a 100 per cent capacity. Third, he allied himself with an air company that was now named Court Line. It had ditched its medium-sized planes and had, with Gullick's promises and financial backing, acquired numerous TriStars that had capacities of over 250 seats per plane (as opposed to Britannia's Boeing 737s, which had a capacity of 132 each).

Court Line were the inexpensive charter airline *par excellence*. One example should suffice. They introduced a concept called 'seat-back catering'. Instead of having cabin crew deliver meals on trays to passengers, the food (sandwiches, cheese and biscuits, the occasional piece of fruit) was ingeniously stowed behind the seat-back table in front of each passenger. This, as you can imagine, saved money. There were no hot dinners to serve, and it reduced the need to employ as many stewards or stewardesses. There was, nevertheless, a problem with this arrangement. The system provided these packed meals for both the outgoing and the returning journeys. I understand that on numerous occasions, the outgoing passengers would consume not only the meal meant for them but also the meal intended for their returning counterparts – the cause of some considerable aggravation.

The heavy losses sustained by Clarksons (in the interest of gaining market share) continued through the early 1970s. The company seemed to adopt the old joke principle of 'We lose money on every client, but our turnover is enormous!' – but they were taking it seriously! This was very bad news for the rest of us. We had to cut margins drastically in order to compete. Horizon Holidays was to learn the bitter lesson that, by and large, the travelling public was not interested in brand loyalty. A holiday from a competing firm that was just a few pounds cheaper was all it took for a client to switch, even if the holiday might involve a slight drop in quality. A hard core of clients

Figure 9.1   Tom Gullick, of Clarksons.

who had travelled with us over the years did, of course, remain loyal, but their numbers were never going to be big enough to see us through the problems that were rocking the industry.

Clarksons, by now, had merged with their airline Court Line. The company was still in the hands of Shipping and Industrial Holdings, which was run by Sandy Glen (later Sir Alexander and subsequently chairman of the British Tourist Authority) and Peter Parker (later Sir Peter, and head of British Rail). Sandy and Peter were men of outstanding probity and intelligence but had complete confidence in Tom Gullick's masterplan of virtually cornering the inclusive tour market and then raising prices to provide the first ever profit for his company. Their eyes were not opened until it was too late.

The years 1972 and 1973 saw the price war in package tours as unabated as ever. A number of smaller operators collapsed. The mighty Thomson Holidays was losing money, but were fortunate to be sustained by their rich parent company, the International Thomson Organisation. Horizon Holidays continued to make losses. Not only was this onerous in itself but it was beginning to affect our presence on the travel scene altogether.

In order to trade, each company had to renew its tour operating licence with the CAA every year. To do so, year-end accounts had to be submitted – and woe betide any firm that showed a red bottom line. If this was the case, the CAA demanded not only fresh injections of capital but also an increased bond, which was issued either by a bank or an insurance company. This was both difficult and expensive to obtain. Thomson and Clarksons were better positioned in this respect, both of them having 'rich Daddies' in the shape of ITO and SIH respectively. Horizon was not so well placed. I owned 100 per cent of the company and was rather a 'poor Daddy' by comparison.

THE OIL CRISIS AND AFTER

The Fates seemed to be conspiring against the company I had created some 25 years earlier. Not only were we in the throes of a vicious price war triggered by what I considered to be the megalomaniac and potentially self-destructive policies of an overambitious individual, but I was caught between the rock of the CAA and the hard place of my bank, which demanded solid guarantees and collateral before it would underwrite the required bonding.

Then came the *coup de grâce*, in the shape of the oil crisis. The whole country was plunged into a period of uncertainty, culminating in the three-day week, electricity cuts and other horrors. We at Horizon, like many other firms at the time, worked by candlelight more often than not. But even slaving over a flickering flame did not stave off the impending doom. I was faced with a stark choice: give up, pull the plug, or throw everything I possessed into the kitty to keep Horizon alive. 'Don't throw good money after bad', I was advised by countless people. But for me there was only one way to act – to liquidate every personal asset I had accumulated over the past quarter of a century and try to keep Horizon afloat for the good of all our staff (including myself!).

All of my possessions had either to be sold or pledged to the bank. The most important asset of all, the family home (in my case our beautiful house in Chelsea Square) was put on the line. The bank, as banks do, wanted cast iron personal guarantees signed by me and also by my wife – in case, I suppose, I tried to put any assets in my wife's name. Nothing was further from my thoughts at the time. All I wanted was Horizon's survival, and everything was expendable. 'Would you like me to place my children in your vaults?' I asked the bank manager (no longer, alas, Mr Whitbread of our early days) on one occasion. He didn't seem to find this funny.

In the event, it was all in vain. The capital input and the horrendously high bond required by the CAA was just too much for me to meet, and the company was unable to carry on in time for the 1974 season, even though our brochures were already on the market and bookings had started to come in. Horizon Holidays had not, however, gone to the wall. Although the company had been forced into receivership with a certain amount of debt, Court Line (owners of my nemesis, Clarksons) had stepped in and taken Horizon under their aegis. This happened on 28 February 1974. Thankfully no jobs were lost – except, of course, mine. I could not possibly consider working in tandem with Clarksons, even though by that time Tom Gullick had been dismissed by his board who had finally realized that his price war tactics had brought their own organization to the brink of ruin.

I was told that with Court Line now controlling two large tour operators (and in the process displacing Thomson as the number one), everything in the garden would be rosy. I wanted desperately to believe this. I wanted Horizon to survive, even under someone else's ownership. Above all, I wanted my loyal staff, now numbering over 600, to hang on to their jobs and their livelihoods.

I had to plough through many disagreeable tasks with bankers, solicitors and administrators. One of the most painful of all was having to preside over a creditors' meeting where I had to face a number of foreign hoteliers whom we had been unable to pay. It was a great disappointment to me that none of my other directors bothered to turn up for this meeting, leaving me on my own to make speeches of regret and contrition. I suppose that it was, above all, my responsibility. I had founded the company, made all the hotel bookings in the early days, and had taken most of the main decisions over the past 25 years. But it would have been a comfort to have the moral support of my directors, who had benefited under my chairmanship and from me personally. I was to experience a great deal of that sort of behaviour in the next few days and weeks.

March and April of 1974 came and went. As did my house, my car and a lot of other things. It was at this time that I began to find out who were my true friends. I was in for some considerable surprises. I have no intention of listing the good, the bad and the indifferent, or those revelling in *schadenfreude* – that delightful German word meaning to take pleasure in the misfortune of others. My wife, mother and daughters, of course, were rock solid. My mother was paying the school fees of my three daughters at the French Lycée. Their knowledge of French seemed to help them out. My eldest daughter, Lucy, who was 14 at the time, told me 'I know there are lots of people called *nouveaux riches*; I suppose we're the *nouveaux pauvres!*' I shall only single out one individual who helped me through thick and thin, both materially and morally. He was Gordon Brunton, my old fellow student from the LSE, whose offer to buy Horizon in the early 1960s I had turned down.

With the help of Gordon and other friends, I moved into a rented house. I was at the nadir of my existence. I was listless, downcast, and drinking even more than Tom Gullick. One day, I was glancing through the weekly *Travel Trade Gazette* when I chanced upon the following item:

> While the holiday industry is going through traumatic times, Vladimir Raitz, head of the failed Horizon Holidays Group, has left these shores and is sunning himself in the garden of his villa in the south of France.

Figure 9.2 The cover of Horizon's silver jubilee (and final) brochure, 1974.

I nearly had an apoplectic fit. Left the country? Villa in France? I had never even thought about buying such a thing! Where was this lying rubbish coming from? I knew the editor of the *Travel Trade Gazette* quite well. His name was Nigel Coombes. I phoned him up and a sub-editor answered.

'May I speak to Nigel, please? It's Vladimir Raitz here.'

'What is this concerning, Mr Raitz?'

'It's about the lying libel about me in this week's issue. And I'm not phoning from my mythical villa in the south of France, or from my townhouse in New York, or from my hacienda in Beverly Hills.'

'I'm sorry, I don't think Nigel is available right now.'

'Listen, my friend, if I don't hear from Nigel within the next five minutes, he won't be able to reach me because I'll be at my solicitor's, issuing a writ against you.'

Within 45 seconds, Nigel Coombes was on the line.

'What is this crock of excrement, Nigel, that you've been writing about me? I haven't been abroad for over six months, and I've never owned a villa in France.'

'I'm sorry, Vlad, the article was given to us by a usually reliable source.'

'I don't care about that, Nigel. Unless I get a full, unequivocal apology on the front page of next week's issue, you'll have a libel action on your hands.'

The next *Travel Trade Gazette* carried a full retraction. I might have made many mistakes, I might have lost the company I had created and I might have lost a lot of money – but I had never cheated anyone, and had pumped every last penny I had into keeping Horizon going. I believed I had earned the right to hold my head high.

COLLAPSE OF COURT LINE

I had serious reservations about Court Line (even with Horizon now riding in tandem with Clarksons) being able to carry on for much longer. The prices of their holidays had at last been raised to an acceptable level, but then Thomson's decided that this was the time to increase the pressure by aggressive marketing and pricing of their own. Moreover, the country was not yet out of its economic mess. Prime

Minister Heath had lost his confrontation with Arthur Scargill's National Union of Mineworkers and was forced into a General Election which he proceeded to lose. I was keeping my fingers crossed that Court Line might survive but the outlook was grim.

One day in August 1974, I received a phone call from a newspaper reporter.

'Good morning, Mr Raitz. What comments do you have on the collapse of Court Line?'

'What? What collapse? Is this some kind of joke?'

'It's far from a joke, I'm afraid. It's just come through on the Press Association wire. Court Line has gone down, along with Clarksons and Horizon.'

'Well, if it's true, all I can say is that it's a bloody tragedy.'

'Thank you, Mr Raitz. We'll call you again when you've had more time to digest the news.'

After that I must have been contacted by every national paper. But what comment could I make? I couldn't really say that I had long feared this would happen. I just said that I was anxious about the fate of so many employees, and that I hoped that none of the clients would have their holidays disrupted and that they would be brought home safely at the end of their stay abroad. This was, after all, the absolute height of the holiday season, and a huge logistical exercise would have to be undertaken by other airlines. At least I knew that the funds for such an operation were in place, by virtue of the bonds lodged with the CAA.

This was very nearly the end of the Horizon story – but not quite. Horizon Midlands (our Birmingham-based offshoot, which I had managed to hive off as a public company some five years earlier) had managed to survive with considerable assistance from West Midlands municipalities. It was, ultimately, to prosper, and to change its name from Horizon Midlands to Horizon Holidays. It was later bought by Bass, the brewers, and then by the Thomson Organisation which, in 1995, decided to discontinue the brand.

ALBERT MIZZI

The Court Line collapse caused me to sink ever deeper into depression. I hardly ever left my rented house. I stopped watching the television or listening to the radio. And I couldn't bear to look at a newspaper (this from a man who had been a compulsive reader of the papers ever since my time at Reuters). I was hardly eating, I was drinking copious amounts of vodka, and spent most of my time playing a ridiculous version of patience that I had invented myself. My family and friends began to despair of me, especially as I stubbornly refused to see a doctor.

Then, out of nowhere, my white knight appeared. I received a phone call from a Mr Albert Mizzi – chairman of the newly founded Air Malta and, as I later found out, one of Malta's most important businessmen who was active in many sectors of the island's economy.

'We want to start a tour operation to Malta from the UK, to assist our airline,' he told me. 'We're looking for a Managing Director. I admire the way you do business, and I hear (there was an artful pause at this point) that you may be free. Might you be interested?'

Might I indeed! We met the very next day at the Churchill Hotel in the West End. I didn't even bother enquiring about the salary, and accepted the job right away. All of a sudden, I had a job again. I could afford to buy a car. Money started to come into the household. I stopped drinking, started eating proper food again and read every newspaper I could lay my hands on. But most of all, I wanted to concentrate on making a success of Medallion, the name of Air Malta's tour operation.

I stayed as Medallion's Managing Director for some years, until a Maltese took over from me at that job. But my association with Air Malta (and with Medallion as a Director) continued for over 20 years. Unfortunately, Bertie Mizzi departed in the early 1990s – and so did I a short time later, having fallen victim to the Byzantine politics endemic in Maltese business. It had been a long and happy partnership, though, and one that had saved my sanity if not my life. I shall be eternally grateful to Bertie.

Since becoming part of the travel industry again, thanks to Bertie Mizzi, I have never had a quiet (or unemployed) moment. Alongside my work for Air Malta, I have carried out numerous consultancies within the industry. My latest venture, which I have put together with my good friend Colin Trigger, President of ABTA, is a tour operation to Cuba for aficionados of Havana cigars. For me, working is too much fun even to consider the concept of retiring.

10

The 1970s: prices tumble, bonding is born

ROGER BRAY

Traumatic though they may have been for Vladimir and many other entrepreneurs who had ridden the post-war wave of popular tourism, the first years of the 1970s brought major benefits for consumers, in the shape of more competitive package prices and much tighter protection for their money. The collapse of Clarksons, described in detail in a separate chapter, acted as a kind of cleansing by fire. The bonding of tour operators had already been introduced when the then market leader foundered in 1974, but it remained flawed. Now the most gaping loopholes in the safety net would be closed. The crash had other long-term effects. When a young Roger Davies, later to become managing director and chief executive of Thomson, arrived at its West End headquarters in 1969, he could hardly have foretold that Clarksons' demise would clear the field for his new employer to take over as Britain's biggest tour operator. And when Victor Matthews, head of Trafalgar House, told Harry Goodman in 1971 that he would 'never be more than a counter clerk', he could not have foreseen how the vacuum left by the failure would allow Goodman to set up Thomson's great rival, Intasun.

The decade was only 23 days old when the first Boeing 747 Jumbo jet, operated by Pan American and fitted with 362 seats, landed at London Heathrow. Inevitably, there were teething troubles. The flight was late leaving New York because an engine had to be changed, and bad weather stopped its onward journey to Frankfurt. But the Jumbo's

172

entry into service was to change the face of long haul travel dramatically. It was not only the new jet's relatively low operating costs that helped airlines hold down prices. Faced with filling an aircraft roughly twice as large as its biggest predecessors, they were forced to come up with more innovative deals, particularly in the quiet months of midwinter. Just as travel to Mediterranean beaches and Alpine ski resorts had opened up to the mass market, so the real cost of holidays in exotic reaches such as the Caribbean and California, seen by most Britons only on cinema and television screens, would fall dramatically. By the end of the century, the price of a bargain, winter return ticket between London and New York – about £130 before the addition of taxes – would be approximately the same as the excursion fare charged by Pan Am 40 years earlier. In a ceremony at Washington's Dulles International, that first Boeing 747 had been named Clipper Young America by President Nixon's wife, Pat. The name rang with irony. While the Jumbo would bring people together around the world, acting as a catalyst for greater international understanding, young America was bleeding and dying in Vietnam, and outraged at home that spring when the National Guard shot dead four students during an anti-war protest at Ohio's Kent State University.

To much of the post-war generation in Britain, such events seemed eerily remote. Few had endured combat. None had been obliged to do National Service in the forces. The overwhelming majority had known nothing but peace. Of all frivolities, nothing cut a sharper contrast with the grim realities broadcast by the news bulletins than the latest fashion fad, hot pants. Other people's wars, in Cyprus, the Middle East and Africa, would all have an impact on the travel industry in the 1970s but for the present the trade seemed to be sunning in an endless summer of expansion. Though there had been big pay rises in the preceding six months, many entrepreneurs saw the Tories' surprise June election victory as the icing on the cake.

THE HOLIDAY SPENDING BOOM

Spending on holidays had risen more rapidly, in percentage terms, than the number of holidays taken. Between 1951 and 1968 the total spent on UK holidays rose by 80 per cent, that on holidays abroad by 400 per cent. In 1951 a British break cost an average of £11, compared with £41 for a foreign holiday. By 1968, the averages were £20 and £62 respectively. A British Travel Association report said those sunning themselves on foreign sands were now younger and generally richer than those staying home. From this it might be assumed that there was demand for last minute getaways. However, while it was practised in Scandinavia, the late sale of holidays at knock-down prices in Britain was still in the future. When an industry working party was set up in 1972 to consider it, operators were divided over whether it was a good idea. Harry Chandler conceded there was no unanimity of opinion. 'I think some operators would be in favour. Some think it would lead to chaos.' The argument against has been aired many times since. Sceptics argued that passengers sitting next to each other on the aircraft would have paid different amounts for their holidays. One noted that 'some people might resent the fact that someone had paid £30 when they had paid £50'. Wilf Jones, the head of Cosmos thought it might even push up prices overall, because people would be tempted to leave booking until the last moment, making it hard for tour operators to plan ahead. Colin Collins, who was in charge of public relations at Clarksons, thought there was little chance of such a system gaining acceptance.

Spain's share of the foreign holiday market had risen from 6 per cent in 1951 to 30 per cent in 1968. Torremolinos was already well established, though its 1800 or so hotel rooms were barely keeping up with demand. Marbella, where only five years earlier there had been nowhere worth mentioning to eat or to stay, now had the first hotels and nightclubs which would transform the village into Spain's smartest resort.

There were still coastal areas of Europe which had not felt the full blast of tourism, but everywhere the developers were stirring. The Greeks had by now recognized the potential of Crete as a holiday honeypot. To get there in 1970 it was still necessary to fly to Athens and complete the journey by steamer. But its airport was about to be expanded. Hotel accommodation amounted then to only 600 beds – of which 273 were in the Astoria in Heraklion, which was used by almost all the UK operators brave enough to offer the island in their brochures. But the building of new hotels was encouraged by big long-term loans from the Greek tourist authorities. A further 6000–8000 beds were planned by 1973.

Likewise, tourism to the Algarve had been hampered by a shortage of hotels, but plans were in hand to develop a whole new resort, Vilamoura, with a projected 100 hotels, homes for 14,000 and a huge marina with room for over 1000 boats. One golf course had been completed and another was on the drawing board. The project was backed by three major Portuguese banks with support from Great Lakes Property Inc of Chicago. In the first eight months of 1969, only 151,300 British bed nights were spent in the Algarve — but even that modest figure was up nearly 90 per cent on 1968.

To appreciate the speed with which the Mediterranean tourism infrastructure developed, it is useful to seek out a contrast — not with the ancient, but with the recent modern. Such a contrast is to be found in Hammamet, now Tunisia's most popular resort. Until the 1960s Hammamet had been a quiet village with a couple of hotels and a beautiful, long, sandy beach. A handful of European intellectuals had discovered it between the wars, building homes among the orange trees. One of them was the wealthy Georges Sebastian, who built a villa on the Mediterranean shore. Now an Arab cultural centre, the house is set in slightly unkempt gardens, shaded by rustling eucalyptus and fig trees. Montgomery and Rommel both stayed in it as the fortunes of the North African campaign shifted. You can imagine them holding tactical talks in the sunken bath, curiously designed to seat four people. For a small fee, tourists may still visit it. Probably very few bother, which is a pity, for the place provides a telling glimpse of how Hammamet was before the pouring of the concrete. The resort's first big hotels were built in the early 1970s. Their architects adopted the garden approach, surrounding them with greenery. Later developments have been less unobtrusive. As the new millennium dawned, a massive new complex, Yasmine Hammamet, was close to completion to the north of town, with palatial hotels and a marina and a four lane highway running through it.

The first month of the new decade saw the first travel advertising on colour television. Clarksons took a slot lasting no less than seven minutes. And the Government at last removed the £50 limit on foreign currency. Since most people had by now learned to live within its constraints, the move was probably more a psychological boost than a real one, though there is little doubt that it released pent-up demand for short and second holidays. Vladimir felt it meant customers would no longer be looked down on as 'poor relations' by other Europeans. One of the trade's most colourful characters, Lionel Steinberg, of Sky Tours, said it had encouraged him to look at a programme of packages to the USA.

BONDING

In August the Tour Operators' Study Group, a club of top companies now called the Federation of Tour Operators, called a press conference to announce that, henceforth, its members would be bonded. While arguments continue about who first conceived the idea of bonds – bank guarantees which could be used to rescue or reimburse holidaymakers when an operator went bust – Harry Chandler is credited with getting the first workable scheme off the ground. As the industry expanded, it was feared that the emergency fund which had been established by ABTA in response to the financial failures of the 1960s – and the consequent adverse publicity – would prove inadequate to cover the price of a major collapse. Chandler claimed he had mooted the idea of bonds at an ABTA council meeting in 1967. The Trade Secretary, Roy Mason, had threatened privately that unless operators came up with a better protection scheme, the Government might force them to put all advance payments from customers into escrow accounts, so that the money could not be touched until they had taken their holidays. Chandler's proposal had been rejected, he said, because of the difficulty of getting hundreds of member operators to agree. It was not the only difficulty. Initially, British clearing banks would not provide the necessary guarantees. But Chandler discovered that the Swiss Bank Corporation would do so, provided the company it was bonding deposited an equivalent amount. After lengthy talks, the UK banks were persuaded to cooperate.

In 1972, the scheme was extended to embrace all members of ABTA. That November the new widened safety net had its first test. Sussex based Frontier International went under, with some 200 customers either abroad or booked to travel. The cost of the rescue operation and the refund of deposits was covered by the firm's £5000 bond. That year ABTA also launched its independent arbitration scheme, designed to provide consumers with an inexpensive way of settling differences with its member firms, though at first, all except Clarksons gave it the cold shoulder.

Meanwhile, in February 1971, the Government had announced that the infamous Provision One minimum price restriction on breaks of seven nights or less would be abolished for the following winter. Operators had already announced £10 packages to Spain in anticipation. Bookings flooded in. But the restriction still applied to some destinations, including Paris, Scandinavia, Germany and the Benelux countries – and to skiing holidays. In October the following year, Provision One would be scrapped in its entirety and laid to rest for good.

Other barriers in the way of cut-price holidays remained, however. ABTA's rules still forebade tour operator members to discount their brochure prices, though operators devised ways of getting around this rule. One method was the allocation of accommodation when customers reached their resorts, an idea branded the Square Deal by Thomson. If clients did not know what they were booking, how could they be getting discounts? Before the decade was over, the rule was dropped but even then, ABTA agents were not allowed to cut the price of an operator's packages without its permission. This rule, contained in the standard agency agreement blessed by the association, was to stand until 1984.

ATOL

At the start of the decade, Cliff Paice, a civil servant who had cut his teeth at the Treasury, was given the job of setting up the ATOL (air travel organizer's licence) system which came into being with the launch of the Civil Aviation Authority. Odd though it seems now, licensing was seen as a way of cracking down on bogus affinity groups, clubs formed to skirt the increasingly unpopular regulations curbing the sale of cut-price air tickets. There were many such groups, some genuine, some not. One whose name lives in the memory was the Trowbridge Caged Bird Society.

These groups had been troubling regulators on both sides of the ocean for some time. American tour operators had been getting representatives in Britain to inform the Board of Trade when rivals were flying in illegal groups. Officials had no option but to take action.

Early in 1970, the Civil Aeronautics Board in Washington had accused four transatlantic airlines of breaking the rules. They were Caledonian Airways, Overseas National Airways, a German operator called Atlantis and World Airways. The CAB's director of enforcement, Richard O'Melia said: 'We have uncovered violations involving upwards of 500 charter trips and 75,000 passengers. In numerous instances, travellers did not know the organization with which they were flying and many joined for the sole purpose of the trip.' The complaint, at least so far as Caledonian was concerned, petered out. In 1971, the UK Government threatened a crackdown, with Board of Trade president Roy Mason noting that affinity group organizers were 'not always careful' to make sure passengers conformed to the rule which demanded they be members for at least six months before flying. Department of Trade inspectors had swooped on three suspect charter flights in the previous year – all from Gatwick to New York. One was on charter to the Cinematic Arts Club, the other to the European Emigrant Families Association and the third to the Left Hand Club. The Air Transport Licensing Board in London took fresh action to tackle the issue, setting up a team of scrutineers to vet applications for affinity group flights. But it was clear that more radical steps were needed.

Before long the new-born CAA would render such activity redundant with the introduction of the Advance Booking Charter. At the outset, passengers had to book at least 90 days before flying, though the period was progressively reduced, but ABCs enabled travel operators to come up with astonishingly cheap deals. When applications for licences opened in 1972, first on the CAA's doorstep was Reg Pycroft of Jetsave, with plans to offer a £49 return fare to New York.

However, licensing was also in demand following the series of celebrated scandals in the 1960s, which we have described in earlier chapters, and which had seen holidaymakers left stranded abroad when tour operators ran into insurmountable financial difficulties. British consulates had been forced to help them by lending them emergency cash – but they had not been repaid. Something had to be done. The ATOL system was drafted as part of the 1971 Civil Aviation Act and legislation was enacted the following year. The first crop to be granted took effect in May 1973. There were 670 applications, of which 496 were approved. To get a licence, operators had to be bonded. Initially, the Authority was determined that bonds should be used to bring home passengers already on holiday with firms which collapsed. Only if there was anything left after that would those still waiting to travel receive refunds.

As Paice recalls, the birth of licensing was not without pain. 'ABTA, typically at the time, said that qualification for a licence should be membership of the Association. We said "go away". They said they wouldn't play ball. The CAA – with quite inadequate thought on the matter – said we would require a bond from each travel organizer. This was clearly going to be difficult. One way of getting the system off the ground, of course, was to recognize ABTA bonds as satisfying our requirement. So in order to bring ABTA along with us we decided, as a matter of policy, that its members' bonds could be lower than those of other companies.'

This bounced back to bite the Authority and, in an oblique fashion, subsequent holidaymakers. If ABTA had not been granted the concession, Clarksons might have held a bigger bond when its parent group, Court Line, collapsed in 1974. That bond, as discussed elsewhere in this story, was inadequate to cover the cost of rescuing and refunding all Clarksons' customers. As a result, later package holidaymakers were obliged to fork out a levy to pay part of the bill.

'Even if we hadn't allowed ABTA members smaller bonds, Clarksons' bond still wouldn't have been enough – but it would have been better', says Paice. 'Did we meet with resistance from the industry? Yes we did. We said: no accounts, no bonds, no licence. Some people came to us and said their accounts would be ready at the end of their financial year – in accordance with the Companies Act. I replied "Fine – your licences will be available at the same time".'

Though he wonders whether the travel industry was all that much worse in this respect than many other sectors, he explains: 'The main problem was getting some of these guys' minds round the fact that they had to provide any accounts at all. It was absolutely shambolic. A vast number of them simply didn't keep any and didn't understand the process. In one case, which I shall never forget, we had some accounts in from an operator who had gone off on holiday. The figures showed he was insolvent. When we called him in and told him he was bust he had no idea of the situation he was in.' The Authority was a little green, too. This was illustrated when the bank which owned Apal Travel went under, taking its holiday subsidiary with it. It emerged that the bank had organized Apal's bond.

'When it came to policy on the granting of licences, we had two choices: either we could refuse to let them in unless they were really financially sound; or we could say: "This is a high risk business in which the risk-takers provide great benefits – so we are not going to lock the little people out". We did the latter. The result was that the financial criteria we applied to tour operators were softer than they were for some others and the failure rate correspondingly higher. But it also resulted in a rich choice of holidays.'

Among the small fry allowed in under this policy was David Crossland, whose Airtours empire is now the second largest tour operator in Britain. 'If you had asked me then whether he was going to make all that money', Paice admits, 'I would probably have said no.'

A lot of firms went bust. Most were trying to earn an honest penny. A handful were not. Paice confesses to having been completely duped by one licence applicant, new to travel but recognizing it as a growth area, who produced excellent accounts. The Authority ran the usual checks through Companies House and ensured that the accounts auditors were properly qualified. 'I was therefore somewhat dismayed to discover that the principals had all been arrested for avoiding VAT on gold imports. They wanted to use the travel company for laundering the proceeds. The accounts were totally fraudulent. The auditor existed but had emigrated to South Africa and they had managed to use what purported to be his letterhead. I would like to be able to say I had some suspicions, but I can't: I was completely conned.'

Paice believes that the great merit of the ATOL system was that it forced operators to produce accounts. Nevertheless, if he could have his time at the CAA again, he would have fought against bonding.

'If I had understood then what I understand now about bonding, I would never have gone near it with a bargepole – because a common fund (which can also be used to ensure holidaymakers are not left stranded or out of pocket) is so much easier and cheaper. Individual bonds are an extremely inefficient way of protecting passengers. Bonds are very expensive for small companies and most of them are not called on in any case, so it's an expense which is not needed.'

The system he nursed into life has survived into robust maturity, though it came under threat in the 1980s. Philosophically, Margaret Thatcher's Conservatives would have liked to get rid of it. There was a move to privatize it – but had that succeeded, it might have caused enormous complications when the EU came up with its package holiday directive in the latter part of that decade.

INTERNATIONAL THOMSON EXPANSION

The dramatic events which led to and followed the Clarksons crash in August, 1974, and Vladimir's experiences during that turbulent period, are described elsewhere. Meanwhile new lead players were emerging from the wings: Thomson, Intasun and Laker. In the mid-1960s, the International Thomson group was casting around for potential profit earners with relatively low development costs. One of its directors, Gordon Brunton (see Chapter 7), decided on the package holiday business. As we recalled earlier, its involvement began in 1965 with the purchase of Universal Sky Tours from Captain Ted Langton for £900,000. With it came Britannia Airways. Lord Thomson gave Brunton's decision the thumbs-up despite a warning, from accountants Price Waterhouse, which pointed to the two companies' poor performance and unstructured management style, and to the fact that the Thomson Organisation had no experience whatsoever of the travel business.

The necessary experience was quickly gained. Thomson also bought a smaller operation, Riviera Holidays. Other acquisitions followed. Britannia decided to move into the jet age. In the teeth of fierce resistance from the Government, which wanted the airline to order the British-built BAC 1-11, it plumped instead for the Boeing 737-200, which was to become the workhorse of the UK package holiday business for years to come. But despite this bold entry into battle, the new holiday empire was slow to exploit its advantages. By the end of the decade its component parts were locked in internecine rivalry and staff were depressed and demoralized. Because of bickering over charter seat rates, the heads of its tour operating companies were hardly speaking to executives at Britannia.

The man credited with turning it around was Brian Llewellyn, educated at Charterhouse and Cambridge, who had taught at a school in Paris, worked for Fisons the fertilizer manufacturer, for BOAC as a counter clerk, and for a West End furniture business. After joining Thomson, he rose to become marketing director of the group's regional newspapers division. Appointed Thomson Holidays' managing director in 1979, he came to be regarded as one of the industry's brightest lights. Llewellyn realized, to quote his own words in 1971, that the firm needed 'to establish ourselves in the public's mind as a big, solid, stable operation capable of operating successful holiday programmes...while at the same time creating credibility and trust'. Thomson's quality image, which was to become all the more important in the wake of the Clarksons debacle, was born. By the start of the 1970s, the firm was Britain's second biggest tour operator, but was considerably smaller than Clarksons. In 1971 it was licensed to carry 350,000 customers, while Clarksons carried 750,000. But Llewellyn was already laying foundations which would see Thomson secure and hold its position as market leader, cutting out the duplication of brands and overseas resort reps and aiming specific brochures at particular segments of the market. As the industry grew and became more complex, the need, as he saw it, was to make decisions which would stand a five or ten year test and 'to create the right product at the right price through thorough market research backed up by really punchy, hard-hitting promotion and top service standards'.

HARRY GOODMAN

In March 1971, Cunard decided to take a majority shareholding in Harry Goodman's company, Sunair. It soon regretted the decision. Goodman, who owned 58 per cent and stood to gain £397,000 in cash from the deal, saw it as an opportunity to 'create some competition for the big boys'. He claimed the operator had carried 80,000 customers in 1970 against 45,000 the previous year and that profits for 1970 would be up more than 50 per cent to well over £200,000. 'Don't believe what you hear about Sunair', he was quoted as protesting. 'Just look at our figures. The trade doesn't like success stories unless they are their own.' In June, Sunair took over Lunn-Poly from the state owned Transport Holding Company for £175,000 and moved to number four in the size league table. Lunn-Poly, which was sold to Thomson in

1972, brought with it a significant loss, estimated at £350,000 for the year to October.

Goodman was to loom large on the package holiday scene for two decades. At the peak of his tour operating career, he was a strange cocktail of private and public, shrewd and cavalier, intermittently modest and outrageous. He was described by one acquaintance as 'a huge risk taker who got good people to work for him'. A man of humble background, he once wondered publicly whether the reason he resorted to cocaine was a sense of inferiority in the corridors of business power. 'I used to find myself totally intimidated by the City of London. You walked into a place with paintings of the founders on the walls, into a room where the people were all from Oxford or Cambridge, or Eton or Harrow – and here was this kid with no upbringing and no experience of that.'

Goodman's rise was remarkable. He was born Harry Brown, son of an East End sweatshop machinist, in November 1938. His father died before the birth and his mother remarried. Her new husband, also a machinist in the clothes business, was one Charles Goodman. Harry took his name. The family lived behind the Charrington Brewery in Bethnal Green, decamping to Marylebone during the blitz. Though he spent much of the war as an evacuee in Nottingham, Harry remembers sheltering from German bombs in a London underground station. He was a bright child, passing his eleven-plus examination and going to grammar school, but luck ran against him. His mother died of cancer when he was 13 and his stepfather died not long afterwards. Orphaned, Harry spent the ensuing years of boyhood shuttling between relatives. He left school at 15 without taking O-levels and joined the Cooperative Wholesale Society, where he dealt with theft claims. Two years later he joined a travel agency in London's Hatton Garden as a counter clerk. He was introduced to the manager by an aunt whose passion for opera left him with an abiding distaste for it.

His flat feet failed to save him from National Service. He wound up as a cook in the Catering Corps. When he crossed the Channel en route for Bielefeld in Germany, it was the first time he had seen the sea. When he left the Army, Goodman became 'totally hooked' on the travel business. In 1957 he took his first 'educational' – the industry term coined to describe fact-finding trips arranged by tour operators for groups of travel agency staff. He went to Majorca and the Costa

Brava. 'I thought I had died and gone to heaven', he said, 'being able to travel at someone else's expense.'

Thomas Cook turned him down. He believes he did not get an interview because of his lack of O-levels (fifteen years later he was dining with its directors in the company boardroom). Next, he ran a travel agency-cum-theatre booking operation under the railway arches near London's Ludgate Circus, but all the while he yearned to break into tour operating. So he answered an out-of-date advertisement in *Travel Trade Gazette* for a job with a company called Travel Savings. Harry set up an air charter division there, working up to 19 hours a day, but the company folded. It was time to start his own operation.

This was Sunair, which he formed with two partners in 1966. The three sold their houses to raise the capital. They set up shop in a travel agency in Sidcup, Kent, taking over and incorporating the next door knitting shop to provide more space. Harry lived upstairs with his first wife. They published a brochure which was half black and white because they could not afford full colour. There followed six 'horrific' months of selling door-to-door, dropping off leaflets and going back next night to see if the recipients were interested in booking. Precious few took the bait, so they decided to try selling through travel agents. This turned out to be easy. There was no statutory licensing, no need to raise a bond to protect customers' cash. All they needed was an office and a desk. About half their clients booked summer holidays before Christmas, and a huge number booked in January and February, yet there was no need for them to pay airlines or hoteliers until the holidaymakers returned. 'Here was this wonderful business', Goodman recalled later, 'with cash flowing in through the windows.' It was common practice to overbook and 'take flyers' – accepting reservations and worrying about charter aircraft seats later. Like others in the business, he and his colleagues organized charters which went out on Fridays and came back on Sundays, so they could spend a weekend in the sun. That, he claimed later, was how the ten- and eleven-night holiday began. 'There was nothing scientific about it at all.'

They sold Sunair to Cunard for what Goodman later described as 'a pittance', though it is thought to have been around £70,000. If they had hung on to it, it would have gone bust. The stolid Cunard was the last company one would have associated with such a brash enterprise but this was a time of forced diversification for the passenger shopping industry, which had seen its traditional business plundered by the airlines. In the words of one industry veteran who worked for the line at the time, the sale was a disaster. 'Cunard was sold a complete pup. The company must have seen the figures – but there was no real substance in Sunair.'

Goodman worked with Cunard until the line was taken over by Trafalgar House. Then he was ousted with a deal which kept him out of travel for two years. He filled the gap running an appointments agency. When the two years were up he raised enough capital to buy into three travel agencies called Intasun – and started his next tour operation. In 1973, Intasun carried a paltry 4000 customers but when Court Line went under the following year, he seized the day. Goodman had two private jets on standby to fly to the Costa Brava and Palma, Majorca, where he and his team snapped up beds with lightning speed and at knock-down rates. That year his company carried some 50,000 holidaymakers and made a profit of £300,000. It would soon become a force in the land.

In the early days, the job of making out final invoices for customers was farmed out to housewives but it was not long before Intasun had expanded to a size which demanded more sophisticated processing. It was only five years old when Goodman, now 39, took the biggest gamble of his career, buying three new Boeing 737s and starting Air Europe, the first new British independent airline to be launched for twelve years. Its chief executive was Martin O'Reagan, its commercial director Errol Cossey. Both were formerly with Dan-Air. Goodman, was reputed to have put up £500,000 of his own money to get the venture off the ground.

By now, Intasun was beginning to tweak Thomson's nose as an innovator. Florida, until the late 1970s, was mainly a winter destination. Orlando had yet to take off as the theme park capital of the world. Walt Disney's EPCOT Centre and Universal Studios had yet to open. Few British tourists were to be seen on Miami Beach, let alone the sands fringing the Gulf of Mexico. When Goodman suggested he could send thousands of British holidaymakers to the state of Miami during summer, hotel owners thought he was mad. June to September were hot and sticky – and often rainy. Nobody would want to come then. But Goodman had correctly foreseen a new wave of tourism which would later spread to the Caribbean islands, until then also winter bolt-holes for the privileged few. The British were ready for America. If the price was right, a little humidity and the odd downpour would not deter them. At first, the hotel owners refused to countenance the kind of rates Intasun offered until Goodman found one who said he would not agree ten dollars a head but had no objection if Harry told rival hoteliers that he would. This piece of Machiavellianism prised open the door, enabling the firm to launch a programme of packages with a lead-in price of £59 for one week. The programme was put together in 1978 and the first customers flew to Miami the following year.

There were teething troubles. British visitors took time to adjust to the idea that they could not walk everywhere as they could in Spanish resorts. Goodman recalls: 'In those days British tourists didn't rent cars. They were used to booking a hotel and spending a large part of their time there. We would send 400 clients and they would all come down to eat or go to the bar – and there would only be two barmen. We had to import our own bar staff and persuade hotels to employ more waiters.' One of the early motels in the brochure was decidedly sub-standard but most of the accommodation in the new programme represented astonishingly good value. One even acquired a dartboard for its new clientele. There were big queues outside Intasun's offices, and the Florida operation made £3million profit in its first year.

FREDDIE LAKER

The third key figure of the decade was Freddie Laker. Enough has been written about his rise and fall elsewhere, but our narrative would not be complete if we omitted to include a short profile. While it is as a battler and catalyst for the advent of cut-price, scheduled transatlantic air travel that Laker is best known, he is also credited with devising time charter – the system, quickly to become standard, under which a tour operator would get exclusive use of a jet by guaranteeing a certain number of flying hours during a set period.

A big man in physical stature and presence, with a management style best described as hands on and paternalistic, inspiring devotion in most who worked with him, Laker rarely appeared less than passionately convinced at the soundness of his arguments. Those who dared question his views were usually assailed with a flurry of rapid verbal blows. It was like going into the ring with a champion heavyweight. A supreme publicist, he always had a puckish sense of humour. One official recalls going to see him at his Gatwick headquarters, being collected in Freddie's Rolls-Royce, then being served an in-flight meal for lunch. To credit him, as some commentators have, with single-handedly creating cheap long haul travel is perhaps to exaggerate. Eventually, consumer pressure would have breached the walls built to protect national flag carriers. But there is no doubt that his struggle to launch a walk-on Skytrain service, initially between London and New York, was perfectly timed to hasten the process. And his role as the underdog, constantly nipping away at the establishment, made him a hero figure in the public mind.

Laker's first break had come in 1948, at the age 26, when a friend loaned him £38,000 to buy a dozen Haltons – converted Halifax bombers – from BOAC. In June that year, the Russians blockaded all traffic in or out of Berlin in an attempt to force the Allies to withdraw from the city. It was decided to call Moscow's bluff and feed the population by mounting a massive airlift. Laker did a deal with a company called Bond Air Services to provide some of the aircraft for this operation. His company, Aviation Traders, was suddenly enjoying significant cash flow. By the end of the airlift, Laker had paid for the Haltons and moved into a large detached house in the London suburb of Carshalton. He was on his way.

In 1958, having acquired a large number of different aircraft, large and small, Laker sold his two businesses, Air Charter and Aviation Traders, to an independent airline, Airwork. It was a time of great promise for such carriers. Two years earlier the Air Minister, Harold Watkinson, had indicated that the long frustrated independents were to be allowed greater opportunities to compete for the growing travel business. But with fourteen such airlines vying with each other, the new jam would be spread very thinly. Inevitably, a process of consolidation began. Airwork had already swallowed Transair, which had carried many of Vladimir's early customers. Now it would become the platform upon which British United Airways was to be built. Laker succeeded Gerry Freeman as its managing director.

That BUA became a force to be reckoned with had much to do with Laker's decision to equip it with the BAC 1-11 in 1960 as a replacement for its Viscounts. As launch customer for the aircraft, he insisted on key features of the Rolls-Royce Spey powered twinjet over lunch with Sir George Edwards, head of the British Aircraft Corporation, which would build it. And when BAC subsequently introduced changes to attract US buyers, but which Laker feared would eat into the jets' payload by making it heavier, his panache and bulldozing negotiating technique ensured he got them at an extremely favourable price. Sir George, who could not but admire his new customer, said later: 'A few hundred years ago he would have had brass earrings, a beard, a bit longer hair and a cutlass'. The buccaneer was soon on the bridge of his own ship again. In 1965, partly out of frustration and partly out of a driving desire to move on, he quit BUA. While he denied strenuously that there had been any rift with his chairman, Miles Wyatt, there was little doubt that their relationship, a clash of two strong personalities, had been choppy.

Laker Airways was soon launched with two Britannias as a stop gap, until the delivery of three BAC 1-11s, ordered for about £4 million. The project was unveiled to the press in February 1966. Freddie proposed to rely heavily on holiday charter business but the question was: how to get enough flying to pay for his new jets. The answer was time charter. His first contract was with Wings, which had grown out of the Ramblers Association. The contract, which guaranteed the operator would use a BAC 1-11 for 1700 flying hours, ran for a year from March 1967. Next came a £500,000 deal with Lord Brothers. Laker scored an early goal flying his planes non-stop to Tenerife, which was at the far limit of their range. He set a limit of 70 passengers and 40 lbs (18 kg) of luggage, telling the two tour operators that if they stuck to it, he would foot the bill if adverse weather conditions forced a stop at Lisbon.

Later that year he acquired a tour operation of his own: Arrowsmith Holidays, which had been set up by Harry Smith, one of the travel industry's pioneers. Smith had been considering selling up for some time. The crash of a chartered Argonaut at Stockport, near Manchester, in which many of his customers died, helped to tip him over the edge. And when Lord Brothers got into trouble, threatening the health of Laker's new charter business, he bought a controlling stake in that, too. Six years later in 1974, under the leadership of George Carroll, the quietly spoken, effectively focused lieutenant recruited to run his holiday firms, the Lord Brothers operation became Laker Holidays.

The crackdown on affinity group charters at the start of the 1970s hit Laker hard. Looking for something to replace them, he announced plans in summer 1971 for a walk-on, no booking service called Skytrain. He though it was the best – and probably the most profitable – idea he had ever dreamed up. The epic battle to get it off the ground exposed, more clearly than ever, the paranoid fears of established carriers that they would lose traffic to this upstart operation and the nervous conservatism of some civil servants and their ministers.

Laker's first application for a licence was rejected – though with encouraging noises – by the soon to be disbanded Air Transport Licensing Board; approved on appeal by a commissioner appointed by the Department of Trade; and then rejected again by the Secretary of State for Trade. His second attempt was more successful. The new order at the recently formed Civil Aviation Authority was more adventurous. After a public hearing rich in the kind of verbal sparring Laker loved, the CAA gave its approval. There were strings, however, notably one which demanded he should not fly from Gatwick, as he wanted, but from the virtual unknown airport of Stansted.

Early in 1973, the British Government designated Laker Airways as a carrier under the Bermuda agreements between the UK and the US. The next task was to secure American approval. The Americans dragged their feet. They wanted to reduce capacity on the North Atlantic, not least to help the ailing Pan American by pushing up revenues. In September 1974, airlines from both sides reached agreement on a reduction for that winter but Pan Am and TWA insisted it would become null and void if Skytrain got the go-ahead. Laker was livid. He took legal action forcing the airlines to rejig their agreement so that Skytrain would not be excluded. Worse, he was furious that the Department of Trade should have gone along with the carve-up.

His frustration boiled to the surface that autumn in Majorca, where a large group of travel agents and journalists had been invited to celebrate the launch of Laker Holidays. As his guests munched their way through roast suckling pig and swilled huge quantities of wine at a restaurant outside Palma, Freddie treated them to a vitriolic attack on the Department's senior aviation officials, describing them as 'bums and gangsters' and 'the same old gang of restrictionists'. Even by his standards the rhetoric was extreme.

The established airlines were still struggling to make ends meet on the North Atlantic, however. British Airways asked the CAA to revoke Skytrain's licence. The Authority declined. Then the Government confirmed suspicions, raised much earlier by its imposition of currency limits, that it did not appreciate the importance of mass travel as a vote winner. After a review which divided the operations of BA and British Caledonian into 'spheres of influence', the Trade Secretary Peter Shore told Laker in summer 1975, that Skytrain could not longer go ahead. It was a serious error. Freddie went back to law. The High Court, and subsequently the Appeal Court, ruled that Shore had acted beyond his powers.

With a new and more sympathetic Secretary of State, Edmund Dell, at the helm, it was back to persuading the Americans. This was no longer such an uphill slog. The mood across the Atlantic was changing. US civil aviation, which had been regulated even more tightly than its European equivalent, was on the brink of liberalization. The consumer army had become too powerful to resist. In June1977, President Jimmy Carter approved Laker's permit. The battle was won.

By now Laker's rivals, British Airways, TWA and Pan American, were planning to hit back with cheap standby fares of their own. BA, for example, offered a New York fare of £64 one way. Fearing that flying from Stansted would leave him at a serious disadvantage, Laker sought permission from the CAA for a switch to Gatwick. In mid-September, with the planned inaugural service only twelve days away, the Authority said yes.

On Monday 26 September, Skytrain took off at last for New York. Under the strict rules set for the operation, passengers were not allowed to check in until 4 a.m. that morning. A beaming Freddie was at the till to take payment for the first £59 one way ticket. Among the 270 passengers were a large number of journalists who had queued at Gatwick for seats, like other customers, since the previous day – and British Airways' commercial planning and pricing director Charles Stuart, who said he hoped he wouldn't be seen as a spy. Some brought sandwiches but most paid £1.75 for a meal of pâté, boeuf Bourguignon, dessert and cheese — and a small glass of wine. Luck was on Laker's side. For a while it looked as though murk over Manhattan would spoil the jamboree, forcing a diversion to Boston but a last minute break in the weather saved the day. Though there were to be many stumbles before the concept became an unstoppable trend, the era of no frills travel was born. The impact on North Atlantic charter operators was devastating. In the first six months of the following year their traffic to the USA from Heathrow and Gatwick slumped by 27.7 per cent while the number of scheduled passengers rose by 44.7 per cent. And as travellers from other European countries came to London to catch cheap scheduled flights, charter traffic from Amsterdam, Brussels and Paris also plummeted. As the 1978 summer travel peak reached its climax, passengers queuing for Skytrain tickets — or for the cut-price standby deals introduced in retaliation by BA, TWA and Pan American — were camping out on pavements outside their central London offices, sometimes sleeping rough for several nights.

'CHEAPIES'

We must now wind the clock back. In the run up to the summer 1975 season, Spanish hoteliers, bitten by the events of 1974, were twice shy. They overbooked outrageously and travellers suffered accordingly. Selling beds three times over was not uncommon. An unconfirmed report suggested that one hotel in Palma Nova, which was among the worst affected resorts, was cavalier enough to have overbooked by 500 per cent. The result was a change in ABTA's code of practice for tour operators. Now they were banned from publishing clauses in their brochure small print aimed at protecting them from compensation claims by overbooked clients. They were committed to warn clients as far in advance as possible when overbooking was about to arise and to offer refunds or comparable alternative holidays to those affected. Although this was an improvement, unresolved issues remained. What about a client moved from a beach to a town hotel? Was that comparable, critics wondered? And what about a four star customer shifted to a five star hotel — when they couldn't afford the drinks or didn't have the right clothes? Hotel overbooking was not the only high

Figure 10.1   One of Freddie Laker's Skytrain DC-10s.

profile problem to dog the industry through the 1970s. Two other recurring issues were the sale of cheap seats on charter flights, and surcharges.

With minimum price restrictions only recently lifted, it followed that selling charter flights without accommodation remained, strictly speaking, illegal. But the 1970s saw a rapid erosion of this regulation. As more Britons bought property abroad and others developed the confidence to rent cars and strike out on their own, demand grew for flights cheaper than the scheduled carriers could provide – and to destinations which they did not serve. Though Cosmos was not the first to launch such deals, the deals came to be identified by its brand name for them: Cheapies.

Tour operators circumvented the rules by offering vouchers for basic accommodation, sometimes in multi-bed dormitories, which customers could throw away. Thomson was told the CAA would stop it. So it introduced a convoluted system under which clients contracted their properties in Spain or Greece to the tour operator for £1. The operator then rented it back to them with the seat. Whether or not the customer really owned property was immaterial. It was impossible for the authorities to check.

British Airways was furious. In 1975, for example, it carped to the Authority that Thomson's 'Wanderer' packages to Greece, which were still being sold as flights and vouchers, were a 'total misuse of its licence'. Its objection was easily explained. The packages cost £59. BA's lowest return fare to Athens was £125. They were just a cheap fare under another guise, the airline said. It demanded that Britannia's licence should be varied to include a condition that inclusive tour accommodation must be paid for in advance by operators, and that it should be of a reasonable standard and realistically priced – though just who would judge this was unclear. Britannia retorted that the number of passengers seduced from BA's services was so small as to be insignificant.

Thomson's defiant response to BA's objections was to offer a much wider choice of Wanderer packages, extending them to the Costa del Sol, Costa Blanca, Majorca, Minorca and Ibiza. It offered two weeks on the Costa Brava, for about £30 less than the price of its cheapest alternative holiday there. Even in peak summer, a fortnight in Majorca would cost only £59.

Cliff Paice says: 'I would like to think that I was a thoroughgoing supporter of all this liberalisation, but I have some idea in my mind that I needed persuading at the time. I definitely remember someone offering package holidays where the accommodation was in a cave'.

Roger Davies, then Thomson's marketing director, admitted that the accommodation on offer was hardly 'the last word in home comfort'. Cosmos managing director Wilf Jones openly admitted that his firm's Cheapies would probably be used as a cut-price way of flying around Europe. The firm said most of the accommodation offered would not have hot or cold running water – and bedrooms might have to be shared. Its brochure small print advised customers: 'regulations controlling inclusive air holidays require that accommodation must be provided for the duration of the holiday but, of course, it is up to you what you do when you get there'.

BA fumed helplessly. Its travel division director Gerry Draper said: 'This type of offer makes a mockery of the conditions governing the sale of package tours or charters.' But it was in vain. Popular sentiment was that European scheduled air fares were a rip-off and that the major airlines deserved all they were getting. After BA's original protest, the CAA had come to the view that whether or not the customers used the accommodation on offer was their business. Its tolerance was not infinite. It still prosecuted one company when a client actually wanted to use the accommodation, only to find that it did not exist. But it did not go back on its decision.

Gradually the voucher system withered away. Operators simply did not bother to keep up the pretence. Now and then the Authority had gripes from the Spanish government about these deals, but it turned a deaf ear. Officials in Madrid would threaten to send holidaymakers straight home again if they were caught without vouchers – something which rarely, if ever, happened – but there was an ulterior motive behind this stick waving. Spain wanted a bigger share of the burgeoning charter market for its own airlines. One tour operator launched a programme under the label 'Just the Ticket'. Spanish officials objected, only to be told, with considerable ingenuity, that in English the phrase meant something completely different, something along the lines of 'just what the doctor ordered'. Along with the Spanish, the Greeks kicked up the most fuss about what came to be known as 'seat onlys', ostensibly because they feared the tickets would attract the wrong kind of tourists – young people, for example, who might sleep on beaches or anywhere else they cared to lay their heads.

SURCHARGES AND FORWARD BUYING

Surcharges continually raised the hackles of consumer campaigners. Since the Arab oil embargo of 1973, operators had levied them to cover unexpected jumps in the price of aviation fuel as well as currency fluctuations. Before that, airlines had purchased fuel on long-term contracts at fixed prices. Now, prices changed monthly. Operators pointed out that they needed to set package prices seven months or so before customers paid their final holiday bills and that, in the meantime, they faced the risk of major unforeseen cost increases. Those who argued that surcharging should be outlawed were naïve, for it would almost certainly have driven some firms to the wall. But the cogency of this argument was undermined by wide and embarrassing differences between the amounts levied by different operators. The suspicion took root that some were lining their pockets.

By 1975, sterling was in deep trouble again. On 1 July the pound slid to an all time low in Spain, buying only 118 pesetas at the tourist rate. Four years earlier it had stood at 172. Last minute demand for surcharges was raising serious concern. One agent grumbled to ABTA's national council that they constituted a 'sick and sordid charade'. Some travellers complained they were asked for surcharges at airports, on the aircraft, when they arrived in their resorts – and even after they got back.

Tour firms asked the Bank of England for permission to buy foreign currency further in advance. Forward buying is now standard practice. At that time, even those (such as Thomson) who made use of the facility were unable to buy more than six weeks before departure. Bills were usually processed some time before that, leaving operators vulnerable in the interim. Tour firms wanted the maximum forward purchase period doubled. In August, the CAA waded into the controversy, telling them that they must stop collecting the extra charges after the customer received the final holiday bill. The thinly veiled implication was that they could lose their licences if they persisted. As a solution, the Authority even kicked around the idea of reintroducing minimum prices for packages. Its chairman, Lord Boyd-Carpenter, felt operators had set unrealistically low prices, knowing they could surcharge to make up the difference. British Airways stole a marketing lead by announcing that its Sovereign and Enterprise holidays for summer 1976 would be guaranteed against currency and fuel surcharges, provided customers booked by 16 January. The following year other operators, including Thomson, did the same.

The demographics of the holiday business, meantime, continued to evolve. Cosmos managing director Wilf Jones was a curious character to be heading a leading tour operation, for he was terrified of flying. He was also allergic to taking lifts. On one occasion – an important travel trade gathering in the restaurant at the top of the Post Office Tower – Wilf insisted on climbing the innumerable flights of stairs rather than take the lift. He was, friends say, more interested in his Kent apple farm than in the travel business. Cosmos had its brochures produced by a printer in Germany. Jones insisted they were despatched to England in boxes of a size which could be re-used to pack his fruit.

Wherever his heart lay, he could spot a marketing opportunity. As the decade neared its mid-point, he identified a swing in bookings from the 'poor rich' to the 'rich poor', noting that the proportion of upper- and middle-class Britons taking packages had dropped by nearly 10 per cent between 1970 and 1974, while that of skilled workers had increased by more than 40 per cent. 'The swing towards the working-class traveller, jetting away towards his holiday in the sun – or to visit his cousins in America – has been developing for the past ten years. You will remember the first shock at finding tea like mum made in Benidorm. What has happened in the past twelve months is that the working-class traveller has now become top dog.' So Cosmos offered to return customers' deposits if they were made redundant.

SPAIN

At ABTA's Convention in Miami in November 1975, Lord Boyd-Carpenter warned the industry against the 'enormous danger' of putting all its eggs in one basket. Of concentrating too much, in other words, on countries whose politics were volatile. He was careful not to single out Spain, but the Spanish Tourist Office was becoming extremely sensitive about the idea that the passing of the Franco regime would lead to a bloody break-up of the country. The travel industry had ridden the overthrow of Portugal's authoritarian regime. Memories of the Turkish invasion of Cyprus the previous year were fresh. But neither episode had threatened to bring the industry to its knees. Cyprus, which attracted around 10 per cent of the market was a relatively small player. That Spain, which accounted for nearly 50 per cent, might suddenly become a no-go area, was an altogether scarier thought.

That summer, there had been a growing sense that the old Spanish order was on the way out. In August, the cabinet introduced swingeing anti-terrorist laws outlawing all kinds of opposition. In September, fifteen European governments withdrew their ambassadors in protest at the sentencing to death of ETA Basque separatists and members of the FRAP (Frente Revolucionario Antifascista y Patriótica) anti-fascist movement. As Boyd-Carpenter spoke, Franco, whose death had been announced accidentally by ABC News in Washington on 22 October, lay in Madrid's Ciudad Sanitaria La Paz clinic, having undergone a four-and-a-half-hour operation to remove two-thirds of his stomach. Kept alive by life support machines, he surfaced only to murmur: 'How hard it is to die'. A fortnight later, the tubes were disconnected and the end came. While the Caudillo held sway, there had been hardly any debate in the travel trade about the morality of dealing with such an authoritarian and sometime oppressive regime. But with his passing, fears emerged that the Basques and others, notably the long suppressed Catalans, would seek independence, perhaps plunging the country into a state of civil unrest.

CHINA

In August 1977, it was announced that Thomson would operate the first regular package holidays to China. Lord Thomson, proprietor of the company's parent group, had discussed the idea with Premier Chou En-lai in Peking three years earlier. Previously would-be visitors had to register their names with a travel firm such as Thomas Cook and wait until the Chinese authorities gave their blessing to another tour group.

THE END OF THE DECADE

Regulation and deregulation continued to strengthen consumer hands and pose new problems for the industry. In 1978, the Unfair Contract Terms Act came into effect, denying operators the shelter of exclusion clauses in their brochure small print which had allowed them to escape responsibility for the behaviour of their suppliers when accidents occurred abroad. If clients suffered in a hotel fire, for example, firms were now obliged to show that they had taken reasonable steps to ensure that the hotelier had complied with all local safety regulations. Two months later, under pressure from the Government, ABTA relaxed its restrictions preventing travel agents from offering incentives to book, such as free sun tan cream or transport to the airport. It was a first, tentative step towards complete freedom of retail pricing, which has seen major agency chains take over from operators as the primary source of holiday discounts.

In July 1978, retailers were confronted with another challenge. It was announced that from spring the following year, the Danish tour operator Tjaereborg would start selling holidays to the British market. Tjaereborg had been built up by Eilif Krogager, known as 'the flying pastor' who had branched into travel a quarter of a century earlier, taking parishioners to Spain by coach. Now the company owned an airline, Sterling, and sold packages to some 600,000 Scandinavians and West Germans. It did not sell through travel agents. It was quickly followed by a Stockholm-based operator, Vingresor, which controlled about a quarter of the Swedish package market. Could such direct sell firms really undercut those which sold in the High Street – or would their advertising costs swallow up the savings they made in commission? A furious debate broke out. Other, home grown direct sell brands, such as Portland, would eventually demonstrate that there was room for both kinds of operation. But the foreign invasion proved short lived. Vingresor was soon taken over by Thomson. Tjaereborg, whose holidays were generally well received by consumers, was swallowed up by Owners Abroad in 1987. The following year, Thomson raised travel agents' hackles by announcing the launch of Portland, another new direct sell brand. Portland's first customers travelled in summer, 1980.

The decade ended much as it had begun – in a confusion of hope and uncertainty. The number of Britons taking package holidays had at last climbed back to its level before the Court Line crash. The Conservatives had been returned to power, led by Margaret Thatcher. British society faced abrupt and painful changes. In Spain, Basque terrorists exploded a small bomb on a beach at Benidorm, which was now attracting some three million Britons a year. Though their campaign against the tourist industry did not develop into a serious deterrent, the incident sent a nervous shiver through the industry. The Middle East was a worse headache. The Shah had been driven out of Iran. His country was at war with Iraq. Fuel prices had doubled in a year. For tour operators and airlines, there were further trying times ahead.

11

The Latter Years: from free spirits to flotation

ROGER BRAY

The collapse of Harry Goodman's International Leisure Group in 1992 marked the end of an era. The buccaneers had raised their last hurrah. The price war battlefield, which had already shifted from the tour operating marketing department to the High Street, would never be quite as bloody again. Airtours was poised to become Thomson's biggest competitor but while its founder, David Crossland, remains a brilliant innovator, he proved very different from the flamboyant Goodman – quiet and retiring, emerging rarely into the media glare. His character seems in keeping with the spirit of the times. Rules have emerged from Brussels which would have left the industry's pioneers aghast. The growth of rampant consumerism has been boosted by the importation of two legal threats from the USA – the class action and the 'no win no fee' lawsuit. And for the three largest operators, all quoted on the Stock Exchange by the end of the millennium, there are now shareholders to be considered. As the package holiday approached its fiftieth birthday, freebooting had been curbed by a need for much tighter discipline.

The 1980s saw the emergence of two major trends. Britons began to travel much farther afield and increasingly opted for self-catering holidays. Assessing such changes has been hampered by the irritating unreliability of statistics. Far too often, what has passed for research has been a combination of exaggeration by the industry and wishful thinking by the media, for whom the identification of dramatic shifts in social behaviour has always made entertaining copy. That said, the best figures available show that in the second half of the decade alone, long haul holidays increased, as a proportion of the total sold, from 6.7 per cent to 12.7 per cent. They also show a shift away from the conventional hotel package. As British travellers became more accustomed to foreign food and culture, there was a marked shift towards self-catering. People were becoming much more relaxed about eating independently in resort restaurants, shopping for local produce and cooking for themselves. Figures from Lunn-Poly, which had been transformed by owner Thomson into a leading travel agency chain, suggested that in 1987, a quarter of all Britons buying inclusive holidays were already opting for villas or apartments. Research from the same source showed that by the mid-1990s, that proportion had risen to nearly 50 per cent.

The 1980s were characterized by an epic struggle for market share between the major tour operators. Companies upped their projected summer capacity by incautious leaps and bounds. Going for growth of 20 per cent in a single year was not uncommon. At times, the struggle degenerated into farce. In late 1985, operators began an absurd game of leapfrog, undercutting each other's bargains by turns. Holidays costing as little as £25 were gimmicks, designed to whip up free publicity but behind the headlines the price war was real enough. Smaller firms began to worry that as the big companies offered unrealistic deals in the battle for ascendancy, they would be unable to get the charter seats they needed. The Association of Independent Tour Operators cried foul. The Office of Fair Trading looked into their grievance and decided it was unjustified. Its director general, Sir Gordon Borrie, said there was nothing to suggest that the big operators were 'deliberately losing money at the beginning of the season with the object of driving competitors out of business'. Echoes of AITO's complaint refused to fade away and while time and change of circumstance have altered them superficially, they may still be heard today.

THE EFFECTS OF THATCHERISM

The decade dawned with Britain in the grip of Margaret Thatcher's reforming zeal. It was not just traditional industries which were left to sink or swim. British Airways was to be privatized, a decision which sent ripples of apprehension through its smaller rivals. The state giant was too powerful to allow real competition, they bleated. Scheduled and charter carriers alike were concerned that BA would use its muscle to sweep up all the prime take-off and landing slots. It was all very well lauding the disciplines which shareholders would force upon it. But if push came to shove, did anybody sincerely believe that the nation's flag carrier would be allowed to go under?

It was a tricky issue for the new Tory Government, which was committed to fostering competition in the air. But there were softer targets. Pretty well everybody agreed that scheduled air fares within Europe were too high. Deregulation in the USA had set the pattern, spawning cheap travel. Ministers, who conveniently avoided high-lighting the fact that charter flights from Britain were even cheaper (charters as we know them have never existed in America), set about convincing their opposite numbers in the European Economic Community that something must be done.

Meanwhile, the Government moved to persuade airlines that BA could no longer expect protection. The Secretary of State for Trade, John Nott, nailed his colours to the mast by devastating its monopoly between London and Hong Kong, which was then virtually a domestic route. The Hong Kong Civil Aviation Authority had given locally based Cathay Pacific and British Caledonian permission to compete with BA. Its UK equivalent narrowed that to BA and B-Cal. Nott declared a free-for-all, giving Laker the green light too, though he was to be frustrated by the colony's authorities. BA hit back with a fare of £99 one way.

British package holidaymakers were becoming markedly more sophisticated. This was reflected by a significant shift from full- to half-board deals as they became increasingly confident about making their own lunch arrangements. During the next two decades this confidence would manifest itself in other ways. Between the mid-1980s and mid-1990s, the proportion of package customers willing to cater for themselves in villas and apartments, many inevitably experimenting with the cooking of local food, would rise from one in four to around 50 per cent. The share of inclusive holidays booked through retailers, for example, would fall, from 83 per cent in 1986 to 74 per cent ten years later. And the proportion of long haul holidays booked would more than double from 6.7 per cent to 15.8 per cent of all air packages, though to some extent this rapid jump was probably a symptom of the widening gap between the haves, with their increasing disposable wealth, and the have-nots. In 1980, Cosmos, a company then more readily associated with sun, sea and sand holidays to the Mediterranean, announced it would start offering regular packages to China. In the same year Thomson, the country's biggest tour operator with over 19 per cent of the summer market, released details of a customer survey which showed that 80 per cent of its customers had taken a package at least once during the previous five years. The firm even toyed with the idea that its clients might welcome holidays split into two distinct halves, with one week fully organized and a second in which they would be left to their own devices, renting cars, perhaps and heading off inland.

Another indication of this greater spirit of adventure was the rise in travel to the USA. In the peak holiday months of June, July and August, 1979, the number of Britons going there had soared by 60 per cent compared with the same month of the previous year. The following year Laker Airways, which was already flying to Los Angeles, was granted permission for a third Skytrain route to Miami, but the Civil Aviation Authority rejected Laker's latest wheeze, a grand plan to crack Europe's hidebound system of bilateral air agreements (which usually allowed only one airline from each country to compete for scheduled traffic between the two) with a huge network of cut-price services.

Despite the new atmosphere of *laissez-faire*, ABTA's Stabilizer rules, which forbade operators belonging to the association from selling holidays other than through member agents, and in most instances prevented its retailers from selling packages other than those organized by members, survived legal scrutiny. In 1978, it had become the first service organization to be referred to the Restrictive Practices Court by the Office of Fair Trading but more than five years were to pass before judgment was handed down. The Government, meanwhile, indicated it would remain impartial. In 1984 the Court decided that on balance, Stabilizer was in the public interest. It was little more than a temporary reprieve, however. By the end of the 1980s, European competition legislation was fast making the system untenable. ABTA was to abandon it formally in 1993. And in his judgment, Mr Justice Lincoln made an important proviso. The association could no longer prevent member agents discounting the holidays of member operators. The proviso still did not stop individual operators keeping the shackles on their suppliers and forbidding them to offer price cuts but this practice soon became illegal following an investigation into the industry by the Monopolies and Mergers Commission, which delivered its report in 1986. By then, agents had read the portents. Lunn-Poly had launched its first major discount campaign the previous year.

THE COLLAPSE OF LAKER AIRWAYS

The seismic event of the early 1980s was the collapse of Laker Airways. There was a brutal irony in the fact that Mrs Thatcher's entrepreneurial hero, who had been knighted by the previous Labour Government, should preside over the first truly spectacular company failure since she became Prime Minister. For some time, his expansion plans had looked overambitious. British Caledonian's chairman, Sir Adam Thomson, wrote later that Sir Freddie had pushed the cliff towards the lemmings. The original economics of Skytrain had been based on DC-10 jets which their manufacturer, McDonnell Douglas had become stuck with and which he had acquired, consequently, for a song. But when he ordered more DC-10s later, he paid much the same as other airlines, so his price advantage was diluted. To make matters worse, he had provoked anger from his major rivals by straying from his original walk-on concept and introducing bookable, premium class fares in what he called Regency Class, invading territory jealously guarded by Pan American, TWA and British Airways.

At the end of the 1970s, recession hit the airline industry hard. And a DC-10 disaster at Chicago's O'Hare Airport in May 1979, had led to a worldwide, two week grounding of the jets – including Laker's. The crisis was reckoned to have cost the airline some £13 million in lost revenues. Soon he was being squeezed from one side by a weakening pound, in which most of his fares were paid, and from the other by a strengthening dollar, which accounted for most of his debts. By spring 1981, he realized he would have to restructure them. At the end of the summer, Laker's bankers agreed to a deal which would keep him going. But the airline's plight was worsened when the big carriers slashed their own fares and a succession of airlines put pressure on McDonnell Douglas and the engine manufacturer General Electric, allegedly with the aim of dissuading them from swapping Laker's debt for equity in his airline.

Matters came to a head the following January, always a time of thin business for scheduled airlines. Laker's bookings were worse than expected. The CAA estimated it would need an injection of £10 million to survive. On 4 February Sir Freddie was given a stark deadline by the Midland Bank. If he failed to come up with fresh funds by 9 a.m. the next morning, his overdraft would be withdrawn.

In a desperate last ditch effort to save the airline, Sir Freddie telephoned the Trade Minister, Iain Sproat, who in turn contacted Mrs Thatcher. She called a meeting at the House of Commons, bringing in Ray Colegate, the economic director of the CAA. Others there included Bob Ayling, then a lawyer with the Department of Trade and Industry, later chief executive of British Airways. They discussed whether the Treasury might guarantee £5 million to keep Laker airborne. Colegate recalls how Mrs Thatcher said she could not bear to 'think of my poor passengers being stranded'. But when the Prime Minister was told that even that amount might not be enough, the thought that her taxpayers might be burdened by an open-ended commitment proved even less bearable. Sir Freddie then phoned Harry Goodman, whose International Leisure Group had gone public in 1981, hoping to raise cash by selling him the Laker tour operations. Goodman was attending a travel trade show in Madrid. He flew back to Gatwick and met the beleaguered Laker at midnight at the Hilton Hotel there. Goodman recalls the night vividly. The press had got wind of the meeting. Reporters, he claims, tried to infiltrate it disguised as waiters. 'Someone even tried to get through on the phone saying she was my daughter.' Freddie, he says, was 'totally shellshocked'. He asked Goodman to negotiate with his bankers in a next door suite. They failed to agree terms. The game was up. By 4.30 a.m. Sir Freddie and his colleagues accepted they would have to cease trading. Goodman was to profit, as he had from Clarksons' demise. That same morning he dispatched negotiators to Spain to pick up the accommodation which was now going begging. He would soon be Britain's second largest tour operator.

Sir Freddie refused to sink without a last thrash towards the light. With his friend, the Lonrho head Tiny Rowland, he explored the possibility of bouncing back with a 'People's Airline', but it was not to be. The obstacles, not least those of shattered confidence, were too great.

His tour operations, principally Arrowsmith and Laker Holidays, remained going concerns. The former was bought by brewers Greenall Whitley for £4.2 million along with Laker North. Laker Holidays was bought by the Saga group, which specialized in packages for senior citizens, for £500,000. But the purchasers quickly encountered problems. Some overseas hoteliers had not waited for the takeovers before selling Laker beds to other operators. And the new owners were dismayed to find the Tour Operators' Study Group advertising to disappointed Laker tour customers that 'all you need to do is visit an ABTA Travel Agent who will arrange the transfer of money paid for a Laker or Arrowsmith holiday to a new holiday with another TOSG member whose name appears below'. Neither of the new owners were members of the group.

The collapse caused serious concern among operators who had chartered seats aboard Laker's aircraft. Finding spare capacity for the remainder of the winter might not be too difficult but with the peak, post-Christmas booking period drawing to a close, there was the coming summer to worry about. Peter Drew, of Rank Travel, which owned Wings and OSL, proposed that British Caledonian should take over the operation of two of Laker's DC-10s and fly them on behalf of a mixed bag of tour firms.

That Autumn, while most of the travel industry was attending ABTA's annual convention in a rain sodden Cannes, the CAA awarded Sir Freddie a licence to operate package holidays again. He promised cut-price transatlantic tickets to people who had lost money in the collapse. But the gesture failed to prevent a huge row from erupting in the conference centre as agents, who felt their clients had been badly let down, objected to his application to rejoin. The association took heed of their wrath and turned him down. Its agents would not display Laker's brochures in their shops. The new Skytrain Holidays programme, launched with backing from Lonrho, would have to be sold direct to its customers. Despite a television advertising campaign with a personal message from the veteran pioneer, they proved hard to come by. The new operation quickly bit the dust.

Sir Freddie must have felt a twinge of nostalgia the following May, when a similarly ill fated US airline, People Express, got permission to start flights between Gatwick and Newark, New Jersey, with one way fares from £99. The newcomer was a sort of workers' cooperative. Staff switched between jobs as and when work needed doing.

The true heir to the Laker tradition, however, was Richard – later Sir Richard – Branson. His Virgin Atlantic made its first flight between Gatwick and New York in August, 1984. Much as he admired Sir Freddie, Branson vowed he would not let the intoxicating whiff of aviation fuel tempt him into overweening ambition. Much in the Laker vein, however, he would soon be accusing British Airways of dirty tricks calculated to undermine his business.

Meanwhile, Sir Freddie's shrewd American lawyer Bob Beckman had advised the liquidators, Touche Ross, that Laker Airways looked to have a valid claim that various companies, among them major North Atlantic carriers including British Airways, Pan American and TWA, had conspired to undermine its business, contrary to US anti-trust legislation. Central to the claim was the allegation that the big airlines had offered unrealistically low fares. Nine months after the collapse, the liquidator decided to go ahead with a lawsuit. The subsequent legal battle, which involved prolonged argument about whether a UK airline could be sued in America, dragged on for over two years and delayed BA's Stock Market flotation. The eventual out of court settlement ensured that passengers who had been left holding worthless tickets got their money back. That was not the only legal reverberation. A class action had been brought against British Airways, Pan American and TWA in the USA on behalf of consumers, claiming Laker's collapse had deprived them of cheap air travel. To get this off their backs, the airlines set up a fund totalling some £21 million, which could be used to cover discounts for those travellers on future flights. Taking on Laker had turned out to be a costly business.

BA AND BRITISH CALEDONIAN

As society polarized into those who were doing well and those who were deprived by the closure of industries, so the travel industry began to split. One end of the market demanded very cheap holidays, while the other wanted specialist knowledge and more personal service – even at a significantly higher cost. In between lay a big gap. Thus by

1985 the bruising price war was causing serious problems for medium size operators, which were neither large enough to compete in volume terms nor small enough to command unswerving customer loyalty. British Caledonian was among the first to throw in the towel, disposing of its loss-making tour operations. Arrowsmith, which had been acquired from Greenall Whitley, was sold to Owners Abroad. The Blue Sky brand went to Rank, which already had a half share in the operator's charter business, Cal-Air. Chris Smart, head of B-Cal's leisure, said the move had been prompted by 'predatory' pricing by leading operators. A year later Rank dropped the Blue Sky name, along with another familiar brand, Ellerman Sunflight, from its brochures, selling all its holidays as Wings.

Although it has continued to operate up-market, long haul holidays, British Airways was also becoming uneasy about its role as a mainstream tour operator. There was a growing feeling at the airline that bread and butter packages to Spain were peripheral to its core business. BA needed either to attack the market with renewed vigour, beefing up its loss-making operations by acquiring other tour firms, or get out altogether. It did neither. A compromise was devised. In September 1987, control of its main brands – Enterprise, Flair, Sovereign and the direct sell Martin Rooks – was handed over to Vic Fatah, the 39-year-old son of a travel agent and keen skier, who had built up Sunmed, a niche operation with programmes to Greece and Turkey in summer and the Alps in winter. A new company was set up, in which BA retained a 50 per cent stake. Fatah took the other half. Fatah had proved himself adept at dancing ahead of the big operators, picking resorts when they were still unsung, before they were swamped with Britons. His company now carried around 200,000 customers a year. Running BA's operations, which would add another 650,000, was a huge step up.

At British Airways, minds were in any case focused elsewhere. A month earlier it had emerged that BA was seeking a merger with British Caledonian. In the airline business, as in tour operating, it had become increasingly difficult for medium size companies such as B-Cal, itself the creation of a merger between Caledonian and British United Airways, to compete.

It has not been the purpose of this book to chart the history of scheduled airlines save where it affected the holiday revolution. The

merger falls into this category. It immediately rekindled the same kind
of concerns which had surfaced in the run-up to BA's privatization,
which had been concluded earlier that year. The Government referred
the deal to the Monopolies and Mergers Commission. Britannia, owned
by Thomson and the largest of the charter carriers, was concerned that
such a powerful new combination could squeeze package holiday flights
out of Gatwick. Government policy was that charters might have to be
shifted to Stansted if room could not otherwise be made for new
scheduled services there. Britannia demanded that all flights should be
treated equally. Rival airlines scrambled to bid for chunks of B-Cal,
arguing that to let BA have it, lock stock and barrel, would be to stifle
competition. Among them was Harry Goodman's ILG, owner of Air
Europe, which wanted B-Cal's European operation. It was not the first
time such an arrangement had been mooted. In 1986, ILG entered
negotiations with British Caledonian about merging Air Europe with
British Caledonian's short haul operation to create what was tentatively
dubbed 'an airline for Europe'. Like other scheduled carriers, B-Cal
was going through a torrid time. Its revenues had been depressed by
the Chernobyl nuclear disaster in the Ukraine and a US bombing raid
on Libya. These events had hit transatlantic traffic, on which it relied
for more than one third of its business. Its European routes were far
from healthy. The idea was that the new airline would have costs up to
a quarter lower than those of the major carriers and that, as Europe
was engulfed in an irresistible tide of liberalization, it could offer fares
much lower than theirs. The idea of collaboration between the brash
Goodman and the soft-spoken, sober-suited Sir Adam Thomson, the
wartime Fleet Air Arm pilot who headed B-Cal, seemed a little far-
fetched from the beginning. While Sir Adam was away in the USA,
Goodman offered what the B-Cal chairman described later as 'a paltry
£36 million' for the whole airline. The waters were further muddied
by leaks to the press, which forced Sir Adam to deny that his airline
was in financial difficulties. The talks broke down.

Lobbying by the smaller carriers paid off. The MMC decreed that
the merged airlines must put B-Cal's domestic routes and ten European
routes up for grabs. More important for the holiday industry, BA
agreed to relinquish at least 5000 take-off and landing slots at Gatwick.
And the airlines' charter operations – BA's was called British Airtours
– would be merged to become Caledonian Airways. For a while it

looked as if investment by the Scandinavian carrier SAS might allow B-Cal to keep flying under its own name. But shortly before Christmas, BA upped its bid to £250 million – £13 million more than the price originally agreed and £50 million more than the revised amount which had been on the table while the MMC deliberated. It was an offer too good to refuse.

As British Caledonian vanished, so a new charter airline emerged. Air 2000 was set up by the Owners Abroad group. It began life with two Boeing 757s, operating around 35 flights a week from its base at Manchester Airport. By the end of the 1990s its fleet had grown to 25 aircraft.

Thomson's dominance as the country's largest tour operator was cemented in 1988 when it paid £75 million for Horizon, the third biggest group, which by then included Wings, Blue Sky and OSL and operated its own charter airline, Orion. This Horizon, of course, was not the company founded by Vladimir. It was the former Horizon Midland (floated off by Vladimir as a public company in 1972), rescued from the flames of the Court Line crash by a consortium led by Bruce Tanner. It had changed its name to Horizon Travel in 1979, when memories of the financial problems which had beset the original Horizon had dimmed. It airline was launched a year later. In 1987 it had acquired Wings from Rank and was itself bought soon afterwards by the brewers, Bass, for £94 million. Thomson, which carried around 3.5 million customers a year, controlled some 30 per cent of the market. Horizon's one million represented 10 per cent. Together they would be roughly double the size of their nearest rival, the International Leisure Group. Lord Young, the Trade Secretary, referred the takeover to the Monopolies and Mergers Commission which gave its blessing the following January. The industry's consolidation had been such that 68 per cent of the 14.2 million holidays licensed by the CAA for 1989 (of which 12.6 million holidays were actually sold) were operated by the top five companies. This was exercising the Office of Fair Trading, which had become concerned about the override or bonus commissions the big operators were paying travel agents and the perks they were offering counter staff as incentives to sell their holidays.

CONSUMER PROTECTION

The consumer protection screw, meanwhile, had been gradually tightened. Sometimes the improvements were the result of official intervention, often they were introduced by the industry, responding to the pressures of publicity. Criticism of surcharges, for example, was stilled to a whisper when ABTA ruled that operators must absorb any extra, unforeseen costs up to 2 per cent of the original holiday price. If the surcharge topped 10 per cent, the customer must be allowed to cancel with a full refund, except for any insurance premium or amendment fees which had been charged. Having recognized that the constant rumble of consumer discontent might damage their business, most major operators were already buying some foreign currency on the forward market to avoid the impact of sudden fluctuations. This enabled them to advertise 'no surcharge guarantees'. ABTA's move caused some financial pain as smaller firms, many of which did not or could not take similar precautions, were forced to swallow unexpected costs. But it also reduced the marketing advantage which the largest companies had enjoyed.

Towards the end of the 1980s, the European Commission in Brussels began to formulate common rules to protect holiday consumers across the community. In Britain, their most important effect would be to spread financial protection from those travelling on air packages to those going by land or sea. The regulations obliged anyone selling an inclusive holiday to provide a guarantee that their customers would not lose money in the event that the tour organizer ceased trading. An inclusive holiday was defined as a pre-arranged combination of at least two of three elements – transport, accommodation and any other ingredient, such as tickets to a major sporting event, which represented a compelling reason for the customer to book. After a long period of consultation and much hand wringing in the industry, the rules were implemented by the British Government as The Package Travel, Package Holidays and Package Tours Regulations 1992. They took effect on New Year's Day, 1993. Despite all the previous debate, and the publication of guidelines by the Department of Trade and Industry, many small operators remained either unaware that or unsure whether the law applied to them. Some continued selling holidays without arranging the obligatory financial protection. In some cases this was the result of ignorance, in others of genuine confusion, for the definition of a pre-arranged package was far from cut and dried. What about those who sold accommodation or trips on the ground in foreign countries but only included transport from the UK if customers requested it as an optional extra?

The simmering problems threatened by this confusion soon came to the boil with the failure, in 1993, of SFV Holidays – a company specializing in French villa rentals but offering to arrange ferry crossings as an optional extra. SFV's customers quickly discovered they were not covered by any bond or other form of protection. It emerged that, before it collapsed, the firm's managing director had written to his local MP, John Patten, telling him it would not be able to meet the new requirements. Patten took the matter up with Michael Heseltine, President of the Board of Trade. Heseltine's reply came in a letter dated 18 January. SFV, he wrote, was 'clearly offering pre-arranged accommodation. I do not think, however, that it is offering pre-arranged travel. This is because the customer is required himself to specify what ferry services he wishes to use, without advice or assistance from the company selling the holiday. In these circumstances I doubt if the travel element can be described as "pre-arranged", in which case it cannot be treated as part of a package.'

Whether or not SFV should have organized cover was clearly a grey area. However, guidelines issued more than two years later by Department appeared to clear the fog. They stated: 'Whether or not a package has been created will depend on the facts of the matter in each case. One reasonable test would be to consider what the consumer thinks he is getting.' Nobody who had attended the first meeting of SFV creditors would have been left in doubt about what its customers had thought they were getting. They believed they were buying package holidays.

The new law was unsatisfactory in two other ways. It allowed operators to put holiday payments into trusts, so that they would be unable to touch them until the customer got home. But anybody could act as a trustee and a trust deed did not have to be drawn up by a solicitor. This was so obviously open to abuse that the Travel Trust Association was established, to provide small operators with an avenue of respectability. The Association required its members to use independent trustees such as bank managers, or accountants working partnerships rather than alone. It arranged £12 million of back-up insurance in case of fraud.

The second weakness was that it effectively created two classes of holidaymaker. Those going by air were covered by the back-up Air Travel Trust – formerly the Air Travel Reserve Fund – which could be dipped into if bonds or other forms or protection proved inadequate to meet costs. Those going by land and sea were not. Suppose a firm offering surface transport went under, having milked its trust account? Customers could be left stranded. Argument about how this potential loophole should be shut raged on unabated.

ILG

Meanwhile, an earlier and much more spectacular failure had highlighted another anomaly in consumer protection. By early 1991, Harry Goodman's ILG was in deep trouble. Like Laker, the company was laid low by a combination of ambition and bad luck. Harry had expanded rapidly, setting up his airline, Air Europe, in 1978 and buying Global Holidays in 1985 for an estimated £5 million to expand his coach business and give him a foothold in the Australian and South African markets. The group branched into London hotels, buying the New Barbican, the Charing Cross and the Grosvenor.

Goodman acquired all the trappings of the successful mogul. There were private jets, first a Hawker Siddeley 125, later a Gulfstream. And, although he sold the second of them in 1987, there were yachts, often to be found moored at Palma, Majorca. Typical of the Goodman style was his arrival, out of the blue, at the sixteenth-century house and water-mill put up for sale by Reg Pycroft, who had founded Jetsave. 'Harry just dropped in one afternoon by helicopter', Pycroft recalled later. 'He didn't take more than five minutes to make up his mind. He said he'd take it there and then, furniture and all.' Goodman says an agent had alerted him that the property was available. 'I didn't even know it belonged to Reg.'

Though he kept remarkably quiet about it, he gave some £7 million to £8 million to charities and over one two-year spell his tour operation provided free holidays for around 6000 Barnardos children. In 1985 he was Chief Barker of the Variety Club of Great Britain, the entertainment industry's charitable organization. The comedian Bob Monkhouse, chairman of what was then known as the Stars Organisation for Spastics, told how Harry was invited to a corporate dinner to offer expert advice on how the charity could become more efficient. Goodman committed £100,000 on the spot.

ILG's life as a publicly quoted company ended in 1987, six years after it had been floated. Goodman had never been at ease with the financial establishment. 'I recognize opportunity', he said. 'The City never takes enough risks.' He took his empire into private ownership again at a cost of £103 million.

Although the worldwide economic downturn in the early 1990s plunged the airline industry into the worst recession it had ever endured, Goodman mainly blamed the Gulf War for bringing ILG to its knees. Uncertainties surrounding Operation Desert Storm, which drove the Iraqis out of Kuwait, made people nervous of travelling. Airline load factors – the average proportion of seats sold – plunged from 70 per cent to around 20 per cent. To make matters worse, the floor dropped out of the second-hand jet market, where ILG was negotiating to sell three aircraft for £40 million. If the company hoped to use cash flowing through its tour operations to stay afloat, it was out of luck. Its package holiday bookings for the following summer were at least 55 per cent below the level achieved at the same point in 1990.

In February 1991, the company axed some 150 jobs at Air Europe and announced a desperately needed injection of funds. Harry denied trade rumours of a merger between his airline and Dan-Air. The crunch was a month away. There were suggestions that Lonrho, seen a decade earlier as potential saviour of Laker Airways, might gallop in as a white knight. They came to nothing. The German stores-to-travel group Kaufhof gave ILG the once-over but there was to be no last minute bailout. On the morning of 8 March, ILG announced that its jets had been grounded and that its holding company, Hudson Place Investments, was asking a High Court judge to place the company in the hands of an administrator. But Goodman, speaking from a private London hospital where he was being treated for diabetes, admitted it was unlikely Air Europe would fly again. His pessimism was not misplaced. The Civil Aviation Authority quickly gave notice that it proposed to suspend ILG's tour operating licence. With hopes of saving the company all but gone, the Tour Operators' Study Group decided to call in the company's £63.2 million bond, which it administered, to ensure that ILG holidaymakers were not left out of pocket. Though there was bitterness about the speed with which this was done, the group claimed it had no option. ILG, it said, had been unable to provide satisfactory assurances that it could organize alternative flights for its customers. And rival airlines had decided not to carry them unless they were paid up front.

Some 35,000 customers were abroad with the group's package companies. Of these, about 15,000 had flown with charter airlines belonging to other companies, so there was no problem getting them home at their end of their holidays. Sorting out the others, who had flown with Air Europe, was a nightmare. Alan Flook, the TOSG secretary, recalls that during the job of organizing alternative flights, he received a kilometre of fax messages. But sorted out it was, with most customers suffering only minor changes in their departure times.

Customers who saw their travel plans disrupted included those who had booked package holidays and others who now held useless scheduled tickets. Both would have flown on Air Europe. It was not the first occasion in which the anomaly had arisen but never had it received such glaring publicity. The Government asked the Civil Aviation Authority to devise a system for protecting scheduled passengers. Though the Authority came up with a scheme to establish a fund, its suggestion has never been acted upon. Major airlines did not see why they should foot the bill for a safety net more likely to benefit smaller and more vulnerable rivals. Officials raised the difficulty of bringing foreign carriers into line.

DAN-AIR

The following year troubles ganged up on another airline with scheduled and charter business. Dan-Air was Britain's oldest established independent airline still operating under its own name, which derived from Davies and Newman, a shipbroking company formed in 1922. It launched its first scheduled flights, to Jersey, in 1953. Charters followed soon afterwards. One of its early customers was Vladimir's Horizon. Longevity was no protector, however. Recession had bitten chunks out of its scheduled business. And with big

Figure 11.1   A Dan-Air Comet (left) and 727 (right).

tour firms owning charter airlines, its charter operation had looked increasingly vulnerable. In fat years, it would pick up passengers which the operator-owned airlines could not handle. In lean years the in-house airlines carried most traffic themselves. The end came in October when British Airways took over a dozen of its routes, most of them from Gatwick. If it had been messier, the denouement might have lent power to those seeking protection for scheduled passengers, but from a consumer standpoint it was fairly painless. Though some had to change their immediate travel plans, BA promised that none of Dan-Air's scheduled passengers would be left out of pocket. The summer charter programme, which was almost finished, was allowed to run its course. Package holidaymakers booked to fly that winter were switched to other airlines.

It is tempting to end this story here. The loss of Dan-Air had broken a link with the pioneering days. The mop haired and sometimes outrageous Goodman was, some felt, the last of a species. But a new force was waiting to take on Intasun's role as chief tormentor of Thomson, the market leader. Airtours, headed by David Crossland, had planned to carry about one million customers in 1991. Following ILG's failure it carried 1.3 million.

DAVID CROSSLAND

Crossland was still only in his mid-40s. In 1963, he had started work for Althams, a travel agency in Burnley, the town of his birth. After leaving school with three O-levels, his choices were limited. He stamped brochures and made the coffee. At 18 he was made manager of another Burnley agency called Central Travel. 'Not because I knew everything but because I knew more than the people who worked there – and, I suspect, because I was cheap.' After a couple of years with a company called Silver Wing, which operated holidays to the Channel Islands, he joined a start-up firm called Travelplan. His big break came on Christmas Eve, 1971, when an elderly childless couple offered to sell him their two travel agency shops. Travelplan wanted to buy them out but the couple said they would rather he bought them. 'I think in their own minds they had adopted me and they wanted to see their business go to a good home.'

There was one small snag. They wanted £8000. He had no money. On Boxing Day he went back to see them and persuaded them to lend him half the purchase price. Then he went to Barclays Bank in Nelson in the hope of negotiating a loan for the other half. While he was there the conversation turned to holidays and Crossland suggested something the manager might enjoy. 'When I went back next day he handed me two cheques. One for the holiday and one for the £4000.' He did not tell either side about the other's loan. 'I didn't think it was devious. I just looked on it as a way of raising money.' Next he sold one third of the share in Pendle Travel to his sister and brother-in-law.

Throughout the 1970s he bought shops from elderly agents who were similarly childless, or whose children were not interested in carrying on the business. He was probably adopted, he jokes, seven or eight times over. By the end of the decade he had a dozen or so, all around Manchester Airport, and was beginning to break into tour operating. His first motive was to provide holidays for customers who could not get what they wanted from existing tour firms. He started by chartering 900 seats. The following year it was 23,000 and in year three 100,000.

At first he operated as Pendle Air Tours. He had acquired the Airtours name along with a travel agency outside Blackburn, which was run by a couple called Albert and Ivy Roberts. They used the three letters of those names, added the 'tours' and registered the brand in 1958. Crossland began to use it in the mid-1980s. By 1986 his company was carrying some 250,000 passengers a year. He realized that this was about as far as he could go as a one man band, and decided to bring in professional expertise to run his finances, and his marketing, for example. Within three years the firm's carryings had leaped to 750,000.

Everything now seemed to be happening in a blur. The company was floated on the London Stock Exchange in 1987 with a market capitalization of £28 million. Just as Harry Goodman's Intasun had done in Florida, it persuaded hoteliers in Barbados and Jamaica to accept British holidaymakers in summer, instead of relying heavily on the American market in winter, and then closing. It began offering long haul holidays to the US West Coast and Hawaii. It played a huge part in developing package tourism to the Dominican Republic. Some observers muttered that it was growing too fast. They saw as a symptom the continual problems of a Boeing 747, chartered for its long haul business, which the press dubbed the 'Flying Pig' because of an appalling sequence of mechanical failures.

It was partly the problem of the Flying Pig which persuaded Airtours to launch its eponymous airline in 1990. Not only did the company want another source of profit – it also wanted tighter quality control.

In 1992, Airtours launched a hostile bid for the Owners Abroad group, which was twice its size and already quoted on the Stock Exchange. A long verbal battle ensued as Owners tried to retain its independence. In the end its shareholders opted to stay as they were. Crossland was not happy but he had an alternative strategy. It bought leisure travel agencies from Pickfords and Hogg Robinson and a tour operation called Aspro, which was strong in Cardiff and Belfast. With it came an airline, Inter European, which was absorbed into Airtours.

The Owners Abroad group rebranded itself as First Choice in 1994. Airtours was to make a second attempt to acquire it in 1999, a bid which was thwarted this time by objections from the European Commission.

Crossland had become a multi-millionaire, living in Jersey, swimming, skiing and mountain biking to take his mind off the business but still getting up at four in the morning and working long hours, his quiet skill epitomizing the new spirit of professionalism now pervading the industry.

CONSOLIDATION AND GLOBALIZATION

The rest of this history is a story of consolidation and globalization. The big tour operators have become bigger through acquisition and have moved into foreign markets. Consolidation raised new fears among small firms, whose campaign for what they saw as fairer competition, echoed by consumer lobbyists, finally prompted a reference to the Monopolies and Mergers Commission in November 1996. The cause of these concerns was vertical integration, the ownership of travel agencies, charter airlines and tour operations by the same group. The Office of Fair Trading had looked at this issue in 1993, and had decided a reference was not justified. But power wielded by the major groups had intensified. Five companies found themselves under the microscope: Thomson, which had some 24.6 per cent of the foreign package market in 1996; Airtours, which had 15.9 per cent; First Choice, with 10.1 per cent; Sunworld, which had just been bought by Thomas Cook; and Inspirations, which had 2.3 per cent and was also destined to be swallowed up by Cook's. Of these, only First Choice did not then own a chain of agencies, though Thomas Cook held a stake in it.

The Commission's report was made public in December 1997. To the dismay of the small fry it concluded there was still plenty of competition in the industry and that there was no need to sharpen it by forcing the big groups to shed any of their component parts. Players came, it said, and players went. There was no significant barrier to entry either as a tour operator or retailer. There were some crumbs for those who had bayed so long for a more level playing field. The Commission decided that the practice among agents of tying high priced compulsory travel insurance to bargains was likely to mislead customers into thinking they were getting a bigger price cut than was really the case. It criticized 'most favoured customer clauses' in agreements between operator and agent. These obliged the retailer to cut the price of that operator's packages in line with discounts from other tour firms. The Commission decided they could discourage agents from discounts which they would otherwise be prepared to offer. And it urged that the big groups should make clearer to consumers exactly which operators were linked with which agents. The Government said it would take action on all three, but while the first two practices were quickly outlawed, the third, ensuring greater transparency of ownership, proved stubbornly difficult to achieve.

The report may have landed the industry with a few little local difficulties but it blew open the doors for a rush of takeovers. Cook's, which already had 385 shops, fourteen charter aircraft and the Flying Colours, Club 18–30, Sunworld, Neilson Ski and Time Off holiday brands, linked up with the Carlson Leisure Group, with over 1050 owned or affiliated agencies, tour operations including Inspirations and its airline, Caledonian. Airtours bought Panorama and two other operators, best known for city breaks, Cresta and the Bridge Travel group. Thomson's shopping haul included the Simply Travel and Magic groups, walking and cycling specialist Headwater and the leading ski operator Crystal Holidays. First Choice snapped up long haul operator Hayes and Jarvis and a small wintersports firm, Flexiski.

Foreign ownership was not new to the industry. Thomson, after all, had Canadian parenthood. Inghams and Cosmos were Swiss owned. But when Midland Bank sold Thomas Cook for £200 million to LTU in June 1992, it seemed a turning point. LTU was Germany's third biggest tour operator with 17 per cent of that country's package market. Thomas Cook was a symbol of Britishness. UK companies would soon be operating in other European countries. Airtours moved not only into the German market but into Scandinavia, Belgium, Holland and France. A large slice of it is owned by Carnival Cruise Lines. More recently First Choice bought the Spanish company, Barcelo, announcing it would target markets so far left untapped by its rivals, such as those in Greece and Italy.

Thomson meanwhile, had launched operations in six other countries – Germany, Ireland, Sweden, Norway, Denmark, Finland and Poland. Its move abroad helped to make it, like Cook's, a target of German interest. Still Britain's biggest tour operator, it had been through difficult times since its flotation on the London Stock Exchange in 1998. At one point its share price had slumped to less than half its initial value of 170p. Its knee-jerk reaction to Airtours' bid for First Choice – a warning that it would raise the number of packages it offered and cut prices in order to protect its market share – was hardly calculated to endear it to the City. Chief executive Paul Brett, who had earlier built up Thomson's direct sell operation, Portland, a man whose homely manner masked an astute business brain, had resigned in a management shake-up. In April, 2000, German travel company C&N Touristic, jointly owned by Lufthansa and the stores chain Karstadt Quelle, approached Thomson with an offer of 130p per share. The UK firm, 23 per cent owned by the Canadian Thomson family through its Woodbridge holding company and roughly 20 per cent owned by small shareholders, many lured in by the prospect of cut-price holidays, instantly rejected the approach. But it left the door ajar for C&N should the Germans come back with a better bid. C&N eventually raised its offer to 160p, valuing Thomson at £1.6 billion. Its management thought it had sealed the deal, but it was pipped to the post by German rival Preussag, the former industrial conglomerate which owns TUI, Europe's biggest tour operation, and which had acquired a controlling stake in Thomas Cook. Preussag agreed to pay £1.8 billion.

The deal created a giant. TUI, market leader in Germany, Austria and the Netherlands and strong in Belgium and Switzerland, handled 12.9 million travellers a year, Thomson, whose strength outside the UK was in Scandinavia, Ireland and Poland, handled 7.7 million. Between them they operated 106 aircraft and over 4000 High Street travel agencies. Such a monster could hardly jump into the pool without creating huge waves – and there were immediate signs that the game of musical chairs had not ended. Preussag had to agree to sell its 60 per cent stake in Thomas Cook in order to secure approval from the European Commission. Westdeutsche Bank, owner of one-third of Preussag, was also obliged to sell its state in Cook's. The Association of Independent Tour Operators had demanded that such a disposal should be made a condition of the deal. Chairman John Bennett had said failure to do so 'would leave Preussag, through Thomson and Thomas Cook, with over 50 per cent of the UK package travel market. This would have been totally unacceptable.' The US Carlson group, which already owned 22 per cent of Cook's, indicated it was looking at buying the rest of it, not just Preussag's share but also that held by the German bank. But would C&N dust itself off and bid for Cook's itself? Would it go instead for Airtours? Some observers felt David Crossland and Stefan Pichler, respective heads of Airtours and C&N, would each be so keen to hang on to the reins that such a deal could never work. Or would it court Airtours' elusive quarry, First Choice, which had just established a strategic alliance with Royal Caribbean. The cruise line announced it would invest around £200 million in its tour operating partner.

For the consumer, this wave of consolidations threatened to reduce choice. The risk was that the massive buying power of these mega-operations would make it ever more difficult for smaller tour operators to compete for allocations of hotel beds and apartments and to secure the charter aircraft seats they needed.

SUMMARY

The package holiday has changed the way we live. It has affected what we wear, what we eat and what we drink. Food is available in supermarkets which the average wage earner had never heard of in the 1950s. Wine consumption has soared. Some of this would have come about as a result of greater prosperity but there is no doubt that it has been encouraged by mass travel. Despite occasional loutish behaviour by the British abroad, it is likely that the annual holiday has produced a net improvement in international understanding and a dilution of blinkered nationalism.

Where next? Reports that the inclusive holiday was teetering on the brink of extinction have proved as premature as those of Mark Twain's death once were. But as it celebrated its first half-century, the industry faced new challenges on several fronts. Legal devices imported from the United States, such as the class action and the 'no win, no fee' lawsuit, have gained in popularity. In a class action, one plaintiff brings a case on behalf of a group of fellow travellers. It spreads the cost and usually strengthens the case. Such actions are often prompted by illness among a large number of people staying in the same hotel. Tour operators can now be held liable for the failings of hoteliers and other overseas suppliers such as coach operators — even if they do not own them. Low cost airlines offering rock-bottom fares to European destinations are beginning to erode the financial rationale for buying a package. And above all, the internet is threatening radical changes in the way consumers book their travel arrangements, making it easier for them to compare prices and assemble the component parts of the package themselves.

Eventually the savings to be made by booking with big tour operators, who keep costs low by contracting flights, accommodation and meals in bulk, may no longer be enough to sustain the industry in its present form. Operators are already having to add value to keep the business rolling in, offering access to 'soft adventure', for example, such as scuba diving and mountain biking. And on top of all this is the unpredictable and possibly devastating impact of global warming and fears about the risk of too much exposure to the sun's rays, which could bring a fundamental shift in where we go and when we go there.

But major changes in travel habits do not happen overnight. The convenience and perceived security of the inclusive holiday will ensure the survival of those operators who adapt until well into the new century. It is a fair bet that the package will live to see its centenary. It has been our purpose in writing this book that when it does, the record of its formative years should not vanish with those who pioneered it.

Epilogue, June 2000

VLADIMIR RAITZ

I have never been out of the travel industry since I returned to London from Calvi in 1949 and registered Horizon Holidays as a limited company in October of that year. As referred to earlier, I had a long and happy association with Air Malta and its tour operation, as managing director and later as a board member for over 20 years. Additionally, I had performed a number of consulting jobs, all to do with tour operating and cruising. I had even been called as an expert witness in several lawsuits involving travel agents, tour operators and airlines. In one mammoth arbitration involving a Miami operator claiming huge damages from a Greek cruise line (which was almost two years in preparation), I was on the successful team defending the Greeks. All of this was very interesting, but what I lacked was the dearest thing to my heart: getting back into tour operation with a company of my own (or at least which was partly mine), where I could be responsible for my own decisions. I received a telephone call in early January, 1999.

'Vlad, I've got something here that might interest you.' On the line was my old friend Colin Trigger, chairman of Scantours and the immediate past president of ABTA. 'I've just had a call from the head of Cuba's national tourist office in London, Jorge Perez. He'd like me to start tours to Cuba, with the emphasis on Havana cigars. I thought this might appeal to you.'

Colin explained that during his presidency of ABTA, he had taken members of the ABTA councils to Cuba and had met many of Cuba's tourism officials, including Jorge Perez. Jorge's call came as a result of that meeting, and he went on to tell Colin that the Cuban tourist authority was not altogether happy with the way in which Havana Cigar tours were being organized out of the UK. In fact, he said, while tourism to Cuba was getting stronger every year and a number of companies were featuring visits to cigar factories as part of their arrangements, what the Cubans really wanted was a tour operation that emphasized the making of the best cigars in the world as the principal object of the tour, rather than as a mere adjunct.

'Are you interested in such a project?' Colin asked me.

Was I indeed! I had never been to Cuba, but I loved cigars – having smoked them ever since I gave up cigarettes in my late 20s. I spoke Spanish, I loved the taste of Cuba Libres and Rum Collinses, and I had adored Cuban music ever since I had first listened to Cuban records in Miller's Music Shop in Cambridge.

'Colin, I'm your man. When do we leave for Havana?'

We eventually left towards the middle of 1999, after numerous formalities had been completed – the most important being the deal with the airline which was to fly our clients to Havana. We chose Iberia, who had a daily service to the Cuban capital from Madrid, and several daily flights between London and Madrid. So it was Iberia who flew Colin and I to Havana at the beginning of what we hoped would turn out to be a small but successful venture.

Cuba surpassed all my expectations. The thriving capital city, the heady mixture of rum, music and cigar smoke, the friendly people, the pretty girls, the sparkling sea and the perfect beaches all make for a perfect holiday destination. Add to all of that the fascination of learning about the highly complex production processes of making the cigars (growing the leaves, drying, sorting, maturing, rolling and packing), and I was left feeling profoundly impressed.

Colin and I reluctantly returned to London and set about producing a brochure and making marketing plans. Our combined experience in tour operating had taught us that the first year's results usually proceed with a loss. The second year, with luck, produces a break-even situation, and the third year (with even greater luck) a profit. So far, our cigar tours have followed such a pattern. In the first year, we did indeed make a loss. But we are now, at the time of writing, entering our second season and optimism is running high. I have now been to Cuba several times, and the magic of the place never palls. Our results for the season 2000/2001 are in the lap of the gods. One thing is certain, though: I am back in tour operating and am utterly determined to make a success of it. And I shall have the time of my life doing so.

Chronology of the Industry

ROGER BRAY

1841: Thomas Cook organizes first excursion, by train from Leicester to Loughborough, in an attempt to stimulate support for the temperance movement.

1855: Cook takes first groups abroad, sailing from Harwich and visiting European cities.

1866: Cook's son, John Mason Cook conducts the company's first American tour.

1868: Thomas Cook claims to have organized travel for a total of two million people.

1884: John Mason Cook asked by British Government to organize relief expedition up the Nile to rescue Major General Charles Gordon from Khartoum.

1888: Poly Tours, origin of Lunn-Poly, formed.

1892: Thomas Cook dies.

1898: Dr (later Sir) Henry Lunn organizes his first wintersports package, to Chamonix, in France. The holiday costs around ten guineas (£10.50).

1919: First daily air passenger service launched in February from Berlin to Weimar via Leipzig, using AEG J II biplanes with an enclosed cabin for up to five passengers. First daily international service starts in August, operated between London and Paris by the British company Air Transport & Travel Ltd using a De Havilland 16 aircraft. The one way fare is £21. London's first airport opens on Hounslow Heath. Thomas Cook advertises tickets for the first public trips by plane. International Air Transport Association is born.

1920: Croydon Airport opens. Hounslow Heath reverts to military use.

1924: State-owned Imperial Airways formed.

1932: Imperial Airways launches 16-day air cruises to Greece and the Middle East, including hotels and first class sleeping compartments. Erna Low organizes her first skiing party – to Sölden in Austria.

1933: Captain Ted Langton starts coach tours to Ostend and Paris. Sets up Les Cars Bleus to carry customers on the continent.

1934: Billy Butlin opens first holiday camp – at Skegness on Britain's North Sea coast. Walter Ingham takes his first private ski party to the Alps.

1935: Harry Chandler organizes his first holiday group – to Schwangau in Bavaria.

1938: Parliament passes act giving one week's paid annual leave to all industrial workers. Butlin opens a second camp – at Clacton in Essex.

1939: First regular passenger and mail flights across the Atlantic, by Pan American and Imperial Airways. Imperial merges with the old British Airways to become BOAC.

1945: Incoming Labour government announces two new state-owned airlines – BEA (British European Airways) and British South American Airways – will split routes with BOAC.

1946: Wartime ban on civilian flying lifted. Heathrow opens on New Year's Day with a flight to Buenos Aires, via Portugal by a four-engined Lancastrian, developed from the Lancaster bomber. Civil Aviation Act limits privately owned airlines to ad hoc, rather than whole season charters.

1947: Foreign holidays banned as Britain faces post-war austerity. Thomas Cook nationalized. BEA makes last scheduled flight from Croydon.

1948: Ban on foreign holidays lifted. Harold Bamberg launches Eagle Airways with one converted Halifax bomber.

1949: Vladimir visits Corsica for the first time, founds Horizon Holidays. Sterling devalued.

1950: Vladimir gets permission from Ministry of Transport to take students and teachers on holiday to Corsica – operates first flight in May with 32 passengers aboard. Association of British Travel Agents founded.

1952: European airlines belonging to International Air Transport Association agree to offer tourist class seats at reduced fares. Survey by *Daily Herald* shows only 1.5 per cent of the British population takes holidays abroad.

1953: Shipbrokers Davies & Newman set up a subsidiary airline, Dan-Air, which is to become a leading holiday charter and significant scheduled operator. Captain Ted Langton launches Universal Sky Tours, whose shortened name survived to become a Thomson brand. Eagle Airways starts Mediterranean air cruises. First edition of *Travel Trade Gazette* published. Government decides Gatwick was suitable for extension as an alternative to Heathrow at a cost of £10 million. Vladimir starts tours to Lourdes.

1954: Harold Bamberg buys Sir Henry Lunn Ltd bringing it under same umbrella as Eagle Airways to form airline/travel agent conglomerate. Airlines, travel agents join rush to offer hire purchase deals to customers.

1955: Commercial TV launched. Travel firms slow to take advantage. New permanent short haul terminals, forerunner of today's Terminal 2, opens at Heathrow. Foreign exchange limit set at £100.

1956: Local interests invent the name Costa Blanca for the stretch of coastline which includes Benidorm. Dan-Air starts scheduled services to Jersey.

1957: Great Universal Stores buys big stake in Global Tours. Milbanke Tours launches Flair Holidays. Currency allowances extended to USA and other countries in the Dollar Area. Polytechnic Tours unveils plans for 28-day tours to North America. Vladimir buys Quo Vadis Travel from Charles Forte.

1958: Clarksons starts offering breaks to Dutch bulb fields. Lord Brothers Holidays takes first booking. Newly redeveloped Gatwick opens as London's second major airport.

1959: Croydon Airport closes. One in eight British holidays spent abroad, but only 3.4 per cent of holidaymakers go to Spain. Harry Chandler takes first look at the Portuguese Algarve – which he and wife Rene will play a large part in putting on the map.

1960: Air Transport Licensing Board formed. Caledonian, British United Airways both launched. Cunard shipping line acquires Eagle Airways to form Cunard-Eagle. Early signs of consumer rebellion against poor accommodation and shoddy service by overseas representative. Court of Appeal rules travel agent failed to fulfil contract when it booked clients into a filthy Spanish hotel room.

1961: Heathrow opens £3 million, long haul Oceanic Terminal – later to be known as Terminal Three.

1962: Sir Henry Lunn Ltd takes over Poly Travel. Walter Ingham sells Inghams to Hotelplan, part of the Swiss grocery wholesaling and retail organization, Migros. Liner SS *France* (later the cruise ship *Norway*) enters service.

1963: Labour MP Edward Milne launches attack on hidden extras concealed in holiday prices. Ernest 'Tubby' Garner becomes Association of British Travel Agents chairman. Consumer Association warns purchasing a package holiday can be 'buying a pig in a poke'. Milne introduces Private Member's Bill calling for registration of travel firms. Boeing 727 makes first flight. Bamberg resigns as director of Cunard, buys back control of his airline which will now be called British Eagle. Washing machine tycoon John Bloom launches cheap package holidays. Chandris Cruises launched. Typhoid outbreak in Swiss resort of Zermatt.

1964: Fiesta Tours collapses with some 2000 customers booked to travel. Tubby Garner prime mover behind first collaborative effort by ABTA members to ensure Fiesta customers get their holidays. John Bloom's Rolls Razor company goes under but his holiday programme survives temporarily. Euravia is re-named Britannia Airways – which will become UK's biggest charter airline.

1965: Clarksons Holidays breaks into Spanish package holiday market. Thomson Organisation acquires Britannia Airways and three tour operators: Universal Sky Tours, Britannia and Riviera Holidays. ABTA's Operation Stabilizer, brainchild of Garner's successor, C. D. Hopkinson is agreed. From the start of 1966, ABTA retail agents will be allowed to sell only packages organized by member operators. And ABTA operators would be permitted to sell only through retailers belonging to the association. Members will have to observe accounting rules. A common fund is to be established, to ensure customers did not lose their money. *Economist* magazine survey shows Spain now Europe's most popular holiday destination with 14 million visitors a year. Faro Airport opens. Harry and Rene Chandler's Travel Club of Upminster launch their first packages to Algarve. Roy Mason, Minister of State at Board of Trade, says registering travel firms would be 'too mammoth a task'.

1966: Harold Wilson's Labour Government reintroduces currency restrictions amid economic crisis. Britons limited to £50 foreign exchange, from which hotel and other ground costs must come. Freddie Laker forms own airline, establishes first time charter deal with

Wings. Harry Goodman launches tour operation Sunair. Newly formed British Airports Authority takes responsibility for running Heathrow, Gatwick, Stansted and Prestwick.

1967: Middle East war and industrial turmoil in Britain hit balance of payments. Government devalues sterling from US$2.80 to $2.40. Pan American orders 25 new Boeing 747 Jumbo jets. Laker acquires Arrowsmith Holidays. Monarch Airlines founded.

1968: British Eagle collapses owing £7 million. Laker buys one of his main time charterers, Lord Brothers.

1969: Edwards Report on UK civil aviation recommends creation of Civil Aviation Authority, setting up a 'third force' airline to compete with BEA and BOAC – and the scrapping of some minimum package holiday price controls. First series of BBC's *Holiday* programme, produced by Tom Savage and starring Cliff Michelmore.

1970: Horizon has best financial results, launches Club 18–30. Clarksons operates first series of Mediterranean cruises. Tour Operators' Study group of top firms launches first bonding scheme to protect customers' money. British Caledonian born. First Boeing 747, operated by Pan American, arrives at Heathrow after flight from New York. BEA sets up charter arm, which will become British Airtours.

1971: Civil Aviation Authority formed (assumes full responsibilities from 1972). Government announces Provision One minimum price restriction on breaks of seven nights or less to be abolished for the following winter. Operators launch £10 packages to Spain in anticipation. Bookings flood in. But the restriction still applies to some destinations, including Paris, Scandinavia, Germany and the Benelux countries – and to skiing holidays. Cunard buys stake in Harry Goodman's tour firm, Sunair. Sunair buys Lunn-Poly from state-owned Transport Holding Company. Ted Arison, founder of Carnival Cruise Lines buys first ship, operating it under the name Mardi Gras. Figures show big five operators – Clarksons, Cosmos, Horizon, Thomson and Global – have captured half the package market between them.

1972: Legislation enacted to set up ATOL (Air Travel Organizer's Licence) system. Provision One would be scrapped in its entirety. Bonding extended to all ABTA members. ABTA launches independent arbitration system to settle disputes between members and customers. CAA invites applications for first advance booking charters (ABCs). Tom Gullick the man behind Clarksons' mushroom growth, resigns. Thomson buys Lunn-Poly and with it acquires its first ski operation. David Crossland, founder of Airtours, buys first travel agencies. BEA and BOAC merge to become British Airways. Thomas Cook returns to private ownership, bought by a consortium of Midland Bank, Trust House Forte and the Automobile Association.

1973: Clarksons' parent, Shipping and Industrial Holdings threatens to put the tour operation in liquidation if Court Line does not buy it. Court Line pays a nominal £1 for 85 per cent of the tour firm to protect its charter airline – which gets 40 per cent of its turnover by carrying Clarksons passengers. Arab–Israeli war results in 70 per cent increase in oil prices by Middle East producers. British Government designates Laker Airways a transatlantic carrier.

1974: Three-day week introduced as oil crisis bites. Slump in package bookings. Court Line takes over Horizon's travel business. Near bloodless coup in Portugal. Turks invade Cyprus. Court Line collapses in August, taking Clarksons, Horizon and 4S with it. An estimated 40,000 customers are abroad at the time. Some 100,000 affected altogether. Tour operators' bonds prove adequate to cover rescue but inadequate to cover refunds to all clients still booked to take holidays. Industry Secretary Tony Benn under fire for allegedly reassuring customers – in June Commons speech – that their holidays were safe. Liner SS *France* withdrawn from service.

1975: Two reports – one by Parliamentary Ombudsman, other by Department of Trade, point finger of guilt at Benn and Government for leading Clarksons holidaymakers to believe their holidays would not be hit. They cannot be absolved of all responsibility, says former. Statements before the crash were no doubt inadvertent, says latter, but were not fair and reasonable. Government sets up air travel reserve fund with £15 million loan to repay Court Line customers who lost money. Loan to be repaid by 1 per cent levy on package prices, rising to 2 per cent in 1976. British Airways protests to CAA at Thomson's Wanderer brand, which offers flights and very basic accommodation – but no food. BA says customers are throwing away the accommodation and using the packages simply as cheap air travel.

1976: Association of Independent Tour Operators formed. Thomson announces big expansion of Wanderer holidays, with a fortnight on Costa Brava starting at £39. Cosmos launches a similar programme, under the brand name Cheapies. Concorde makes first commercial flights.

1977: President Jimmy Carter approves American permit for Laker's walk-on Skytrain service across the North Atlantic. Thomson announces first regular package holidays to China, pulls out of cruising. Midland Bank buys out Trust House Forte and the AA to become sole owner of Thomas Cook.

1978: Skytrain launched between Gatwick and New York. Unfair Contract Terms Act stops operators using brochure get-out clauses to evade responsibility for suppliers' actions. Harry Goodman launches own airline – Air Europe. ABTA's Stabilizer scheme referred to Restrictive Practices Court.

1979: Harry Goodman's Intasun takes its first customers to Florida. Danish direct sell operator Tjaereborg starts programme from UK. DC-10 disaster at Chicago's O'Hare Airport in May, 1979, forces worldwide, two week grounding of the jets. Horizon Midland (the former Horizon Midland which was rescued from the debris of the Court Line crash) changes name to Horizon Travel. Thomson sets up direct sell Portland Holidays – which recruits former Labour minister Lord George Brown as an 'ombudsman' to settle disputes with customers. Neilson Holidays ski operation launched.

1980: David Crossland sets up tour operating division, trading initially as Pendle Air Tours, later as Airtours. Peter Dyer and Darko Emersic form ski specialist tour operator Crystal Holidays.

1981: International Leisure Group floated on Stock Exchange.

1982: Laker Airways goes bust. The company's tour operations, Arrowsmith and Laker North, are bought by brewers Greenall Whitley for £4.2 million, Laker Holidays by the Saga group, which specialized in packages for senior citizens, for £500,000. CAA awards Laker new licence to operate package holidays.

1983: Laker launches short-lived new holiday programme, Skytrain Holidays. US airline People Express starts cut-price flights between Gatwick and Newark (New Jersey). Cathay Pacific makes first non-stop flight from London to Hong Kong.

1984: Restrictive Practices Court rules Stabilizer in public interest. Richard Branson's Virgin Atlantic makes its first flight between Gatwick and New York.

1985: Harry Goodman's ILG buys Global for estimated £5 million. Arrowsmith sold to Owners Abroad. Blue Sky brand bought by Rank, which already had a half share in the operator's charter business, Cal-Air.

1986: Rank drops Blue Sky and Ellerman Sunflight brands. Sells all its holidays as Wings. ILG talks to British Caledonian about a merger of its short haul operations with Air Europe's. Heathrow's £200 million Terminal Four opens.

1987: Airtours floated on the London Stock Exchange with a market capitalization of £28 million. Harry Goodman takes ILG private again. British Airways floated on Stock Exchange. Control of British Airways' main holiday brands – Enterprise, Flair, Sovereign and direct sell Martin Rooks – is handed over to Sunmed founder Vic Fatah. BA retains 50 per cent stake. British Airways takes over British Caledonian. Horizon, UK's third biggest group, embracing Blue Sky, OSL and charter airline, Orion, buys Wings from Rank. Brewers Bass then buy Horizon for £94 million.

1988: Thomson pays £75 million for Horizon. Deal referred to

Monopolies and Mergers Commission. Gatwick's North Terminal opens.

1989: MMC clears Thomson's takeover of Horizon. Figures show top five operators account for 68 per cent of 14.2 million packages licensed.

1990: European Union members adopt EC directive on package travel which extends financial protection to all consumers buying package holidays.

1991: ILG collapses in March with 35,000 customers abroad. Some customers with scheduled tickets on Air Europe left out of pocket. Government asks CAA to devise a system for protecting scheduled passengers. Authority comes up with a scheme to establish a fund, but its suggestion is not acted upon. Airtours launches own charter airline. Stansted, redeveloped at a cost of £400million, opens as London's third major airport.

1992: Thomas Cook sold by Midland Bank to Germany's Westdeutsche Landesbank and the German LTU Group for £200 million. Dan-Air collapses. British Airways takes over some routes. Dan-Air's charter programme is allowed to run its summer course. European Commission directive implemented by the British Government as The Package Travel, Package Holidays and Package Tours Regulations 1992. Airtours launches unsuccessful hostile bid for Owners Abroad group. Buys Leisure 333 travel agencies from Pickfords instead.

1993: Package travel regulations come into force on 1 January. ABTA formally abandons Stabilizer. Airtours buys leisure travel agencies from Hogg Robinson and tour operators Tradewinds and Aspro. Office of Fair Trading investigates industry consolidation. Decides reference to Monopolies and Mergers Commission not justified.

1994: Owners Abroad group re-brands itself as First Choice. Airtours acquires first cruise ship, *Seawing*. Thomson takes over UK self catering specialist Country Holidays.

1995: BA sells charter carrier Caledonian Airways to Inspirations. Airtours acquires Scandinavia's largest tour operator, SAS Leisure AB and sets up Scandinavian Leisure Group, incorporating the Ving, Saga and Always brands. The new group has a 50 per cent interest in Premiair, the biggest charter airline in Scandinavia. Deal also nets Airtours the Sunwing Hotel Group. Westdeutsche Landesbank makes Cook's a wholly owned subsidiary by acquiring LTU's 10 per cent of group. Thomson acquires Blakes self-catering property operation and English Country Cottages.

1996: Carnival Corporation, the world's largest cruise company takes a 29.6 per cent stake in Airtours, with Airtours acquires two more Scandinavian tour operators, Spies and Tjaereborg, the Stella Polaris hotel chain and the remaining 50 per cent of Premiair. Office of Fair Trading refers vertically integrated travel companies to Monopolies and Mergers Commission. Thomas Cook buys Sunworld, UK's fifth largest short haul tour operator from Grupo Viajes Iberia, and specialist European city breaks operator Time Off. Thomson buys Budget Travel in Ireland.

1997: MMC report on vertically integrated companies attacks agents' discounts linked to compulsory insurance sales, most favoured customer clauses, urges greater transparency of ownership. Government acts to outlaw first two recommendations, delays action on third. Thomson launches Swedish operation, Thomson Sverige.

1998: Thomson Travel group floated on Stock Exchange, acquires Crystal, Blakes boating operation, Magic Travel Group, Scandinavian operator Fritidsresor. Airtours swallows Direct Holidays, Panorama, city break specialists Cresta and Bridge Travel – all UK-based operators – and Belgium's biggest tour firm Sun International. Thomas Cook announces intention to merge with Carlson Leisure Group, which owns tour operator Inspirations and airline Caledonian and has a big chain of retail agencies. Cook's subsidiary Sunworld take over the Flying Colours Leisure Group, including its airline, and the Sunset and Club 18–30 tour operating brands.

1999: Airtours' unsuccessful bid for First Choice is thwarted by objections from European Commission. Thomas Cook combines Sunworld, Sunset, Flying Colours, Inspirations and Caledonian Airways under new JMC brand. Thomson buys Simply Travel, Headwater and Spanish Harbour Holidays, breaks into Poland with acquisition of Scan group, takes over leisure travel interests from Norway's Via group.

2000: Germany's Preussag buys Thomson Holidays for £1.8 billion. Airtours buys UK-based Greece and Turkey specialist Manos.

INDEX

Note: Page references in *italics* are to illustrations

accommodation vouchers 192–4
accounts of tour operators 179–80
Adamowski, Jan 73
advance booking charters 178, 232
adventure holidays 222
Adventurer 119
affinity groups 80, 177–8, 189; *see also* 'closed
    groups'
Aga Khan 20
air accidents 36, 203, 233
Air Charter 187
Air Europe 185, 208, 212–14, 233–5
air fares 10, 32–3, 36, 38, 40, 49–50, 64, 92, 97,
    173, 192–3, 201, 227
Air France 36, 46
Air Malta 171, 223
Air Transport Advisory Council (ATAC) 16–17, 20,
    37, 56
Air Transport Association of America 47
Air Transport Charter (Channel Islands) Ltd 5, 16
Air Transport Licensing Board (ATLB) 42, 83, 85,
    92, 97, 178, 189, 229
Air Travel Organizer's Licence (ATOL) 159, 177,
    232
Air Travel Trust 212
Air 2000 209
Air Union 58
Airfair 153
airports 43–4
Airtours 115–17, 120, 125, 180, 199, 215–21,
    232–7 *passim*
Airwork 48, 187
Algarve, the 30, 49, 82, 175, 229–30
Alghero 19, 59–60
Alicante 22
Allied Suppliers 152

Alpine holidays 25, 27, 99; *see also* skiing holidays
Ambler, Joyce *19*, 56
American Express 110, 151
Anglo-Soviet Shipping 121
Apal Travel 180
Aquila Airways 49
arbitration scheme 176–7, 232
The Archers 47
Les Arcs 107
Arison, Ted 122, 231
Arrowsmith Holidays 49, 188, 205, 207, 231,
    234
Aspro (tour operation) 217, 235
assisted passage scheme 120–1
Associated Rediffusion 47
Association of British Travel Agents (ABTA) 48, 65,
    77–8, 83–8, 96–7, 153–4, 176–9, 195–7, 202,
    205, 210, 223, 228, 230, 232, 235
 code of practice 84–6, 191
Association of Health and Pleasure Resorts 48
Association of Independent Tour Operators 200,
    220, 233
Association of National Tourist Office
    Representatives (ANTOR) 85
Aston Villa Football Club 52
Atlantis 178
ATLAS group 153
Attlee, Clement 31
Australia 120–1
Austria 106–12 *passim*
Austrian Airlines 109
Autair 144, 153
Aviation Traders 187
Avro Lancastrian aircraft 24
Avro York aircraft 39, 41
Ayling, Bob 204

BAC 1-11 aircraft 127, 144, 153, 181, 188
back-to-back itineraries 20, 41, 60, 118
Bad Gastein 25
Badrutt, Johannes 100
Bamberg, Harold 40–2, 46, 48–50, 66–7, 88, 228, 230
Banco del Noroeste 150
Barber, Anthony 154
Barcelona 22
Barclays Bank 216
Bardot, Brigitte 109
Barker, Ray 42, 84–5
Bass (company) 170, 209
Beckman, Bob 206
'bed deposits' 141–2, 150
Benidorm 49–51, 50, 144, 146, 149, 198
Benn, Tony 141, 158–60, 232
Bennett, John 220
Berchtold, Walter 38
Bergen Line 106
Berlin airlift 187
Bibby Line 48
bikinis 47, 89–90
Birmingham 52
BKS (company) 16, 59, 74, 77
Blackman, Honor 78
Blitz, Gérard 3
Bloom, John 88–9, 230
Blue Cars 34–5, 65–6, 227
Blue Sky 207, 209, 234
Blue Star Line 48
Boeing 707 aircraft 127
Boeing 727 aircraft 88, 93, 215, 230
Boeing 737 aircraft 127, 163, 181, 185
Boeing 747 aircraft 33, 172–3, 217, 231
Boeing 757 aircraft 209
bonding 85–6, 149, 165–6, 170, 172, 176–80, 211–14, 232
booking of holidays 42, 84–5, 90, 144, 150, 222
Borrie, Sir Gordon 200
Boulogne 45
Bouvier, Jacqueline 36
Bovril food group 152
Boyd-Carpenter, Lord 195–6
Brancker, John 52
Brand 155–6
brand loyalty 163–4, 207
Branson, Sir Richard 206, 234
Brett, Paul 220
Britannia (paddle steamer) 23
Britannia aircraft 90, 132, 134, 188
Britannia Airways 41, 90, 127, 132, 134, 152, 163, 181, 193, 208, 230
Britavia 48
British Aircraft Corporation 188; see also BAC 1-11 aircraft
British Airports Authority 231
British Airways 190–5, 201–9 passim, 215, 232–5
British Caledonian 190, 201–9 passim, 231, 234

British Eagle 88, 91, 92, 96, 230–1
British Electric Traction 35–6, 66
British European Airways (BEA) 5, 8, 10, 16–17, 23, 32, 36–8, 42, 46, 49, 52–3, 58, 69, 82, 84–5, 90, 92, 127, 227–8, 232
British Hotels and Restaurants Association 81
British Independent Air Transport Association 37
British Overseas Airways Corporation (BOAC) 36–7, 46–7, 92, 118, 123, 127, 187, 227, 232
British Travel Association 81, 174
British United Airways 127, 187–8, 207, 229
brochures 39
  covers and pages from 35, 50, 71, 89, 105, 108, 145, 168
  for Horizon Holidays in 1970 127–8
Brown, George (Lord) 233
Brown, Jennifer 123
Brunton, Gordon 90, 130–5, 152, 167, 181
Bulgaria 89
Buseti, Pier 77
Butler, R.A. 23
Butlin, Billy 29, 227
Byng, John, Admiral 70

C&N Touristic 220–1
Cadbury, Sir Peter 42
Caetano, Marcelo 156
Caledonian Airways 92, 178, 229
Calella de la Costa 62
Calella de la Palafrugell 62
Callaghan, James 95
Calvi 1–3, 11, 17–18, 59, 69
Canada 115–16
Canberra 124
cancellation of cruises 119–20
Canterbury Tales 25
car travel 28, 36
Carlson Leisure Group 219–20, 236
Carnival Cruise Lines 122, 219, 231
Carr, Robert 155
Carroll, George 189
Carte, Richard d'Oyly 28
Carter, Jimmy 190, 233
Casanova, Mr 15
Castle Holidays 157
Cathay Pacific 201, 234
Catholic Herald 56
Cavenham (company) 152
Ceaucescu, Nicolae 147
Cecchini, Lepanto 60
Chalets Tamaris 18, 69
Chamonix 100, 226
Champness, Ian 141
Chandler, Harry 29–32, 30, 82, 103, 156, 174, 176, 227–30
Chandler, Rene 82, 229–30
Chandris, Anthony 117
Chandris, Dimitri 'Mimi' 117
Chandris Cruises 117, 230

INDEX

charter cruises 125–6
charter flights 39–43, 64–5, 107, 144, 148, 161, 191–2, 201
Chateaux d'Oex 109
Chaucer, Geoffrey 25
'Cheapies' 192–3, 233
chicken farming 146
China 197, 202, 233
Chou En-lai 197
Churchill, Winston 58, 75
Chusan 96
Civil Aviation Act (1946) 41
 Provision One 92, 97, 148–9, 177, 231–2
Civil Aviation Act (1971) 178
Civil Aviation Authority (CAA) 97–8, 158–9, 165–6, 170, 177–80, 189–95, 204, 209, 213–14, 228, 231–5 *passim*
Clark, Alan 64
Clarkson's Holidays 22, 110–11, 113, 119, 140–60, 162, 165–6, 169–70, 172–82, 229–32
class actions 199, 206, 221
'closed groups' 64; *see also* affinity groups
Club 18–30 137–9, 219, 231, 236
Club El Catalan 129, 138
Club El Remo 76
Club Franco-Britannique 3, 8, 11–14, 17–18
Club Méditérranee 3–4
Club Olympique 1–3
Colegate, Ray 97, 204
Collins, Colin 174
Comet aircraft 36, *37*, 39, 82, 127, 144, *215*
Compagnie Generale Transatlantique 107
complaints 148
Concorde 88, 233
'consolidation' 150, 218, 235
Constellation aircraft 24, 90
Consumer Council 85, 96
Consumers' Association 230
Contarini, Agostino 25
Cook, John Mason 27, 226
Cook, Thomas 27, 226; *see also* Thomas Cook (company)
Coombes, Nigel 169
Co-operative Travel Service 85
Cormack, Bill 90
Corsica 17, 21; *see also* Calvi
Cosmos 96, 119–20, 156, 174, 192–6, 202, 219, 233
Cossey, Errol 185
Costa Blanca 49, 229
Costa Brava 18, 20, 50–1, 59–60, 67, 69, 129, 193
Costa del Sol 74
Costa Line 120
Costa Smeralda 20
Courchevel 109
couriers 26, 142
Court Line 113, 140–1, 146, 152–60, 163–6, 169–70, 179, 232–3

Crédit Hotelier 18
credit selling of holidays 45–6
Credito Hotelero 68
Crete 174
Cristaltour 150
Croft, Eric 81
Crossland, David 114, 180, 199, 215–18, 221, 232–3
Croydon Airport 58–9, 227–9
cruising 116–26, 148
Crystal Holidays 111, 114–16, 219, 233
CTC Lines 121–2
Cuba 223–4
Cunard 88, 110, 123, 135, 182–5, 230–1
Cunard Eagle 80, 109–10, 229
currency allowances 38–9, 45, 48, 52, 93–5, 104, 111–12, 122, 146, 175, 190, 229–30
currency, forward buying of 195, 210
Cyprus 156, 196, 232

Daily Express 65, 149
Daily Herald 34, 228
Dakota aircraft 11, 16, 39, 55
Dan-Air 144, 155, 185, 213–16, *215*, 228–9, 235
Davies, Roger 172, 193
Davis, Joe 29
Dawson, Roy 99, 103
DC-4 aircraft 44
DC-10 aircraft 155, *192*, 203, 205, 233
De Haviland aircraft 24, 227; *see also* 'Elizabethan' aircraft
deferred payment for air tickets 46
Defoe, Daniel 25
Dell, Edmund 190
Delos and *Delphi* (cruise ships) 118
deposits paid to hotels 68, 141–2, 150
Derby Aviation 52
devaluation of sterling 32, 95, 112, 231
Dial Corporation 114–16
Dickens, Charles 23
direct selling of holidays 65, 144, 198
discounting 177, 202–3
Draper, Gerry 194
Drew, Peter 156, 205
drinking on flights 47
Duffett, Bob 123
Dulles International Airport 173
duty-free shopping 129
Dyer, Peter 111, 112, 114–16, 233

Eagle Airways 88, 99, 228–9
Eagle Aviation 39–40, 50, 66–7
Eason's of Grimsby 39
The Economist 91–2, 230
Edmonds, Mike 74–6, 129
Edwards, Sir George 188
Edwards Report (1969) 97–8, 149, 231
Efthymiadis Line 119, 148
El Al 90

INDEX

Elizabeth II, Queen 59, 125
'Elizabethan' aircraft 53, 74
Ellis, Doug 51–2, 54
Emersic, Darko 115, 233
Encesa, Señor 63
Engelberg 106
Escarrér, Gabriel 155
escrow accounts 176
Estartit 129, 138
Euravia Air 132–3, 230
European Union package holiday directive 181, 199, 210, 235
Evening Standard 157, 170
Everest, Connie 6, 7, 9–10, 14
Everest, first ascent of 36
Exchange and Mart 100–1
exchange controls *see* currency allowances

failure of travel companies and airlines 82–3, 86–8, 96, 178–80, 204–5, 211–12; *see also* Court Line
Falklands War 121–2
Faro 82, 156, 230
Fatah, Vic 207, 234
Fatima 58
Fields, Gracie 29
Fiesta Tours 86–8, 230
Filipacchi, Mme 3
Filipoff, Dimitri 1, 3
First Choice 217–21, 235
Flaine 109
Flair Holidays 51, 229
flight times 24, 39
'floating resorts' 126
Flook, Alan 214
Florida 185
fly-cruise packages 117, 123, 125
Flynn, Errol 75
Fodor's guides 21
Folkestone 47–8
Ford Motors 36
Forte, Sir Charles 77–9, 135, 229
France (liner) 123–4, 229, 232
Franco, Francisco 22, 141, 157, 196
Freeman, Gerry 55–6, 58, 187
Friedrich III, Kaiser 25
Frontier International 176

Galapagos Islands 118
Galaxy Queen 119–20
Garner, Ernest 87, 230
Garstang, Cecil 84
Gasteiner Perchten festival 25
Gatwick Airport 43–4, 49, 59, 189–90, 208, 215, 228–9, 235
Gay Tours 90
General Electric 203–4
George III 26
Gerlos 112
Glen, Sir Alexander (Sandy) 165

Global (company) 16, 47, 51, 96, 118, 212, 229, 234
Goldsmith, Sir James 151–2
Goodman, Harry 159, 172, 182–6, 199, 204, 208, 212–17 *passim*, 231–4
Grand Tour 25–6
Great Lakes Property Inc. 175
Great Universal Stores 51
Greece 82, 194
Green, Hughie *35*
Greenall Whitley 205, 207, 234
Griffin, B.W., Cardinal 56
Griffiths, Eldon 160
Grindelwald 101
Gulf War 213
Gullick, Tom 22, 119, 142–52 *passim*, 162–7, *164*, 232
Guthrie, Sir Giles 92

Halifax bomber 24
Hambros Bank 151
Hammamet 175
Happiways 34
Harbord, Noreen 17–18, 129
Harskin, Maurice 139
Haws, Duncan 42
Heard, David 138–9
Heath, Edward 170
Heathrow Airport 44, 58, 228–9
Heseltine, Michael 211
Hickie Borman (company) 92
hidden extras 96
Higgins, Francis 156
hire purchase 45–6
Hochsölden 99
Hogg Robinson 217, 235
holiday camps 29, 227
holiday prices 9–10, 50, 64, 92, 97–8, 110, 140, 149, 173, 193, 233; *see also* discounting
war over 162, 165–6, 199–200, 207
holiday reps 63–4, 75
holidays, demand for 21, 23, 34, 40, 43, 48, 53, 81–2, 155, 175, 213, 228
holidays with pay 22–3, 29, 227
Holland America Line 123
Hong Kong 201, 234
Hooper, Michael 110–11, 143–4, 147, 150
Hopkinson, C.D. 87, 230
Horizon Holidays
    at its peak 127–39
    clientele of 69
    end of 161–71
    first brochure 9–10
    first flight 10, 228
    first office 6, 7, 18, 127, 228
    name 7
    1970 programme 127–30
    take-over of 155, 232
Horizon Midlands 128, 170, 209, 233

INDEX

Horizon Travel 209, 233–5
'hot bed system' 147
Hotelplan 103, 229
hotels 27
  Aliancia, Faro 82
  Astoria, Heraklion 174
  Banff Springs, Alberta 27
  Costa Brava, Majorca 17–18
  Dux, Palma 75
  Escandinava, Torremolinos 76
  Ferrocarril, Soller 67
  de la Gavina, S'Agaro 63
  Grand, Adelboden 101
  Hilton, Park Lane 88
  Hochgurgl, Austria 110
  Kulm, St Moritz 100
  La Lepanto, Alghero 59–60
  Lloyd, Torremolinos 76
  Margherita, Aleghero 59–60
  Mediterraneo, Palma 4
  Metropolitan Beach, Arenal 96
  Ofir, Portugal 73
  Reid's, Madeira 28
  Rif, Tangier 129–30
  Santa Clara, Torremolinos 76
  Santa Luzia, Portugal 73–4
  Savoy, London 28
  Torremora, Torremolinos 129
  Las Tronas 59
Hudson Place Investments 213
Hunting-Clan Air Holdings 48, 51
Hurn Airport 44

Iberia (airline) 224
Ibiza 49, 70, 71, 147
Idlewild Airport 44
Imperial Airways 28, 227
Ingham, Walter 102–3, 227, 229
Ingham's Travel 99–115 passim, 105, 219
Innsbruck 110
Inspirations 218–19, 236
Institute of Travel Agents 48
Instone Air Transport 5
Intasun 172, 181, 185–6, 215, 217, 233
Inter European (airline) 217
International Air Transport Association (IATA)
  32, 37–8, 40, 52, 64, 77, 85, 92, 97,
  227–8
International Leisure Group (ILG) 139, 159, 199,
  204, 208–9, 212–14, 234–5
International Ski Federation 101
internet, the 222
Italy 112, 155

jet aircraft 36, 39
Jetsave 116, 178, 212
Johnson, Samuel 26
Jones, Doris 19
Jones, Wilf 120, 156, 174, 193–6

Karstadt Quelle 220
Kaufhof group 213
Kennedy, John F. 36, 92, 140
King Flight 50
Kirker, Christopher 140, 158
KLM 118
Kloster, Knut 117, 122–4
Korean War 36
Krogager, Eilif 198
Kuoni 116

La Plagne 106, 107
Laker, Sir Freddie 49, 67, 92–3, 186–91, 203–6,
  230–1
Laker Airways 159, 188–9, 201–6, 232, 234
Laker Holidays 181, 189–90, 205
Langton, Ted 34–6, 65–6, 68, 90, 119, 132–4, 181,
  227–8
Latcham, Paul 137–8
Lauro Lines 119
Leeward Island Air Transport 153
Leroy Tours 85, 157
Levi-Tilley, Gaston 5, 9, 16, 60
licensing
  of air routes 5, 7–8, 16–17, 42, 69–70, 77
  of tour operators 149, 165, 177–80, 209
Lincoln, Mr Justice 202
Lindblad Voyages 118
Lindsay, Peter 109
Llewellyn, Brian 134, 181–2
Lloyd, Selwyn 63
load factors 161–3, 213
Lockheed see Constellation aircraft; TriStar aircraft
long-haul holidays 199–201, 207, 217
Lonrho 204–5, 213
Lord Brothers (company) 82, 92, 154, 188–9, 229,
  231
Lourdes 55–8, 57, 228
Low, Erna 99, 103–6, 109, 111
Luciani, François 13–15, 17–18
Lufthansa 220
Lunn, Sir Arnold 101
Lunn, Sir Henry 16, 100–1, 102, 226; see also Sir
  Henry Lunn Ltd
Lunn-Poly 92, 110, 113, 182–3, 200, 203, 231–2
Luxitours 90
Lyons Tours 157

McCarthy, Joseph 36
McDonald, Father 55–6
McDonnell Douglas 203–4
MacGregor, Oliver 11
Mackenzie, Norman 11
Macmillan, Harold 23
mailing lists 31–2, 65
Majorca 4, 17, 42, 50, 67, 69–70, 129, 189–90
Malaga 77
Manchester Airport 209, 216
Mansour 118

Marbella 174
Marcu, Lionel 3
Mardi Gras 123, 231
market research 53, 91
Marre, Sir Alan 159
Masefield, Peter 32
Masia family 60
Maskell, Dan 29
Mason, Roy 87–8, 176, 178, 230
Matthews, Victor 172
Maudling, Mrs Reginald 88
Maxwell, James 41–2, 48
Medallion (tour operation) 171
Melina 148
Méribel 109
Miami 123, 185–6
Michelmore, Cliff 96, 231
Midland Air Tour Operators 52
Midland Bank 45, 204, 219, 232–5 *passim*
Midland Counties Railway 27
Migros 103, 229
Mikhail Lermontov 121
Milbanke Tours 51, 118, 229
Miller, William H. 122
Milne, Edward 86, 96, 230
Ministry of (Civil) Aviation 7–8, 16, 41
Minorca 70–3, 137, 148
Mizzi, Alberto 170–1
Molyneux, Elizabeth 56
Monkhouse, Bob 213
Monopolies (and Mergers) Commission 88, 203, 208–9, 218–19, 234–6
Montgomery, Bernard, Field Marshall 175
Morris, Aubrey 133
Morrison, Joe 133
'most favoured customer' clauses 218–19, 236
Mürren 101, 104

Nabarro, Gerald 94
Neilson, John 114
Neilson Ski 114, 219, 233
New Statesman 9
New York Times 46
Newbold, Charles 116
'niche' operations 135–7, 207
Niederau 112
Nixon, Pat 173
'no win no fee' lawsuits 199, 221
Norlin, Per 38
Norway 106–7, 229
Norway (cruise ship) 124
Norwegian Cruise Line (NCL) 123
Nott, John 201

Odessa 121
Office of Fair Trading 200, 202, 209, 218, 235–6
oil crises 155, 157, 165–6, 194, 198, 232
Olympic Airways 82
O'Melia, Richard 178

Operation Stabilizer 87, 202, 230, 233–5
Oporto 73–4
O'Reagan, Martin 185
Oriana 84, 124
overbooking 191–2
Overseas National Airways 178
Owners Abroad 198, 207, 209, 217, 234–5

P&O 96, 124–5, 135
Paice, Cliff 158–9, 177, 179–80, 193
Palma *43*, 59, 75, 212
Palma Nova 191
Pan American 24, 36–7, 46, 52, 88, 93, 172–3, 189–91, 203, 206, 227, 231
Paracelsus 25
Parker, Sir Peter 165
Parris, John 19
passports 45
Patten, John 211
People Express 205–6, 234
Perez, Jorge 223
perks for staff 77–8, 209
Perpignan 20, 50, 59–60
Perrin, Andy 115
Petrofina 142
Phippin, Eric 118
Pike family 10, 15
Pilgrim Tours 56–8, *57*
pilgrimages 25
Pisa 42
Poly Tours and Poly Travel 85, 106, 109–10, 226, 229
Polytechnic Tours 16, 52, 229
Port Mahon 70–2
Portland Holidays 198, 220, 233
Portugal 73–4, 156, 196, 232
Presley, Elvis 46
Preussag 135, 220, 237
Price Waterhouse 133, 181
prices *see* air fares; holiday prices
Project Gemini 124–5
protection of consumers 83–8, 95–6, 160, 197, 210–14, 235
Public Schools Sports Club 101
Pycroft, Reg 178, 212

Queen Mary 23
Quo Vadis Travel 77–8, 229

rail travel, development of 26–7
Ramblers' Association 188
Rank Organisation 207, 209, 234
Regent Street Polytechnic 110
Regina 118
regulation of travel firms 84, 86–8, 96, 230
Rein, Maria-Luisa 76
representatives *see* holiday reps
reservation systems *see* booking of holidays
Restrictive Practices Court 202, 233–4

INDEX

Riviera Holidays 90, 133–4, 181
Robertson, Bill 140
Rolls Tours 88–9
Romania 147
Romantica 117, 118
Rommel, Erwin, Field Marshall 175
Ros, Señor 62
Rowland, Tiny 204
Royal Caribbean International 123, 126, 221
Royal Daffodil 45
Royal Mail Lines 121
Ruskin, John 26
Russian cruise ships 120–2

Saalbach-Hinterglemm 112
Sabena 46
Saga group 205, 234
San Feliu de Guixols 62–3
Sandklef, Ulla 39
Sant'Elia, Conte di 59–60
Santiago de Compostela 58
Sardinia 18–20, 59–60, 69
Sarnen 31
Sassoon, Mr 103–4
Saunders, Fred and Edith 76
Sauvage, John 152
Sauze d'Oulx 109
Savage, Tom 96, 231
Scandinavian Airlines System (SAS) 38, 46, 209
Schwarzler, Hubert 104
Scottish Television 131
'seat-back catering' 163
Sebastian, Georges 175
self-catering holidays 199–201
Serfati, Aimée 130
Servicios del Sol 150
SFV Holidays 211
Sheddon, John 114
Shipping and Industrial Holdings (SIH) 151–3, 157, 162–5, 232
Shore, Peter 158, 190
short breaks 142
Silver City Airways 37
single rooms 147
Sir Henry Lunn Ltd 39, 42, 45–6, 64, 66–7, 84–5, 106, 109–10, 228–9
skiing holidays 99–117, 177
Sky Tours 35, 36, 49, 66–8, 90, 132–4, 176, 181, 228
Skytrain 93, 187–91, *192*, 202–5, 233–4
Skyways 48
Slater, Jim 152
small print in contracts 197
Smart, Chris 207
Smith, Harry 188–9
snow guarantees 114
Snowjet 110
Societa Aerea Mediterranea (SAM) 155

Société Générale de Transports Départementaux (SGTD) 60
Sölden 103, 227
Spain 21–2, 43, 67–8, 91–2, 141, 174, 194, 196–7
Spain International Travel 85
spas 25
Spencer-Churchill, John 75
spending on holidays 23, 94, 173–4
'spheres of influence' 190
Sproat, Iain 204
Stalin, Joseph 36
Stansted Airport 189–90, 208, 235
Starward 123
Steinberg, Lionel 176
Steinheil, Nicholas 1, 3–4
Sterling (airline) 198
sterling crisis (1966) 93–5, 111, 146
Stevens, Captain 16–17, 77
Stuart, Charles 190
'students and teachers' restriction 8, 16
Sun Cruises 125–6
Sunair 182, 184–5, 231
Sunday Express 158
Sunday Times 119
Sunflight 51
Sunmed 207
Sunotel 150
Sunward 122–3
Sunworld 218–19, 236
surcharges 95, 113, 154–5, 192–5, 210
Swan, Ken 135
Swan Hellenic 124, 135–6
Swan's 39, 112, 115
Swiss Bank Corporation 176
Swissair 38
Switzerland 106

Tait, Alan 73–4
Tait and Company 73
Tangier 129
Tanner, Bruce 209
Tavistock Institute 148
Teddy Boys 46
television advertising 47, 175, 205
television holiday programmes 96, 231
Tenerife 188
Terrington, Lord 16
Thatcher, Margaret 181, 198, 200, 203–4
Thomas, Sir Miles 39
Thomas Cook (company) 16, 27, 32, 39, 42, 52, 64, 82, 90, 106, 109–10, 139, 184, 218–21, 227–8, 232–6
Thomson, Roy (Lord) 131, 133–4, 181, 197
Thomson, Sir Adam 203, 208
Thomson Holidays 41, 113, 116–17, 120, 125–6, 134–5, 140, 151–6 *passim*, 162, 165–6, 169, 177, 181–3, 192–8, 200, 202, 208–9, 218–20, 232–7, 237

Thomson Organisation 90, 131–2, 135, 165, 170, 181, 230
Thomson Publications 130–1
Tignes 108–9
time charter system 186, 188
Tjaereborg (tour operator) 198, 233, 236
Topaz 125
Torremolinos 74, 76, 129, 174
Touche Ross 206
Tour Operators' Study Group 154, 176, 205, 213–14, 231
tourist air fares 36, 38, 92
Trade Descriptions Act 96
Trans World Airlines (TWA) 52, 189–91, 203, 206
Transair 55–6, 58–9, 127, 187
Transalp 109
Transglobe 96
Transmediterranea line 70
Transport Holding Company 182, 231
Travel and Holiday Clubs Ltd 86
Travel Club of Upminster 29, 82, 156, 230
Travel Savings 184
Travel Trade Gazette 36, 39, 81, 90, 167, 169, 184, 228
Travel Trust Association 211–12
Travelplan 216
Trigger, Colin 171, 223–4
Trippe, Juan 93
TriStar aircraft 153, 155, 163
Tropical Places 116
Tupini, Umbero 81

Unfair Contract Terms Act (1978) 197, 233
Unilever 152
United States
 Civil Aeronautics Board 47, 178
 travel to 52, 92, 115–16, 185–6, 202
Universal Sky Tours *see* Sky Tours
The Universe 56

V forms 93–4, 111–12
Val Thorens 109
Van Horne, William Cornelius 27
Variety Club of Great Britain 212–13

VC10 aircraft 127
VIAD (company) 116
Vickers aircraft *see* VC10; Viking; Viscount
Victory, Juan 71–2, 137
Viking aircraft 16, 41–2, 50, 74, 99, 144
Vilamoura 175
Vinceschi, Mr 14–15, 17–18
Vingresor (tour operator) 198
Virgin Atlantic 206, 234
visas 43
Viscount aircraft 32, 144
vouchers for accommodation 192–4
Voyager of the Seas 126

Walthamstow Chamber of Commerce 142
Watkinson, Harold 187
Wayfarers 109
Westropp, Edward 45
Weymouth 26
Whitbread, Mr 15
Whitehall Travel 64, 157
Whitfield, Henry 86–7
Williams, Jed 133
Wilson, Harold 93–5, 111, 141, 146, 230
Windstar Cruises 123
Wingate Wiggett, Ben 90
Wings (tour operation) 49, 92, 188, 207, 209, 231, 234
Women's Institutes 142, 144
Workers' Travel Association 31
working-class travellers 196
World Airways 178
World Cup 146
Worlock, Derek 56, 57
W.R. Grace (corporation) 151
WTA (company) 39
Wyatt, Miles 188

Young, Lord 209

Zemette, Jean and Christine 11, 14, 17–18, 69
Zeppelin LZ126 23
Zermatt 88, 230